Landscapes of Desire

The publisher gratefully acknowledges the
generous contribution to this book provided by the
Lisa See Fund in Southern California History.

Landscapes of Desire

ANGLO MYTHOLOGIES
OF LOS ANGELES

William Alexander McClung

UNIVERSITY OF CALIFORNIA PRESS
Berkeley   Los Angeles   London

University of California Press
Berkeley and Los Angeles, California

University of California Press, Ltd.
London, England

Library of Congress Cataloging-in-Publication Data

McClung, William A.
   Landscapes of desire : Anglo mythologies of Los Angeles / by William
Alexander McClung.
      p.   cm.
   Includes bibliographical references (p.   ) and index.
   ISBN 0-520-21827-2 (alk. paper).
   1. Los Angeles Region (Calif.)—Civilization—19th century.   2. Los
Angeles Region (Calif.)—Civilization—20th century.   3. European
Americans—California—Los Angeles Region—Psychology.   4. English
language—Social aspects—California—Los Angeles Region—History.
5. Landscape—California—Los Angeles Region—Psychological aspects.
6. Architecture—California—Los Angeles Region—Psychological
aspects.   7. Los Angeles Region (Calif.)—In literature.   I. Title.
F869.L85M33   2000
979.4'94—dc21   99-23426

Manufactured in the United States of America

08   07   06   05   04   03   02   01   00   99
10   9   8   7   6   5   4   3   2   1

For Stephen Orgel
O et præsidium et dulce decus meum

Contents

Illustrations

Preface

◉

This book is a study of only one of the several major cultural forces that have shaped Los Angeles: its appropriation by mostly white, English-speaking visitors and immigrants from about 1850, when California entered the Union, to about 1985, a date that approximates the incorporation of Anglo sensibilities into broader patterns. By *Anglo* I mean what is usually meant in California: people of, for the most part, European descent whose first language was English or had become English by the time they reached the Pacific Ocean. By *Los Angeles* I mean what is usually meant locally, not only the city proper but Los Angeles County, with its eighty-odd incorporations and its unincorporated areas stretching from Malibu to Claremont, and the region under its cultural and economic sway, including primarily the counties of San Bernardino and Riverside and, to a lesser extent, those of Orange and Ventura.

There are many cultural studies of L.A. as so defined, and the chapters that follow will take note of them; in the background is Carey McWilliams's *Southern California: An Island on the Land* (1946 and many later editions), from which all modern examinations of the subject begin. The present book, however, is not a political or sociological history of Los Angeles; its subjects are architecture, landscaping, literature, photography, painting, and other vehicles of the imagination, specifically the Anglo imagination. It will argue that anglophone Los Angeles sought to reconcile two contradictory visions of ideal place and space: an acquired Arcadia, a found natural paradise; and an invented Utopia, an empty space inviting development. Arcadia and Utopia (one of which is also—and the other of which sounds as if it ought to be—a city in Los Angeles County) are, of course, very generally inherited cultural properties, but in the Anglo imagination of the late nineteenth and earlier twentieth centuries they interacted in ways peculiar to this region and to the civilization that invoked and celebrated them. The consequences of their contradictions, failures, and triumphs have outlived the Anglo hegemony and help explain what Los Angeles is today and what it is likely to become.

The first chapter, "Inventing Utopia," examines the tensions between conflicting visions of what kind of city and culture should and would emerge under the Anglo dominion. "City of Metaphor," the following chapter, focuses on literary celebrations and condemnations of L.A. The third chapter, "A Usable Past," explores connections between Anglo uses of historiography and of architecture. The fourth, "The Shapes of L.A.," identifies six conceptual models for the region's topography and argues that present-day L.A. is a product of their overlap. The last chapter, "Inventing Arcadia," looks primarily at painting and conceptual art for evidence of efforts both to affirm and to question Los Angeles's mythic image of itself as a found natural paradise. Finally, an afterword offers my personal explanation for this undertaking.

The literature of and on Los Angeles is broad, but rarely deep; in fact, the persistence of fixed ideas in the face of evidence to the contrary is one of the subjects of this book. Reyner Banham, who radically revised perceptions of the region in his *Los Angeles: The Architecture of Four Ecologies* (1971), remarks with amusement on the reaction to his researches by some young Angelenos, who observed that there were already plenty of picture books on L.A. Reviewing Mike Davis's *Ecology of Fear: Los Angeles and the Imagination of Disaster* (which unfortunately appeared too close to my deadline for consideration in this book), the *New York Times* noted the originality of Davis's work within "the all-too-limited literature of the nation's second-largest city." I hope, by searching out the roots and strata of the city's imagination of itself, to expand those limits and to give a clearer picture than has existed of what lies within them.

Note: An asterisk in the text refers the reader to the Explanatory Notes, a section of expansions on particular points found after the body of the text. Documentation of sources can be found in the Reference Notes; these are silently linked to the text by keywords in italic at the head of the reference.

Acknowledgments

❦

I was encouraged to begin this book by Dan Calder, who brought me to UCLA as a Visiting Scholar in 1985 and afterward as a Visiting Professor at intervals until 1989. In inviting me to offer a course on Los Angeles in literature, he remarked that he would not let it be taught by anyone who did not love L.A. It is a great sadness to me that he did not live to see his trust fulfilled.

A fellowship from the American Council of Learned Societies allowed me to do much of the research for this book. The high cost of assembling the illustrations and permissions was substantially met with assistance from the Office of the Provost, the Office of Research, the College of Arts and Sciences, and the Department of English of Mississippi State University. I am happy to express my thanks to all these parties.

For sheltering the manuscript during my travels to and from Tokyo, I am forever grateful to Naomi and Bob Brofman, residents in that most singular of notional L.A. addresses, B.H.P.O.

For advice on the manuscript I am indebted to Robert Winter and William Deverell, who read it for the University of California Press. Most of the research was done at the Huntington Library; at UCLA's University Research Library, Department of Special Collections, Maps and Government Information Library, and Library of the Graduate School of Architecture and Urban Planning; at the California Historical Society's photographic archives housed at the University of Southern California; at the University Arts Library of the University of California at Santa Barbara; and at the Getty Center (now Getty Research Institute) for the History of Art and the Humanities. To the directors and staffs of these collections I express my gratitude for infinite assistance and kindnesses.

Julius Shulman, who has kindly allowed the use of several of his photographs in this book, gave me a memorable tour of his house (by Raphael Soriano, 1950) and grounds, a microcosm of the best in high modern architecture and timeless landscaping. Ian Whitcomb was a sympathetic consultant on L.A. as viewed from his own perspective and that of his British compatriots, and Carolyn See, a valued colleague, shared with me her extensive knowledge of L.A. in literature. Finally, to my students at UCLA 1986–89, who taught me at least as much about L.A. as I taught them, my affectionate thanks.

1 Inventing Utopia

Make this valley full of ditches.
For thus saith the Lord,
Ye shall not see wind, neither shall ye see rain;
But that valley shall be filled with water.

2 KINGS 3:16–17

The concrete blocks of Lloyd Wright's 1926 Sowden House in Los Feliz (Fig. 1) "came alive," an architectural historian writes, "in the sharply contrasting sun and shadows of pre-smog Los Angeles." His words sound like an elegy for a lost atmosphere of clear and brilliant air, one repeated in countless other complaints about Los Angeles. It is surprising, then, to read William Faulkner's 1934 description, in his L.A. short story "Golden Land," of how "the sun, strained by the vague high soft almost nebulous California haze, fell . . . with a kind of treacherous unbrightness." Both writers are bearing witness to some sort of betrayal, but the former is regretting a paradise lost, with the clear implication that we are at fault for polluting nature's gift of light, whereas the latter, writing a decade before smog seized the public imagination, reads the L.A. light as being by its nature ambiguous and menacing.*

FIGURE 1. Sowden House by Lloyd Wright, East Hollywood, 1926 (photographed in 1985).

Inconsistent testimonies about the climate are nearly as old as Los Angeles itself; they contribute to the uneasy overlay of conflicting mythologies on which the city and its chroniclers have fed. Such testimonies are efforts to make sense of the city in space and time by locating its present state, however incompletely seen or understood, as a point on a time line defined as much by myth as by history. Whatever coherence one observer can find in, or impose upon, a place so vast is necessarily selective and usually figurative. Los Angeles has been most often read and seen metaphorically, as a manifestation of something else—a midwestern city, a small town, a rancho, a playground, or a park, to name a few models—and criticism and analysis have reflected the values found in those models. Maps of Los Angeles are not simple sheets but large loose-leaf compendia of detailed fragments, or series of pamphlets with vaguely helpful labels like "Central and Western Area"; concerned analysts produce other kinds, like the L.A. Department of City Planning's wildly dissimilar maps of what residents of different districts imagine the city's dimensions to be, or a diagram of the city as a system of one kind of entity, like the "archipelago" of powerful cultural institutions sketched in Mike Davis's *City of Quartz*. They are all partial, in both senses of the word. I mean to show that although the "real" city is in fact so complex as to be unmappable, it nevertheless overrides any reductive model, whether hostile or flattering. This book seeks to map one of its largest dimensions, its space as imagined by generations of predominantly English-speaking immigrants. Their efforts both to discover and to fabricate a desired landscape established the terms of the debate over L.A. that we live with today.

The contours of their landscape emerge through the efforts of writers and designers to give it a name, an origin, and a purpose. If the divisions in the mythologizing of L.A. are evident anywhere, they are so in the different tracks followed by those who treat the city as a text and those who treat it as a body. For essayists, journalists, and writers of fiction, Los Angeles has more often than not been a collection of messages to be decoded; for planners, architects, and builders it has often been undifferentiated matter to be shaped into meaningful forms. Faulkner, for example, describes a canyon wall of villas, a characteristic Los Angeles panorama, as "halfhidden in imported olive groves or friezed by the sombre spaced columns of cypress like the facades of eastern temples." His rhythmic language suggests what is alien, mysterious, even sinister, and is representative of the metaphorical weight that burdens much literary treatment of Los Angeles, and that is seized upon by literary critics as evidence of the city's "real" nature—the text, so to speak, behind the body.

A photo of a Sunset Hills tract in 1939 (Fig. 2) offers an excellent opportunity for such a "reading," grounded in mythologies not of the pathology of style (as in Faulkner's exotic and therefore suspect and enervating Moorish architecture) but of the natural sequence of structures. It is all too easy to say that the street and the lighting are finished, the houses incomplete, and the land unimproved, in an evident inversion of cultural priorities. This interpretation is nothing more than a facile exercise—my own—in literary criticism transferred to landscape, and its strategies include artificial hierarchies, unexamined assumptions, and a glib elision from descriptive to metaphorical to judgmental language. Readers of *The Day of the Locust*, often cited as the definitive Hollywood novel, would do well to question the steps by which Nathanael West persuades them to a "reading" of Hollywood as artificial, insubstantial, and perverse.

FIGURE 2. Sunset Hills tract, 1939.

As a body of material culture as well as a text of meanings and messages, Los Angeles, since the latter half of the nineteenth century, has been
shaped by several traditions of imagined, ideal societies. At a crucial period in its growth, these traditions spoke to a dominant Anglo culture,
some of whose visions have been literal and serious, even deadly serious,
while others have been playful or ironic. Some have subscribed heavily
to the physical properties of ancient myths of the good place and the good
life, like a golden climate and trees in perpetual fruit; others have been
figurative and abstracted, finding essences of myth and popular fantasy
translated into suitable equivalents. An 1899 real estate brochure (Fig. 3),
for example, covers its products in an envelope of allusion to ancient
dreams of Arcadia, a found natural paradise. The premise of its imagery
is that the built environment defers to the unbuilt, at most completing or
fulfilling its implicit structure. When the land transactions were completed, however, the iconic image was not of a piping boy in an orchard

FIGURE 3. Cover of the real estate promotional brochure *Los Angeles California Illustrated* by Cyrus M. Davis and T. Newman, 1899.

but of something more conventional (Fig. 4), an image of upper-class ease and repletion. Was the conjunction of these images a leap of imagination, through which prosaic midwestern values could be saturated with Edenic idealism, or was it merely a shallow and cynical exercise in marketing? Such is the structure of the debate over whether Anglo L.A. ever enjoyed a season in paradise.

The opposite of Arcadia is Utopia. In its purest form it would be a spaceship, where the environment is as much a construction as the society itself. A Utopian designer customarily treats the landscape as raw material to be shaped for human purposes and is never shy about asserting the dominance of the built over the unbuilt. Los Angeles, which has de-

FIGURE 4. Longstreet House, Los Angeles, 1900.

veloped on so many different scales and at so many different paces, offered plenty of blank canvases upon which futures could be built. Van
Nuys in 1911 (Fig. 5) appears to be waiting not only to be populated but
to be conjured into existence out of a non-space. Local condescension toward this community and its neighbors, all lying to the north of Hollywood, Beverly Hills, Bel Air, and Brentwood, may have something to do
with the fact that scenes of proto-*arrivisme* like this came late in the San
Fernando Valley and are better documented than the groundbreakings
to the south and southeast. The long and overlapping histories of development, improvement, and destruction in the region found a narrative
shape in L.A.'s greatest annexed space, its sidecar, so to speak; the general Utopian pattern of the fashioning of a city out of mere raw materials, implicit throughout the region but obscured elsewhere by varying
scales and rates of change, finds, in the Valley, readily accessible coordinates of space and time.

The Valley further epitomizes failures characteristic of a Utopia that
can be less conveniently pinned upon other parts of the city. In the regret
for what-might-have-been, the Valley is L.A.'s muffed Second Chance at

FIGURE 5. First tract office in Van Nuys, February 1911.

building an ideal city; its rapid growth into a national prototype of Anglo suburbia is vaguely understood to follow from the supposedly shady
circumstances of its birth and delivery into Los Angeles, brought about
by Owens Valley water in a Promethean gesture enshrined in the imagination of Los Angeles as its Original Sin. Whatever the facts of the matter, they have been superseded by a will to understand the bringing of
water to the Valley as the rupture with both Nature and Law that irrevocably brands L.A. as a type of Babylon.* In the Utopian pattern of thought
characteristic of the region, the "future" is desperately sought as the rem-
edy for this unacceptable present; in making all new, some future state
will restore a lost innocence.

Sophisticated planners in the twentieth century have cited the Spanish regulations for colonial towns as an authorization for abstract and au-
thoritarian planning: "They shall try as far as possible to have all of one

FIGURE 6. Von Sternberg House by Richard Neutra, Northridge, 1935.

type for the sake of the beauty of the town." Carefully planned cities-within-cities, however, did not take hold in L.A.: the Park–La Brea complex of the 1940s and Century City (1969–present) are unusual. The former has many fans, although it looks eerily like something on the margin of the inner and outer boroughs of New York, but Century City gives ammunition to advocates of the low-rise and the idiosyncratic in L.A. design. As Robert Winter remarks, it seems "planned not for people but for architectural photography."

A partial Utopian city, however, can be pieced together from a number of remarkable structures, whose power is as much a factor of their siting, or of how they are photographed, as of their design. They announce their Utopian status either by overpowering an undistinguished site or by appropriating the characteristics of a distinctive one to their own uses. In an early photograph, Richard Neutra's Von Sternberg House in Northridge, built in 1935 (Fig. 6), appears to float in negative space; a 1947 shot (Fig. 7) does justice to the mature planting that came to reconcile site to

FIGURE 7. Von Sternberg House by Richard Neutra, Northridge, 1935.
Photograph (1947) Julius Shulman, Hon. AIA.

structure but without erasing the deliberate line—drawn in both images
by walls and the moat—between the house and the Valley landscape. The
earlier photo does justice to certain totalizing characteristics of the design,
which included a site selected because it was, in Von Sternberg's own
words, "barren and forlorn." On the other hand, Julius Shulman, who shot
the later image in Neutra's company, testifies that the architect was attracted to the land because it was "cheap by the acre[;] . . . the first act of
Von Sternberg was to remove the onus of the 'naked land.'" The two photographs send different but not inconsistent messages. Perhaps the independence of the house—its Utopian or "spaceship" quality—is more obviously read in the details of its equipment, which included various
specially designed enclosures for, among other features, dogs and a Rolls-
Royce; a ship's searchlight at the entrance; and a futuristic sprinkler system around the curving wall that "produced varied effects from a gentle
mist to a battering rainstorm."

FIGURE 8. Strathmore Apartments by Richard Neutra, West Los Angeles, 1937.

Similarly subtle gradations of perception are registered by different photographs of Neutra's 1937 Strathmore Apartments. The earlier shot (Fig. 8) appears to proclaim not only the formal triumphs of modern architecture but also that architecture's command over the apparently irreducible hills of West L.A. It takes an act of will—aided by the study of architectural drawings, models, and photography—to isolate these buildings from their urban context and read them as a kind of supercity, but that kind of mental and visual exercise is sanctioned by architectural tradition, as, for example, in the eighteenth-century perception, evident in treatises like Marc-Antoine Laugier's *Essai sur l'architecture*, of a "real" Paris of significant neoclassical buildings and a merely contingent one of forgettable and (it was to be hoped) ephemeral constructions.

However, Shulman's 1939 shot of the same structure from about the same angle, but now *with* mature planting and *without* attention drawn to the bare landscape behind (Fig. 9), goes a long way toward documenting

FIGURE 9. Strathmore Apartments by Richard Neutra, West Los Angeles, 1937. Photograph (1939) Julius Shulman, Hon. AIA.

a harmony between structure and landscape that may lie as much in the artistic choices of the photographer as in the conditions of the site. Frank Lloyd Wright objected in the twenties to the easy complacency of the physical environment of L.A. (see chap. 4); buildings like Neutra's, which are doubly works of art, both as architecture and as photographic images, have made strenuous demands on local sensibilities, forcing a heightened esthetic of severe grandeur while at the same time projecting luxury and sophistication. Photography not only mediates this dialogue between the found or given and the achieved or constructed city; it largely establishes its terms and drives its conclusions: whereas the two earlier photographs deliberately emphasize the disjunction between structure and background, the two later ones read the compositions as esthetic unities.

Imagining Los Angeles has been, to a greater extent than with other U.S. and European cities, a process of aligning a model of a hoped-for Utopian future with one of an allegedly Arcadian past that cries out to be

redeemed. Rapid growth has simultaneously aided and frustrated its citizens' efforts both to find what has been lost and to make something altogether new. Attitudes toward the city, adoring, optimistic, ironic, cynical, and bitter, are more often than not the consequence of the incongruities
between the two visionary models, each of which attempts to stabilize and
perfect our lives by reordering the unsatisfying conditions of historical
existence and by either reinstating or inventing some idealized system of
social and environmental relationships. These are the contradictory models for the Los Angeles said by an urbanist to represent both "the emergence of a populous, urbanized, and industrialized settlement" and "the
rejection of the metropolis in favor of the suburbs." The imaginative history of Los Angeles is a record of efforts to improve upon Arcadia without acknowledging that to interfere with a found or given natural paradise is to introduce an element of dissatisfaction that can be eradicated
only when the transformation to a Utopia is complete. Since that transformation has occurred only imaginatively, in works like the paintings of
David Hockney, the mentality of Los Angeles is trapped in anxious aspi-
ration, simultaneously striving to go forward and to turn back.

Narratives that make sense of experience by giving it an origin have
arisen to lend structure to L.A.'s malleable sense of self. At the beginning
of the mythic sociology of L.A. is an imagined lost civilization of harmony
between human beings, their crafts and arts, and nature. The stability of
the Spanish and Mexican culture of Southern California, which from a
post-1860s perspective appeared impervious to change, has qualified it
as a kind of Arcadia. So enthusiastically has Anglo culture endorsed this
myth that it was enshrined in a Disney comic book (Fig. 10). This reading
of history has fallen into disrepute, to be replaced by the less popular exaltation of an ecological paradise that only the American Indians, victims
of Spanish conquest, might legitimately inhabit. Both perspectives share,
however, an anxiety over the transformation of the land into a commodity. If we can imagine a time when the terrain of Southern California was
"beyond" value—as evidenced, for example, by its being exempt from
taxes before the Americans assumed power—then a classical declension
of ages on the model of those described by ancient writers comes into play:
a Golden Age, whose stability appeared invulnerable to change from

FIGURE 10. A page from *Donald Duck in Old California*, 1951.
© Disney Enterprises, Inc.

within, yields to a Silver Age, like that described by Ovid in the *Meta-morphoses* (I.113–24), in which the introduction of the arts of civilization was paralleled by a decline in morals, health, and happiness. In 1848 the new American governor prophesied from Monterey, "The arts and sciences will flourish, and the labor of the agriculturalist, guided by the lamp of learning will stimulate the earth to the most bountiful production."

A dispassionate analysis of the bases of the success of the Latin rancho order—its freedom from taxes, its indifference to efficiency, its command of forced labor, and principally its isolation from the outside world—does not erase the compelling analogies to ancient imagined societies where land, the basis of existence, was synonymous with its use and with the life lived on it, and could not be conceptualized as an alienable commodity. Like air, land could be imagined as a medium of existence rather than a raw material to be transformed. Agriculture was a Silver Age innovation in ancient myth; for Los Angeles, the cultivation of the ranchos is, from one perspective, the beginning of the process that changed land into real estate. The famines of the early 1860s that forced the sale of the ranchos to pay taxes and their subdivision for profit set in motion the acceleration of property values that is so popular a topic of conversation in L.A. today. Between 1850 and 1880 the value of agricultural land multiplied twenty times; the wheat harvest of 1850, for instance, was less than 3 percent of that in 1880. The collapse of the "bucolic" (a word whose Greek root means "cattle") era was recorded in statistics of the same period, "for of all the major products, only cattle did not record a substantial increase in value."

Robert M. Fogelson has set these facts forth in *The Fragmented Metropolis: Los Angeles, 1850–1930*. He ponders, but does not resolve, the mystery of why Los Angeles came so rapidly to be a metropolis. A materialistic explanation—that industrial and commercial attractions were created to satisfy the needs of both an existing and an anticipated population—is not enough; the explanation contains, however, the seed of something more satisfying in its emphasis on the element of invention and anticipation characteristic of the city's culture and growth, or, indeed, of its culture *of* growth. Invention is the hallmark of Utopias, but the word in its root Latin sense means "discovery," with the implication that what is invented was already there. The mythologies that have governed Los Angeles are ultimately Arcadian; they are quests for what was already there and what somehow, implicitly, remains: a remembered paradise not only of leisure but of fruitful, fulfilling labor. Such quests, however, have been only fitfully rewarded by the vision and experience of an El Dorado, a fabulous country of repletion and reward. From very nearly its first years as Anglo territory, the promised land of Southern California has extracted a

FIGURE 11. Irrigation canal, Riverside County, from *Art Work on Southern California* by Lou V. Chapin, 1900.

Utopian commitment. It has been necessary to cultivate and shape the landscape, to tease its implicit amplitude from the reluctant soil, whether literally, by adding water, or figuratively, by painting, filming, and designing an L.A. adequate to the demands of desire. "This fantastic, colorful, light-hearted civilization," said a writer in the *Atlantic* in 1930, "depends for its very existence on irrigation ditches." The biblical citation at the head of this chapter points to the analogy, often drawn in booster literature, between Palestine and Southern California, and it furthermore gives divine authorization for improvements. In the Arcadian mythology of California, however, such acts of "improving" (Fig. 11), epitomized by, but not limited to, the funneling of water from the Owens Valley, have become its primal error.

Late-nineteenth-century publicity for Los Angeles, such as A. T. Hawley's *The Present Conditions, Growth, Progress, and Advantages of Los Ange-*

les City and County (1876), is full both of praise for the climate and of cli-
matological tables and charts; as mechanisms for reducing the subjective
and ineffable properties of the environment to calculating uses, these impose a narrative and a system of differentiation where chronology and
structure had been missing. Besides describing conditions, however, tables could be used to redefine them. J. M. Guinn, speaking to the Historical Society of Southern California in 1890, both eulogizes the salient advantage of Los Angeles and teaches how to manage the tables for its better
marketing: "If there is one characteristic of this state, of which the true
Californian is prouder than another, it is its climate. With his tables of mean
temperature and records of cloudless days and gentle sunshine, he is prepared to prove that California has the most glorious climate in the world.
Should the rains descend and the floods prevail, or should the heavens
become as brass, and neither the former nor the latter rains fall, these cli-
matic extremes, he excuses on the plea of exceptional years." From objective description to promotion was one step; the next was the suppres-
sion of inconvenient facts, such as the desertlike conditions of at least some
areas; and the last was such flagrant misrepresentations of L.A. as "posters
in the east and in Europe [that] showed gaily decorated excursion steam-
ers plying up and down the Los Angeles River." In the conceptualization
of statistics as an armature against experience we can recognize the
Utopian over the Arcadian impulse, the refusal merely to accept the land
as found, and the will to master it to use. The process quickly degener-
ates, however, into the sharp practice that is at the root of Anglo L.A.'s
bad conscience about its origins, and that by extension has compromised
the very notion of "improvement."

Because the economics of Los Angeles centered on struggles to define
the meaning and proper use of its land, the tables and charts mark yet another stage—soon followed by the irrigation ditches—of the transformation of terrain into property. This process, of course, took the form of spec-
ulation in land, with communities in the 1880s boom platted almost
overnight, but it also meant the development or exploitation of the earth.
In the latter half of the nineteenth century, writes Glenn S. Dumke, "practically every means of utilizing the land's resources was tried at least once
in southern California," including not only the famously successful cit-

rus crops and the nearly forgotten silkworm industry, but also digging for minerals and drilling for oil. Self-invention is more than a metaphor in L.A.

The coordinates of mythic Los Angeles cannot, however, be found in statistics about cattle or orchards or the prices of lots in new subdivisions. An ideal Los Angeles of the recent past is continually reconstructed in imagination, despite complaints at almost every stage since 1850 that paradise had already been lost. Air, the element that can't be avoided, has become the reference point of struggles to command the high ground of L.A. rhetoric. A comparison of two photographs of the landscape (Figs. 12, 13) makes a telling case for the contradictions at the base of much judgmental rhetoric about atmosphere in Los Angeles, and by extension about its history of gains and losses as well. Superficially, the two images might appear to illustrate the contrast between the overbuilt landscape we know and the Arcadian one of idealized memory. It is somewhat of a jolt to discover that the later image (Fig. 12) dates to as far back as *1910,* and that the horizon in *both* is murky, although the earlier picture (Fig. 13) was shot about 1875. John D. Weaver, writing in *California History* in 1981, cites an unidentified source from the summer of 1912 who states that from the summit of Mount Lowe, "the effect of Los Angeles smoke on the surrounding pellucid air is evident and apparent as a gray-brown veil hanging over the city." Before it became a scarlet letter on the body politic, smog was a fact of the esthetics, if not the pathology, of the region; revulsion against it has fostered the delusion of an imagined L.A. of long ago, a crystal city whose atmosphere was not only clean but absolutely transparent. Color photographs today, shot during Santa Ana conditions, when the normal flow of air from the Pacific is reversed and hot desert winds blow the haze out to sea, reinforce the unrealistic conviction that the air over the immense Los Angeles basin and its adjacent mountains and valleys is supposed to be as clear as glass.

Contradictions in the imagination of Los Angeles reflect contradictions among the kinds of spaces L.A. is implicitly understood to be, such as, for example, a metropolis, where stress is accepted as the price of grandeur, and a resort, which is organized for pleasure. Apologists for Los Angeles have stressed the continuity between the simple rewards promised in its

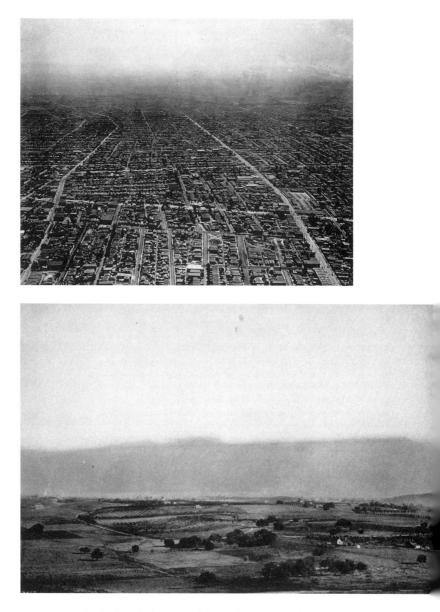

FIGURE 12 *(top).* San Pedro, east of Central Avenue and south of Eighth Street, as viewed from a balloon, 1910.

FIGURE 13 *(bottom).* General view of South Pasadena, about 1874–75.

early days and the complex ones sought in its maturity. In what follows I shall try to account for both the motivations for idealizing place and space and the strategies by which that is done, considering that extension in space and movement forward in time are ultimately contradictory, even antagonistic, kinds of experience, and that the quixotic intention of both Arcadian and Utopian idealism is the subsuming of time within space and, therefore, its conquest.

Two early views of American Los Angeles seem to gesture in opposite directions. The earlier (Fig. 14), dated 1853, illustrates a War Department survey of California shortly after the transfer of government and presumably is intended to be objective. Taking in the entire town from Fort Hill, it sketches an inconsequential settlement—one even less as-sertive than a similar Disney image (Fig. 15) intended to call attention to the pueblo's insignificance. The "streets" are merely vague spaces between structures, which themselves have little clear relationship to one another, neither dominating nor organizing the spaces around them. The "vista" reduces the whole scene, even the Plaza and church at the settlement's core, to unimportance.

The Kuchel and Dresels perspective (Fig. 16) of 1857, by contrast, takes matters firmly in hand. It was one of many commercially produced views of cities, remarkable mainly for having, in the case of L.A., about as little as possible to work with, even by comparison with other west-ern towns like Salt Lake City. The direction of the central image is to the north—what, with the drama of its backdrop, would come to be the pre-ferred angle for subsequent nineteenth-century views. Although the prospects are indefinite (even, except for the mountain barrier, endless), the streets look straight and fast—an effect imprinted by the baroque con-vention of galloping horses. There is no conventional "view" of the cen-ter of town: the Plaza and its environs are in the distance, and the fore-ground gives a detailed overview of residential compounds. Yet this

FIGURE 14 (above).
General view of Los An-
geles in 1853 by Charles
Koppel, from *Reports of
Explorations and Surveys,
to Ascertain the Most
Practicable and Economi-
cal Route for a Railroad
from the Mississippi River
to the Pacific Ocean . . . ,*
1855.

FIGURE 15 (right).
Detail from *Donald Duck
in Old California,* 1951.
©Disney Enterprises, Inc.

FIGURE 16. Promotional lithograph showing Los Angeles in 1857.

image projects something more important—the idea of the town as shaped and orderly, but also as dynamic and extensive. The vista is a kind of transparency through which an implicit, assertive grid can be easily read.

Little imagination is required to make of this plate an embryonic model of booster L.A.: the "Utopian" city of men that controls the space of its site and foreshadows the metropolis to come. Having in the principal image virtually schematized a western city, the artists pay homage to commerce and community with representations of the principal businesses and their owners' houses, positioned nearly equally around the border, like the squares on a Monopoly board. These vignettes were customarily furnished for a fee or a commitment to purchase quantities of the print. The fixed image of the Plaza has vanished, and the moment for the first of its several romantic revivals has yet to arrive. Present, rather, in the plate as a whole are what many will find true of L.A. today: an orderly, impersonal urban infrastructure with characteristically efficient transportation arteries; a predominance (in the bordering images) of commercial over civic

FIGURE 17.   The Plaza, Los Angeles, from *Art Work on Southern California* by
Lou V. Chapin, 1900.

or ecclesiastical structures, which in fact are wholly absent; and substantial private homes that appear, in the central image, protected, even nes-
tled away, from the public sphere and that stand, in the bordering images,
as the confident equals of the commercial structures. The main image even
anachronistically evokes post–World War II flat-roofed ranch-style tract
development.

Each "take" on the city testifies to a different artistic temperament and
to different expectations on the part of the intended audience. The earlier,
however gracefully amateurish it appears, is a government document,
whereas the latter is a sales pitch, adroitly balancing the objectives of aggressive and obsequious presentation. Each implicitly articulates a notion
of the relationship between the built and the unbuilt environment that re-
verberates to the present day. In their extreme forms, these images remain
separated, and it is still possible to imagine a Los Angeles characterized
by the diffident charm of one or by the confident assertion of the other.

FIGURE 18. View in the Glen Rosa section of Pasadena, near Orange Grove Avenue, about 1880.

In various guises Los Angeles has been thus marketed, both as a tranquilizer and as a stimulant. Literally Arcadian imagery (Fig. 3) may seem extreme, but a 1900 view of the Plaza (Fig. 17), by now sedately subtropical and waiting to be occupied by the viewer, is scarcely less wishful. As an obligatory commemoration of the traditional heart of the city, this view is curiously oblique, in that it excludes the structures for which the Plaza is (to the extent that it is at all) historically and architecturally important. The priorities of the photograph are those of Anglo L.A. on a Victorian Sunday. Other pictures from the same volume (Figs. 11, 49, 99, 104–7, 131, 138), a lavish publication, set forth an even wealthier, lusher, and emptier metropolis, but the Plaza photograph itself exalts palms over architecture in a manner that links the image to other ahistorical, evocative vistas characteristic of the period. There is, for example, an area of Pasadena about 1880 (Fig. 18) that to us evokes the gardens of the then nonexistent Huntington estate, or a scale-distorting juxtaposition of house and cactus (Fig. 19) that minimizes the former as much as it inflates the latter, and that doubtless conveyed to a homelier audience the appeal of this accessible Eden. Perhaps the desired balance is most characteristically struck in promotional literature that ranks vegetables as the equal of constructions, as

FIGURE 19. Giant cactus,
Los Angeles area, late nineteenth
century.

in the plate labeled "Tropical Plants and Historical Buildings" from an
1880s brochure (Fig. 20).

By contrast, Julius Shulman's glamorous and thrilling photograph
(Fig. 21) of Pierre Koenig's Case Study House #22 (1959) speaks to the
contrast of mountain and plain captured in the 1857 picture, but from
the heights: the elegant pavilion, overlooking and overtopping the vast
gridded flatland, echoes its linearity and brilliance. Floating in their successive wraps of evening gown, crystal box, and illuminated space, the
luxurious young women complete an image of a vast and dramatic natural
setting transformed and perfected by the arts of design. Less accessible
than a frame house and a cactus, Case Study House #22 is nonetheless a
democratic, Utopian vision of the heights to which money, technology, and
the International Style can convey a citizen in L.A. There is here no nostalgia for orange groves; Koenig even rejected the use of wood, considering it "an archaic material."

EIGHT MILES FROM LOS ANGELES, FOUNDED 1776.

MAIN STREET, LOS ANGELES, FOUNDED 1886.

SAN GABRIEL MISSION.

MISSION CHURCH.

PALM TREES(TWO LARGEST IN THE CITY

DATE PALM.

YUCCA TREE.

MISSION SAN JUAN CAPISTRANO, 30 MILES SOUTH, FOUNDED 1776. SAN LOUIS REY MISSION 40 MILES SOUTH, FOUNDED 1798.

TROPICAL PLANTS & HISTORICAL BUILDINGS.

FIGURE 20. "Tropical Plants and Historical Buildings," from *Views of Los Angeles and Vicinity, Cal.*, about 1887.

FIGURE 21. Case Study House #22 by Pierre Koenig, Los Angeles, 1959. Photograph Julius Shulman, Hon. AIA.

The Case Study designs of 1945–67 projected thirty-eight houses, of which twenty-seven were actually built. These were not only a high-minded experiment in reforming architectural taste to the canons of high modernism; in a city whose buildings lacked organization, density, and consistency, they were also an effort to create an archipelago of ideal forms, to which the bulk of the city, derivative and inconsequential, would be ancillary. Utopian schemes in their purest forms summon up entire cities all at once out of the void and typically have an easily recognizable shape; such cities, with their drawing-board plans and sculptured elevations, are signs of and for themselves. In the Los Angeles of mixed styles and half-achieved projects, however, such totalizing gestures are snuffed out not only by the sheer quantity of the ordinary urban envelope but also by the layering of intended and envisioned alternative cities. L.A. is a palimpsest of such cities, most of them intermittently visible in the survival and revival of its characteristic architectural styles and in the unfinished logic of maps and plans. The true Utopian gesture in L.A.—the declaration of the city and its culture as a complete object and a sign for itself—is likely to be blunt and naive, like a classical column, topped by an eagle, put up in 1895 and composed of 13,873 oranges.

Representing or advertising Los Angeles has depended for the most part on a blending and balancing of Arcadian and Utopian elements. One of the hardiest of Southern California's industrial arts, the citrus box label, often strives for such a synthesis; the Questa lemon-box label (Fig. 22) of the World War I period, for example, is virtually a diagram of a Southern California of idealized juxtapositions. There are four approximately equal zones, starting at the mountains, which are wilderness (the land as it was and can, without damage to profits, be allowed to remain), and progressing to the citrus groves, an orderly and proper exploitation of nature. A boulevard next announces a modern city and its technological panache, displaying the imagery not of mass (i.e., rail) but of leisured transportation—open cars, a horseman, and a carriage or pony cart. Finally a lady appears on foot, hatted and handbagged, as if going to pay a call. The sidewalk and planting unite the smooth curves and bright surfaces of the impeccably engineered avenue to the lushness of the watered San Gabriel Valley suburbs; the lady's presence redoubles the basic dualism of the en-

FIGURE 22.   Citrus label showing zones of the San Gabriel Valley, about 1915.

tire picture, which implicitly asserts that nature and civilization are per-
fectly in scale, and that the pace of the planted Arcadian city is simultaneously that of the motorist and of the pedestrian.

If we erase oily machinery and migrant laborers from the picture, we
might find the Questa daydream within the bounds of possibility, at least
for the eastern valleys of Los Angeles County in the heyday both of the
citrus industry and of the sunny winter resort and health capitals: Riverside, Pasadena, and (for the local establishment only) San Marino. Something similar was in the works from the 1880s on, when much of the region seemed to unite leisure and labor in a way that dissolved the
distinction between them. Viewed from the wishfully named town of Ramona (Fig. 23), Pasadena, as it is identified in the picture's original cap-
tion, appears to be completely contained in the great resort hotel, the Raymond, here fronted by vast citrus groves that look like part of the garden

FIGURE 23. View of the San Gabriel Mountains, Pasadena, and the Raymond Hotel, from *Southern California: Its Climate, Trails, Mountains, Canyons, Watering Places, Fruits, Flowers, and Game. A Guidebook* by C. F. Holder, 1888.

enjoyed by the woman and child in the foreground. The reality of the climate and the mystique of the orange combine in a reverie of existence that satisfies the biblical command to labor while reaping the rewards of an irrigated Eden.

Less persuasive is the "Pacific Coast" of a mid-twentieth-century citrus label (Fig. 24), a pastoral Southern California neatly accommodating the family (citrus) farm, a superb highway, and the pleasure facilities of the coast. This both is and is not Los Angeles; the contours of the land and the bold pier allude to L.A. but invite us to reshape it as an idealized enclave—one that also offers sybaritic indolence with the justification of implied honest labor. Characteristically ambiguous in its statement of values, the picture promises the rewards of technology, by means of the overscaled highway that guarantees unlimited access; the (literal) fruits of old-fashioned labor; and the luxury of an idyllic resort. Trying to satisfy all these imperatives accounts for many a Southern California neurosis, not the least of them the problem of what to do with the millions

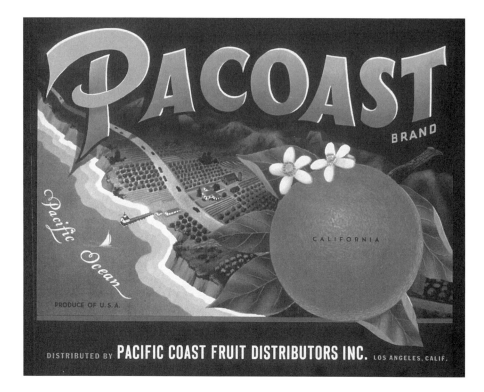

FIGURE 24. Citrus label showing an idealized Southern California, about 1950.

who accepted the invitation of the superb highway and so overwhelmed the solid little farm and the daintily independent sailboat.

Solutions to the competing claims of Arcadia and Utopia have often been, in the style of this region, idiosyncratic. Los Angeles is the world capital of the detached private house, and perhaps nobody sought so sensitively to reconcile its metaphors as Rudolf Schindler in his 1921–22 house for himself in West Hollywood. Described by Schindler as a "camper's shelter: a protected back, an open front, a fireplace, and a roof," it looks even today somewhat like desert architecture in a more forgiving ambiance. The King's Road House may be faulted for excessive idealism about Los Angeles's climate; it lacked a mechanical heating system and offered sleeping porches rather than indoor bedrooms. But the sleeping arrangements continued an established local tradition, sanctified by the image of the region as a health resort and the medical concepts of the time, and in any case Schindler appears to have conceived of it as a vacation house. In fact it was used year-round and must have been uncomfortable during Hollywood's frequent chilly nights and damp mornings— an instance of the discrepancy between a perfect and a merely excellent climate.

In setting the language of wood craftsmanship beside that of machine technology, however, Schindler created a powerful Southern California symbol. Whereas both the material and the penetration of the interior by exterior space evoked the idealism of nature and the natural life of the West, the esthetics of the new European architecture spoke, paradoxically but convincingly, to the freedom of choice and from prejudice supposed to characterize the new culture of Southern California. The novelty of his design also symbolized the identification of the city with innovation and progress, all the more effectively in that the house is sited not in an isolated canyon or on a difficult hillside but neatly within the urban grid. Arcadia and Utopia as implicit impulses could hardly have been more adroitly joined.

In their contrastingly unassertive and theatrical sitings, the Schindler and Koenig houses pose questions about how we visualize any part of Los Angeles in relation to its tremendous whole. The city is notorious for the absence of a hierarchy of surface streets and neighborhoods—the sort of hierarchy determined, for example, by the spine of Manhattan from Madison Square to Central Park, or laid down by the compass in the rims and spokes of an English garden-city. The search for a city may be as mundane as the search for the "right" or "real" city, the portion that (literally or figuratively) lifts itself above the rest and thereby epitomizes and dominates it. The residential towers of Fifth Avenue and Central Park West make such a clear visual and social statement, translating the élan of the skyscrapers where money is made into the luxury and privilege of the skyscrapers where, in the service of private life, it is spent. Los Angeles has not developed this way. Desired areas have tended either to define themselves as enclaves, like Beverly Hills, or to follow the lead of the topography, like the Hollywood Hills. The Schindler House epitomizes

that dimension of Los Angeles that identifies the city with the most intimate of enclaves, the house; the Koenig House gives the impression of being the focus of the city, and of not only profiting from, but also depend-
ing upon, the unsurpassable view.

Shulman's image is the record of a perceptual act by which the enormous city below is annexed to the house above it. Visitors to Los Angeles often remark on the lengths to which the quest for status carries its citizens; those lengths are frequently the literal ones of distances that must
be crisscrossed and locations that must be discovered or invented in a city
that has never had an unassailable fortress of prestige, a Beacon Hill or a
Faubourg Saint-Germain. Speculators in real estate and the young hunt-
ing down the latest unadvertised club share the Los Angeles assumption
that, in this city of floating objects and ideas, a center exists somewhere.
The image of pinnacled centrality achieved in Shulman's photograph represents one way of "getting to the top" in L.A., yet like an image in a film,
it may exist only within the limits of this frame.

Utopian planning, which might have enforced the centrality of a particular location, is absent in Los Angeles except on the vastest of scales;
the region has long been gridded into the hydraulic systems that dictate
the rhythm of life throughout California and the West, and it now is harnessed to the freeways, which determine patterns of traffic and growth
on a less grand but still overpowering scale. Within the interstices (some
of which encompass entire cities), the question of planning is always alive
somewhere. Trying to get a grip on the entire region while actually settling, developing, or exploiting a manageable part characterizes the history of the postpueblo city. The clash in scales and orientation between
the settled area surveyed by Lieutenant Edward Ord in 1849 and the remaining pueblo lands as surveyed in 1857 (Fig. 25) helps explain the patterns of idiosyncratic development that have resulted in neighborhoods
and entire cities laid out on unaligned grids and sometimes colliding in
a tangle, as at the junction of Venice and Robertson Boulevards in Culver
City. Vast developments might occur spottily both near and far from the
historic core, as the 1869 sale map of the enormous Abel Stearns Ranchos
shows (Fig. 26). The pueblo and its pendant seaport, Wilmington, seem
comically inadequate as centers or points of reference for the offered prop-

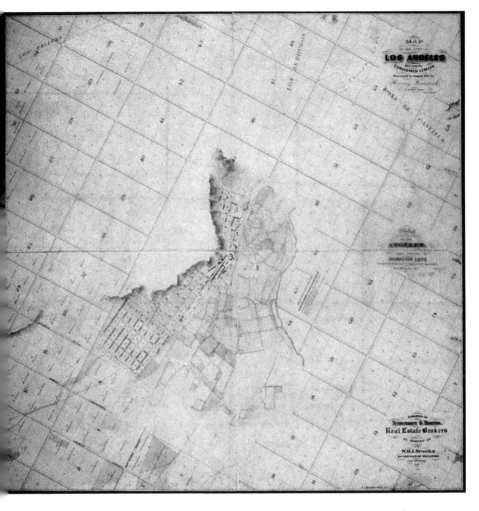

FIGURE 25. Map synthesizing the 1849 and 1857 surveys of Los Angeles.

erties, which at the time were still part of Los Angeles (rather than Orange) County. Such imbalances between the existing administrative capital and its apparatus of government on the one hand, and the vast private enterprises on the other, upset conventional organic metaphors of
"growth." Los Angeles did not so much grow as sell itself into existence.

    The Utopian impulse to offer up a fully designed environment is more

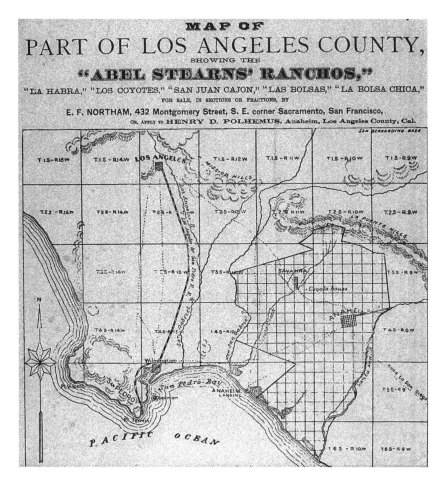

FIGURE 26.   Sale map of the Abel Stearns Ranchos, July 1869.

evident in L.A. at the stage of promotion than of actual development. Hollywood at its very beginning, the creation of the Wilcox family, appears
as a classic L.A. diagram of a wild natural terrain "improved" into geometric order (Fig. 27). At the same time, the map makes the characteristic L.A. promise that in buying a part, one will buy into the whole—a
promise often heard from communities that are selling the intangibles of
climate and other "found" amenities. An 1877 map (Fig. 28) similarly devotes fully half the terrain to undeveloped land—not surprisingly, since

FIGURE 27 *(top).* Real estate promotional map of Hollywood, 1887.

FIGURE 28 *(bottom).* View of Los Angeles from Boyle Heights, 1877.

that is the land these particular mapmakers were trying to sell. But what has remained characteristic of L.A. modes of representation is the effort to telescope the whole into the part, to suggest that in acquiring a lot one is acquiring a landscape. In the Brooklyn Land and Building Company's "View of Los Angeles from the East"—in fact from Boyle Heights in East L.A.—the entire basin has been radically foreshortened, so that the Pacific Ocean appears to lap the western blocks of downtown.

Concurrent with that sort of "real estate opportunity" is the phenomenon of local sensibility that always sees the present as falling just short of the city's intended shape, its state of "perfection" in the Aristotelian sense of "completion." This frame of mind is reflexively Utopian and can be mapped in such statements as, "It was a city . . . which never really felt urban and rarely, except for a small patch of stone-and-brick-built office blocks in the Downtown financial area, even looked it." The reference is to the period 1910–50 and resembles a statement in the *Los Angeles Times* of 17 April 1989 that L.A. was only *then* evolving into a "real" city. The creation in recent years of a relatively dense downtown of new skyscrapers and public buildings has not fulfilled such hopes but has instead provoked a new order of complaints. Because most of these complaints are, from one perspective or another, laments over threatened or lost amenities associated with an earlier, less populated, city, the message by the end of the century is that Los Angeles is incapable of building itself into a Utopia because the very act of construction is understood to be a further disruption of the rhythms and proportions of some idealized city of the past.

The philosopher E. M. Cioran has heaped contempt upon the concept of Utopia, arguing that it is based on the delusion that the future is a replete state of being, qualitatively different from the past and the present, and in possession of its own principles of order. He is fascinated by "the role taken, in the genesis of events, not by happiness but by the *idea* of happiness": rejecting what the present offers, people absurdly seek happiness in the chimera of futurity. Yet Cioran also acknowledges a necessity: the quest for the future, which is the essence of Utopian activity, is both an anxious and an ecstatic condition without which a society would stagnate and collapse.

If the truest Utopia is a condition of complete novelty, absolutely free

FIGURE 29. Lobby of Pantages Theatre by B. Marcus Priteca, Hollywood, 1929.

from the contingencies and qualifications of the past, then it can probably exist only as a mental act. There are no boundaries we can place upon such designs and constructions. But in the public realm, Utopia in Los Angeles is probably going to be found only in an *interior*, in some space that is either vulgarly or sublimely otherworldly. The movies once offered an approximation of this, distinguishing the entertainment they provided from the mundane business of life by shaping and decorating spaces of imagination and fantasy, like the lobby of Pantages Theatre in Hollywood (Fig. 29). The photograph itself, however, reveals imperfections in the concept: our position—which is the camera's—will not allow us to become one with the composition, parts of which are invisible behind us, and which gestures to other-spaces under arches and up the staircase. It cannot be *our* space; it tells us to keep moving—a nice equivalent for that state of desire and frustration so often associated with Hollywood.

Utopianists know that the ideal place is both elsewhere and immune to outside influence. The interior of the Bradbury Building downtown,

FIGURE 30. Interior
court of the Bradbury
Building by George H.
Wyman, Los Angeles,
1893.

the unique masterpiece of the forgotten George Herbert Wyman, has long
been venerated in L.A. as a kind of sacred space. Here the photograph
documents a space that is at once thrilling and reassuring (Fig. 30). Nested
within the cast-iron harmonies of columns and lifts and railings and stairs,
the visitor is simultaneously diverted and excited by their intricacies. It
is one of the few constructions to which the old architectural metaphor of
"frozen music" seems unembarrassingly applicable. Yet its facade is dull,
even more so than the unremarkable exterior of Pantages; the Bradbury's
interior court not only takes us by surprise but also appears unconnected
to anything beyond itself. An inside without an outside, it overrides all

givens of place because it is not linked, visually, esthetically, or experientially, to the containing skin. It may seem perverse to defend a pedestrian design, but by not meriting a second glance *and by appearing to have nothing to conceal,* the facades of the Bradbury Building effectively insulate the interior, muffling any visual or conceptual transition from the street to this cage of light.

2   City of Metaphor

After winding through the willow hedge rows
for a couple of miles we drove suddenly out from
among the vineyards and gardens & in among
rows of flat one-storied adobe houses with long
corridors in front covering the side walk. Melted
bitumen was dripping from the flat rooves to the
danger of careless pedestrians. Turning a corner,
the rows of houses took the shape of streets of
shops. One street, this street, led to the plaza,
whence two or three others branched, and this
was the city of Los Angeles.

EDWARD OTHO CRESAP ORD, *The City
of the Angels and the City of the Saints, or, a Trip to
Los Angeles and San Bernardino in 1856*

❧

Innocently observing that L.A., "climatically insulated,"
was "a sort of island on land," Helen Hunt Jackson in 1883 echoed a curious old misconception about California. The name had been adopted
from Rodriguez de Montalvo's *Las Sergas de Esplandián* (1510), a romance
about an island near the Earthly Paradise, full of gold and Amazons, and
although early-sixteenth-century Spanish and English explorers had
mapped California, with increasing accuracy, as firmly attached to the continent, it was redrawn in the early seventeenth century as an island. The
credit for this error goes to a Carmelite friar, Fray Antonio de la Ascen-

40

sión, who accompanied an expedition of 1602–3 and whose memoirs, printed in a compendium of missionary and exploration activities in 1613, were widely read. His apparently sincere but misguided interpretations of geography were understood, as John Leighly has set forth in detail, to correct previous naive errors about the shape of California. The literary image itself, from de Montalvo's fiction, may have shaped the perceptions of Brother Antonio and of cartographers who, despite challenges in the early eighteenth century, continued to perpetuate the error as late as 1785, four years after the founding of the pueblo. The "correction" was, of course, itself an error and was itself eventually corrected.

This is a structural parable about California, and about Los Angeles. The misleading maps show how newcomers coped with a terrain they had only begun to explore by giving it a vivid, imaginary shape rich with metaphorical associations. Furthermore, the authority for that imaginary shape was literary, deriving possibly from the association of the name of the province with the magical island of de Montalvo's fable, and certainly from the pious reportings of Brother Antonio. Drawing on the elegiac imperatives of Jackson's 1884 novel *Ramona*, Anglos shaped Los Angeles into the material equivalent of their desire; but since the 1920s their imagined city has disintegrated in the face of an obsessive and repetitious discourse of disillusion and betrayal. That discourse, a new map of the island, deserves as severe a scrutiny as the discredited "Ramonaland."

Maps have hidden agendas of their own, those of the "Island of California" perpetuating the region's nominal origin in a Utopian fantasy of sex and power. When maps of the United States of America are read anthropomorphically, with the Midwest understood as "the heartland," the East and West Coasts are literally "marginalized" in such discourse as the definition of what is essentially American. L.A.'s role in this drama of competing metonyms begins with the map of the Utah Territory (Figs. 31–32), whose blank zones are as informative as its markings. It is a political diagram of the future of the United States, projecting an established nation into a realm treated as undefined, empty, and expectant; in its scheme, Los Angeles is on the rim of a void and at the terminus of a journey. As such, L.A. occupies "the future," both in space and—because it is an unrealized, or unexploited, land that must be made as well as found—in time.

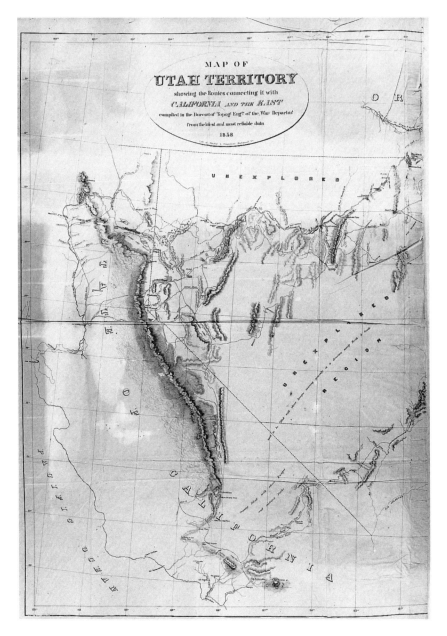

FIGURE 31. United States War Department map of the western territories and California, 1858 (detail, western area).

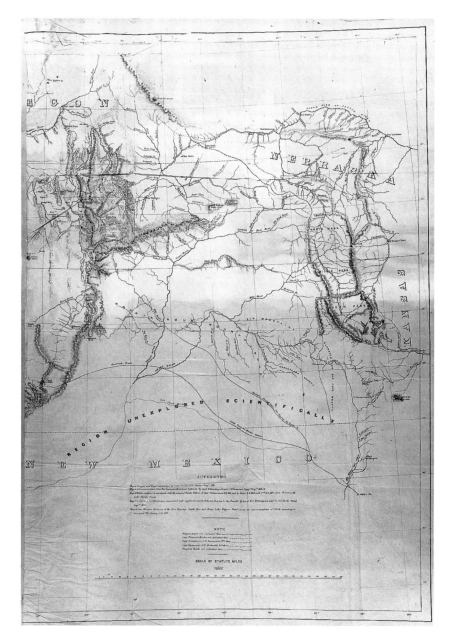

FIGURE 32. United States War Department map of the western territories and California, 1858 (detail, eastern area).

The Lieutenant Ord whose short journey into Los Angeles is quoted at the head of this chapter is the man who first surveyed the pueblo in 1849. Ord's is an embryonic L.A. narrative, and not merely because it sketches a city whose planting is more impressive than its architecture. Through his words, as in his drafting, he gives the place a shape; the careful, twisting stages of his cadenced prose mimic a search, as through a maze, for a center, which turns out to be a recognizable heart or core, the Plaza. Long before the "Hollywood novel" would ritually introduce L.A. from the perspective of somebody who had just stepped off a train, Ord presents Los Angeles as a destination pursued in careful but accelerating steps; then, before building to the climax, he mildly deflates the drama of arrival with a downbeat observation on the town's insubstantial physique. It is a brief, but highly structured, experience.

He was not the only early observer to temper his presentation with irony. In reporting to the United States Senate on the natural characteristics of California, Philip Tyson in 1850, noting the northwest winds and fogs, comments that "most of our countrymen . . . expected a universal prevalence of soft breezes and bright skies." Even documents with an overt design on the reader, like Charles Nordhoff's *California for Health, Pleasure, and Residence* of 1872, incorporate warnings against overstatement into their pitch, while adding fuel to a famous rivalry: "The Puebla [*sic*] de Los Angeles—the town of the angels—is not, in its present state, a very angelic place. It is irregularly built, the older part having but one principal street, at one end of which, however, stands a building which is, both for size and excellence of architecture, worthy of San Francisco or New York. If you walk down this street, you will be surprised at the excellence of the shops and the extent of some of the warehouses, and will see abundant signs of a real and well-founded prosperity, which will surprise you if you have listened to the opinion of San Franciscans about this metropolis of Southern California." Addressed to prospective tourists and settlers, Nordhoff's publicity also invokes the implied structure of a journey and a destination, while using a rhetoric of correcting false images to define a Los Angeles adequate to the demands of the future. As his title states, he speaks as much to those who will stay as to those who visit. His observations, like Ord's, are part of a chain of appreciative documents that tem-

per anticipation with candor, or that even ridicule the claims of climato-
logical and real estate boosters. In his 1878 account of Los Angeles, *Between
the Gates*, Benjamin Franklin Taylor rhapsodizes about "wealth of color,
clouds of fragrance, [and] luxuriance of vegetation" but observes that for
all their glossy beauty, orange groves are workaday places, not suitable
for pastoral repose. He describes L.A. in summer: "Palm trees are as gray
as an elephant's ears, and portions of the landscape have a disused air, as
if beauty was about going out of business and moving away, while the
heat dances a hot-footed hornpipe upon the top of your hat." Jane E. Weeden's 1884 versified "yellow pages" of L.A. businesses and services warns
that those coming to partake of the "angelic oranges" had better have

> a reliable purse
> Or a practical brain or muscular force;
> For on climate and crackers most people can't live.

Taylor seems to have written without ulterior motives,* but Nordhoff, as
David Streatfield notes, wrote on commission and Weeden was obviously
puffing local trade; these two may wish to strike a skeptical note in order
to sound more convincing. Nevertheless, their tone helps sketch a plausible map of Los Angeles, with demystification written from the beginning into the rhetoric of salesmanship.

Yet for much of its recent history, Los Angeles has been narrated as
an "other-place," an island of the mind if not of the map, to be, at best,
visited, appreciated (or exploited), and abandoned. Early in one of the pro-
totypical "Hollywood novels," *Queer People* (1930), the main character
"alighted from a Santa Fe transcontinental train, dusty and bored with
three days of staring at Kansas, New Mexico, and Arizona"; the tale ends
in a flurry of departures from railway stations and piers, as if Los Angeles, like the fraudulent Emerald City imagined by Angeleno L. Frank
Baum, were not a place, but a fable of experience and a rite of passage. A
substantial body of writings, both fiction and criticism, views the Los Angeles both of today and of the early Anglo period as shaped by only the
grossest sort of self-promotion. Just as Dorothy was not fooled by the Wiz-
ard, they affirm, neither should we be. Even the title of Horace McCoy's
1938 novel *I Should Have Stayed Home* is reflexively scornful, and epipha-

nies come cheaply and easily, as if written on the map: "Ahead of me, on top the Newberry store, a big neon sign flashed on and off. It was an outline map of the United States and these words kept appearing: 'ALL ROADS LEAD TO HOLLYWOOD—And the Pause that Refreshes. ALL ROADS LEAD TO HOLLYWOOD—And the Pause that Refreshes. ALL ROADS LEAD TO HOLLYWOOD—'"

"Dissolution" is one way of characterizing the unifying theme of the Los Angeles novel of the 1930s,* and to the extent that the term is helpful, it is valid for fiction written well after 1939. Understood generally as the displacing of sound by corrupt principles and institutions, "dissolution" usefully sums up what writers often seem to discover in L.A.; they convey it not only by action and subjective response but also by a series of metonyms that include climate, transportation and circulation systems, architecture, and landscaping. To its credit, the literature of Los Angeles is exceptionally committed to the material culture of the city, finding in its body, so to speak, the causes, equivalents, and consequences of human behavior. Less admirable is a mechanical correlation between the phenomena of the city and its citizens' supposedly shallow values and vicious behavior. Because it was only a venture, a place reached by a journey, L.A. is easily dismissed: "Los Angeles," as Alison Lurie concludes her novel *The Nowhere City*, "had disappeared into a bowl of smog."

⊙

> Not too long ago, L.A. was a nice place to live.
> LETTER TO THE *Los Angeles Times Magazine*, 21 MAY 1989

> We who lived here for some time, although still not enticed away, find the area constantly less attractive.
> FROM THE *Annals of the Association of American Geographers*, 1959

> I used to like this town. A long time ago.
> RAYMOND CHANDLER, *The Little Sister*, 1949

Eudora Welty has said that love of a place, to the extent that other places are devalued or repudiated, depends on that place's being not found but chosen, and chosen for being what the seeker is not, but hopes to become. The Los Angeles of literature—with some notable exceptions—is a chosen place loved or hated according to how well it has satisfied the traveler's expectations. Because it lies at the end of a journey, L.A. is expected to give immediate gratification—to justify the long trip—yet at the same time it is usually understood to be the beginning of a new life whose rewards will materialize later. By effectively identifying its American readers both as insiders who would desire the bucolic culture of Southern California and as outsiders responsible for its destruction, *Ramona,* in a sophisticated way, defined California as both an end and a beginning. Readers responded to the novel somewhat simplistically, however, understanding its elegiac tone as an authorization not of guilt but of nostalgia. In the quasi-colonial environment of Southern California in the late nineteenth century, *Ramona*'s fans validated their obliteration of the old culture by making a cult of its memory.

Ramona offered a recoverable past, one imbued with nostalgia yet capable of resuscitation. One reason was its iconic presentation of the constituents of ideal landscape, all of which, however dignified by association with a vanished order, would be accessible to a fresh plantation. A locus classicus is the prospect, from the Moreno residence, of an earthly paradise, like the gardens of Alkinoos in *The Odyssey* or Eden in *Paradise Lost,* where flowering spring comes at the same time as fruitful autumn:

> Between the veranda and the river meadows, out on which it looked, all was garden, orange grove, and almond orchard; the orange grove always green, never without snowy bloom or golden fruit; the garden never without flowers, summer or winter; and the almond orchard, in early spring, a fluttering canopy of pink and white petals, which, seen from the hills on the opposite side of the river, looked as if rosy sunrise clouds had fallen, and become tangled in the tree-tops. On either hand stretched away other orchards,—peach, apricot, pear, apple, pomegranate; and beyond these, vineyards. Nothing was to be seen but verdure or bloom or fruit, at whatever time of year you sat on the Senora's south veranda.

More than a set piece, the passage is an internal stage direction, establishing that lovely and abundant condition away from which romance and tragedy will carry both Ramona and history. In the ecology of this novel, the passage defines the threatened sphere of the vanishing order; to its readers, it holds up the image of what can be salvaged or reconstituted.

The success of Anglos in not so much discovering as inventing such a California laid the basis of the literature of discontent and disillusion that has since represented Los Angeles to an educated public. From one perspective, we might admire the Anglos' will to remake the landscape and the city according to the mentality of their desire; from another, we might deplore their bad faith in appropriating only those parts of the past they found convenient—only, indeed, those dimensions of *Ramona* they found convenient. The rhetorics of landscape and of architecture are two of literature's many tools for demystifying the benignity cultivated by the *Ramona* image-makers; they should be seen as part of a campaign to control the representation of Los Angeles by discrediting the Anglo mythology— narrated in romanticized local history and made visible in neo-Hispanic architecture—of a successfully appropriated past. The premises of this anti-Ramonaland rhetoric are either that the land and its climate are perverse, and that architecture extends or compounds that perverseness, or that the land is innocent or benign but is violated or betrayed by architecture and other "improvements." Architecture itself is characteristically represented as, at the very least, insubstantial or illusory, like a stage set, and even as ridiculous when it apes the styles of remote times and cultures. In the latter case, the fault is compounded if the techniques and materials of construction are "inauthentic."

In its radical denial of legitimacy to virtually every modern act of cultural invention in L.A., this rhetoric discloses its structural affinity with "Ramonaland." Both perspectives acknowledge the concept of an authentic or legitimate culture, but whereas the former locates it in transferable and recoverable images, the latter relegates it irrecoverably to the past. Because L.A.'s present is (at the time, or for the audience, of this literature) Anglo and its past something else, the city can never, from the latter's perspective, claim to perpetuate that past, and so its romanticism (most apparent after 1900 not in literature but in architecture) is judged bogus. By the same token, however, because its earlier centuries were in various degrees provincially Spanish and Mexican, it cannot now find any indigenous precedent for an "authentic" architecture, much less for an entire culture. Thus the city, not to mention all Southern California, has been routinely damned both for reconstituting the material cultures of its past and for inventing ones that are altogether new.

The root argument is ecological. Evelyn Waugh, in a preparatory sketch for *The Loved One*, dismisses Los Angeles as little more than a desert encampment: "In a thousand years or so, when the first archaeologists from beyond the date-line unload their boat on the sands of southern California, they will find much the same scene as confronted the Franciscan Missionaries. A dry landscape will extend from the ocean to the mountains. Bel Air and Beverly Hills will lie naked save for scrub and cactus, all their flimsy multitude of architectural styles turned long ago to dust, while the horned toad and the turkey buzzard leave their faint imprint on the dunes that will drift on Sunset Boulevard." Christopher Isherwood, a famous expatriate, puts a similar case from the perspective of George, the hero of his 1964 novel, *A Single Man*, who has come up to the Santa Monica range above L.A. for the first time in quite a while: "The area is getting suburban. True, there are still a few uninhabited canyons, but George can't rejoice in them; he is oppressed by awareness of the city below. On both sides of the hills, to the north and the south, it has spawned and spread itself over the entire plain. It has eaten up the wide pastures and ranchlands and the last stretches of orange grove; it has sucked out the surrounding lakes and sapped the forests of the high mountains."

Although he is an immigrant to L.A., George appears not to feel any responsibility for its growth; instead, he demonizes the city as a mindless, insatiable, primitive life-form, while implying that the prior uses of the land (pasture, ranches, orchards) were immemorial and legitimate, unlike, apparently, housing. The scale and rate of the city's decline (and, paradoxically, of its growth as well) are simply a part of his own adult life, inasmuch as he had visited these hills often in his early days in L.A. Then, he had "felt the thrill of being a foreigner, a trespasser there, of venturing into the midst of a primitive, alien nature." There is no way, despite an occasional flourish of ironic distancing in the prose, to distinguish George's emotions from his author's; in the manner of much modern fiction using a kind of personalized third-person narrative, "comment" or evaluation is the property of the subjective narrating or narrated consciousness. The reader must judge the validity of his prophecy: "And yet [Los Angeles] will die. . . . It will die of overextension. It will die because its taproots have dried up—the brashness and greed which have been its only strength. And the desert, which is the natural condition of this country, will return."

The cycle he has sketched, from wilderness to cultivation to urbanity to suburban dispersal to wilderness again, seems both inevitable and avoidable, a matter of, on the one hand, the earth's resuming its rhythms after human beings' interruptions, but of, on the other, a vengeful response to, as he puts it, greed. What its "natural condition" is, the classic question in Los Angeles ontology, is not clear. As Rodney Steiner points out, not only the indigenous culture but also those of the pueblo (an agricultural settlement) and of the citrus plantations managed to do without imported water. Los Angeles without its millions and without its aqueducts would be a modest ecology indeed, but hardly a desert.

Isherwood closes the passage with a slippery equation of technology and falsehood—"the lights snap on in their sham jewel colors all over the plain"—that begs the question of why traffic lights should be viewed as ersatz jewelry, something neither their inventors nor those who depend on them have ever imagined. If not exactly in bad faith, Isherwood's characterization of L.A. seems self-referentially literary, dependent on habits of accepting metaphors and analogies as arguments. Both in literary criticism and in more general cultural commentary, this strategy is widely accepted as legitimate: "[One] can draw wholly valid assumptions about a place from those discernible patterns of consistency and recurrence that run throughout a regional corpus. That is to say, though writer A, for aesthetic (or polemic) reasons, may portray a skewed reality, when writers B, C, D, and E portray in so many respects the same reality—as Southland writers do—marked not only by the same objective characteristics but the same states of mind, one can with assurance begin to draw inductive insights into the place." Tom S. Reck, piecing together only the passages describing sordid episodes and repellent individuals in the novels of Raymond Chandler, similarly concludes that L.A. must be a sordid and vulgar place, and that "it is not necessary to verify the accuracy" of what he calls "the Chandler vision."

One can imagine the same argument being made about 1700 to assert that California must be an island if so many reports agree that it is. Such a habit of thought seems to shape the received opinion that the past was better because L.A. had fewer people. As long ago as 1960, a local historian, Remi Nadeau, used "Tourist Go Home!" as the title for the first chapter of his *Los Angeles: From Mission to Modern City,* and as an epigraph he offered these words, supposedly spoken by a freeway commuter in a traffic jam, "My solution is to make everybody in L.A. draw lots to see who packs up and who moves out." Such attitudes, Nadeau states, would have been "unthinkable . . . a generation ago," but "life in Los Angeles, once famed for its leisurely pace, has become a perpetual jostling match."

In *Clichés of Urban Doom,* Ruth Glass argues that cities are likely to be perceived as too large according to relativistic or subjective standards, such as comparisons with "rival" cities and concern with the rate of growth, rather than according to actual numbers. Its 1871 inhabitants thought of London, for example, as larger than did those of 1971. It is certainly risky to accept the rhetoric of disillusion that extends through Los Angeles literature as transparent reporting of facts; more plausibly, such rhetoric expresses the futility of what David Wyatt has called "the belief that happiness can be found in natural space." Although the Los Angeles novel spurns such a supposedly naive belief, its substitutions are not necessarily wiser.

World War I Hollywood may seem like a quaint place to us, but in 1921 Stephen Vincent Benét, in images of exoticism, unreality, promiscuity, and perversion that link exterior forms and interior values, and that have never ceased to be popular, evoked "the whole arabesque and painted world . . . [of] artificiality and easy money from studios that were steel and stucco copies of Renaissance chateaus to febrile, sex-precocious little girls who drew salaries in the thousands and lived in the conjugal intimacy of a bedroom farce. . . . There were any number of overdressed young men, and most of them used scent, either in private, where it was a vice, or in public, where it became a disease." The imagery and strategies of the movies seem to have been a revelation to writers and intellectuals; the deliberate theatricality of "Ramonaland," symbolized by such structures as the Mission Playhouse in San Gabriel, became, from this time on, their great theme. The novel *Queer People,* a picaresque adventure in Hollywood, establishes a supposed distance between the real and the fake through descriptions of "a hybrid species of Spanish architecture" and a "pseudo-Spanish hillside home"; the question of what architecture might be pure or genuine is, characteristically, not addressed.

Benét's observations on the Hollywood of 1917–18 could have been the publicity for William Faulkner's 1934 story "Golden Land," a tale of a realtor who exploits his starlet daughter's wild behavior to publicize his business. As one would expect from the author of *The Sound and the Fury,* the setting is as important as the plot: "The terrace, the sundrenched terra cotta tiles, butted into a rough and savage shear of canyonwall bare yet without dust, on or against which a solid mat of flowers bloomed in fierce lush myriad-colored paradox as though in place of being rooted into and drawing from the soil they lived upon air alone and had been merely leaned intact against the sustenanceless lavawall by someone who would later return and take them away." The tiny, characteristic corner of L.A. here described is burdened with a language of perversion and betrayal unrelated to any plausible experience of the elements themselves. Faulkner calls attention to the absence of dust as if that somehow compounded the failure suggested by "bare," rather as Richard Gilbert, in *City of the Angels* (1964), complains about the "unnaturally clean suburbs." One might expect to be impressed by the soil's capacity to generate blossoms out of barrenness, but Faulkner "reads" the flowers as mockeries of stability and vitality, hinting at an analogy to funeral displays even as he overtly figures the landscape as a movie set. His mistaken notion that L.A. sits on volcanic rock ("lavawall") is less surprising than his apparent feeling that air plants—one of which, the Spanish moss, is a symbol of his native state—are unnatural or implausible.

Thirty years after Faulkner's story was published, Alison Lurie's description of an L.A. streetscape is still decoding images and drawing morals: "All the houses on the street were made of stucco in ice-cream colors: vanilla, lemon, raspberry, and orange sherbet. Molded in a variety of shapes and set down one next to the other along the block, behind plots of flowers much larger than life, they looked like a stage set for some lavish comic opera. The Southern California sun shone down on them with the impartial brilliance of stage lighting. And though it was late in the afternoon and late in the year, the temperature was that of a perfect windless June day." Trivialized by the allusion to childish treats (ice cream) and by the suggestion that all are worked into shape from a common, simple substance, the houses are, like toys, "set down" in an environment whose unnaturalness can be inferred from the size of the flowers, the strength and consistency of the light, and the strangeness of the temperature, by comparison with, presumably, that of Harvard Square, whose neighborhood the protagonists have just left.

Faulkner, who worked as a screenwriter in Hollywood for much of the 1930s and 1940s, for his own reasons contributed to the legends of how great writers were degraded in Tinseltown. In fact the many tales of his troubles with the studios do not stand up to examination; he even worked on *Absalom, Absalom!* in Beverly Hills and read its proofs in Pacific Palisades. His Los Angeles, like the Yoknapatawpha of that highly wrought novel, is the product of a writer's desire for correspondence between action and setting, and just as "Golden Land" is a narrative of treachery and, by his standards, perversion (the protagonist's son Voyd likes to wear a brassiere), so are its structures and landscape reduced by imagery of insubstantiality and illusion (eliding from description to metaphor to judgment) to the status, first, of film sets: "the city in the bright soft vague hazy sunlight, random, scattered about the arid earth like so many gay scraps of paper blown without order, with its curious air of being rootless—of houses bright beautiful and gay, without basements or foundations, lightly attached to a few inches of light penetrable earth"; and then of film itself: "that city of almost incalculable wealth whose queerly appropriate fate it is to be erected upon a few spools of a substance whose value is computed in billions and which may be completely destroyed in that second's instant of a careless match between the moment of striking and the moment when the striker might have sprung and stamped it out."

Edmund Wilson in 1940 asserted the categorical abnormality of *all* of California, where "the purposes and passions of humanity have the appearance of playing their roles in a great open-air amphitheater which lacks not only acoustics to heighten and clarify the speeches but even an attentive audience at whom they may be directed." As if to account for such a

failure to connect, he terms the sunlight "empty," "a golden and bound-
less sunlight that never becomes charged with [human] energies," a "non-
vibrant air," a "nothing": this language generates concepts of absence or
void like the "void of the vast Pacific," which inexplicably "seems ex-
pressionless and purposeless after the moody assaults of the Atlantic."

Agreeing that it is important "to find a language for the reality of the
[Californian] experience," he nonetheless reverts to demonizing Los Angeles, which he calls "gigantic and vulgar, like one of those synthetic California flowers . . . [it] tend[s] to drain the soil of the imaginative life of
the State." Presumably, if the flower is capable of "draining" anything,
"synthetic" must mean "hybrid" rather than "artificial," although it is
difficult to take such a figure of speech seriously. It is equally difficult to
know why, if talent exists in California and if it is recognized and rewarded
in L.A., the vampire metaphor is appropriate; it was probably irresistible,
however, as a veiled reference to Los Angeles's importation of water. The
real force of the metaphor comes from a guilty conscience about the Owens
Valley, which is not Wilson's subject at all.

Wilson's effort to give significance to the sunlight—or, actually, to
empty it of significance—recalls the ambivalent language near the close
of "Golden Land": "[The sun] was still high, still afternoon, the mountains stood serene and drab against it; the city, the land, lay sprawled and
myriad beneath it—the land, the earth which spawned a thousand new
faiths, nostrums and cures each year but no disease to even disprove them
on—beneath the golden days unmarred by rain or weather, the change-
less monotonous beautiful days without end countless out of the halcyon
past and endless into the halcyon future." Both Faulkner and Wilson implicitly contrast the "something" of weather in other places to its supposed
vacuousness or absence in L.A. It is to them and to others that Joan Didion must be responding when she argues that the climate, far from being "numbingly bland," is unpredictable and dangerous. Yet the weather,
at least when it is being criticized, remains a kind of objective correlative
of the city's character. A nonliterary event, an exhibition celebrating the
palm tree in Los Angeles, reveals how effectively the moralizing tone and
rhetorical strategies of literature have adapted to other media.

Los Angeles and the Palm Tree: Image of a City was an exhibition held in connection with the 1984 Olympics in L.A. Because of the occasion, it spoke more than ordinarily to the city's image of itself. Among the contributions to the exhibition catalogue, Michael Kurcfeld's is a touchstone of anti-L.A. rhetoric. He finds evidence in the palm tree for the depravity of the city, choosing it, apparently, because in modern iconology it has replaced the orange tree as the symbol of local promise; unlike the useful citrus groves, which are felt to be victims of "progress," the decorative, idle palm tree stands for the breaking of that promise.

Contemporary criticism in literature and the arts glories in a rhetoric of triumphant exposure. If a novel "about" or a painting "of" L.A. fails clearly to call attention to the gap between promise and performance, a critic is likely to supply the requisite irony and announce the demystification of whatever images the work has presented. Such are the cases of Nathanael West's 1939 novel *The Day of the Locust,* which explicitly ridicules Hollywood, and of Raymond Chandler's fiction, into which such ridicule has been mistakenly read. Kurcfeld shares with other critics the assumption that there has been a mystification—in the case of L.A., that the city has stimulated false hopes and ungratifiable longings—and that works of art deliberately or unconsciously correct that delusion.

The palm, in fact, is a kind of miniature paradise garden equipped with serpents in the form of rats. The trope of rats nesting in the palms, which occupies a terrain somewhere on the border of folklore and jeremiad, is predictably deployed today as yet another instance of L.A.'s decline. In Jay Gummerman's *Chez Chance,* a 1995 "L.A." novel synecdochically and cleverly restricted to Anaheim, the protagonist has lost the use of his legs after falling from the palm tree he was trimming when assaulted by a startled rodent. The rats' behavior, however, is not apparently a consequence of urban development; in 1883, R. W. C. Farnsworth described Pasadena in *A Southern California Paradise, (in the Suburbs of Los Angeles)* as full of strange effects: "Squirrels live in the ground and rats in the trees." "Those who will not learn from the past are condemned to repeat it" would be a helpful caveat not only for people who hang around palm trees but for writers and critics in pursuit of the incisive metaphor.

One of Kurcfeld's topics is Edward Ruscha's 1971 small volume *A Few Palm Trees,* part of the exhibition, whose sequences of isolated images (see,

FIGURE 33. Page from *A Few Palm Trees* by Edward Ruscha, 1971.

for example, Fig. 33) are termed "ironic" and "mordant." The irony and mordancy depend upon our reading certain characteristics of the image and its context as metaphors, for example, that the blank background implies the meaninglessness of the tree, or that their deadpan sequential presentation mirrors the monotony of the formless cityscape—"like Los Angeles weather," observes Peter Plagens of these same palms, "slightly different but indifferent."

Plagens's language refers implicitly to a normative climate of alternating seasons, whose "difference" presumably forestalls the charge of "indifference." Local perceptions of weather may be equally skewed to the norms of "back East," a condition that is corrected by lessons not in meteorology but in experience. Didion defines one of the uniquely Los Angeles states of mind and body in her passage on the unpredictable, dreaded winds: "There is something uneasy in the Los Angeles air this afternoon, some unnatural stillness, some tension. What it means is that tonight a

Santa Ana will begin to blow, a hot wind from the northeast whining down through the Cajon and San Gorgonio Passes, blowing up sandstorms out along Route 66, drying the hills and the nerves to the flash point." Though no advertisement for life in Lotusland, the Santa Anas as she invokes them are "weather," of a kind that stiffens the fabric of local experience. Understood as a kind of equilibrium maintained precariously between the atmospheres of ocean and desert, the Los Angeles climate may seem less paradisal than provisional. As in Frank Fenton's 1942 novel, *A Place in the Sun,* the balance can tilt suddenly: "The lingering mist of morning fog was rising and in the fog there was the salt flavor of the sea. Then the shreds of fog melted and the great yellow and white city lay at the mercy of the sun." There is no question in either Didion's or Fenton's observations of the "normative"; the region establishes its own norms, and its climate, like its ecology, is adequate to the demands of experience. Didion, for example, continuing the passage just cited, makes the Santa Anas as personal as a headache and as communal as an earthquake: "For a few days now we will see smoke back in the canyons, and hear sirens in the night. I have neither heard nor read that a Santa Ana is due, but I know it, and almost everybody I have seen today knows it too. We know it because we feel it. The baby frets. The maid sulks. I rekindle a waning argument with the telephone company, then cut my losses and lie down, given over to whatever it is in the air. To live with the Santa Ana is to accept, consciously or unconsciously, a deeply mechanistic view of human behavior."

Richard Gilbert, who complained about suburbs that are too clean, complains in the same sentence that downtown is too dirty. It is a characteristic of L.A.-watchers to be irritated by both a phenomenon and its opposite, and just as uniformity supposedly invalidates the climate, so variety makes a mockery of the architecture. Tod Hackett, the hero of *The Day of the Locust,* is a Yale graduate whose ambitions to be an artist (while he works in Hollywood as a set designer) do not cloud his ironic perception of incongruities. Through his eyes we visit a canyon in the Hollywood Hills:

> The edges of the trees burned with a pale violet light and their centers gradually turned from deep purple to black. The same violet piping, like a Neon tube, outlined the tops of the ugly, hump-backed hills and they were almost beautiful.

But not even the soft wash of dusk could help the houses. Only dynamite would be of any use against the Mexican ranch houses, Samoan huts, Mediterranean villas, Egyptian and Japanese temples, Swiss chalets, Tudor cottages, and every possible combination of these styles that lined the slope of the canyon.

The redeeming dusk is itself undercut by being characterized as a lighting "effect." West's critique depends, however, not on the supposed falseness of the film set, but rather on the correct Modernist position on architectural style. In conflict with one another, and borrowed from other cultures, the styles of this neighborhood violate the organic and antihistoricist dogma of advanced thought of the day. They are structurally improbable as well: "When he noticed that they were all of plaster, lath and paper, he was charitable and blamed their shape on the materials used. Steel, stone and brick curb a builder's fancy a little, forcing him to distribute his stresses and weights and to keep his corners plumb, but plaster and paper know no law, not even that of gravity." Like the ephemeral houses remarked upon in "Golden Land," these structures are meant to be read as metonyms for an illusory, insubstantial culture. Fantastic architecture, in fact, does not depend on the manipulation of cheap, insubstantial materials; the greatest examples were built of masonry and brick in nineteenth-century Europe. Nevertheless, Tod's final verdict is that they are monstrous (a word properly designating not the horrific but merely the unnatural), and therefore truly sad.

Tod himself lives in a cheaper edition of what he surveys in the canyon, "a nondescript affair called the San Bernardino Arms. It was an oblong three stories high, the back and sides of which were of plain, unpainted stucco, broken by even rows of unadorned windows. The facade was the color of diluted mustard and its windows, all double, were framed by pink Moorish columns which supported turnip-shaped lintels." Alison Lurie introduces a similar piece of residential architecture, but situates dishonesty in the name rather than the facade ornament: "Vista Gardens: a long row of two-story plaster apartment buildings backing on to the San Diego Freeway. There was no vista, of course, and no gardens, Katherine thought. This whole city was plastered with lies: lies erected in letters five feet tall on the roofs; lies pasted to the wall, or burning all night in neon."

Katherine subsequently fixes upon a revolving doughnut—an enormous piece of "signage"—as the best symbol for L.A., its "big empty hole going around and around up in the air, with some name painted on it . . . that's what this city is . . . a great big advertisement for *nothing*."

Tod's and Katherine's responses express cultivated literary opinion about L.A. architecture and the civilization it represents. This attitude is "literary" not only because it is found in texts but also because it treats the city as a text with messages coded in its phenomena. Modernist pronouncements on the virtues of organic form, the obligation to express structure through surfaces (or to make structure and surface synonymous), and the irrelevance of historical styles dictate an "educated" response to the architecture that, by extension, implies the unenlightened tastes and values of Los Angeles.

Thus the "Hollywood" novel, which is likely to wander into other zones of the city where "Hollywood" types are found, characteristically establishes the narrator's (or protagonist's) superiority through descriptions of houses, the most important of L.A. building types. Liam O'Flaherty, in *Hollywood Cemetery* (1935), introduces a Hollywood house "done partly in the adobe of Indian pueblos and partly in the English Tudor style, with mahogany beams that had come from the southern part of Mexico. The terrace, however, was copied from a house built in Jamaica by an Italian woman that had married an English planter." Inside, "a Roman arch" leads to a "vast drawing room, which was astonishingly furnished in the Persian manner." The description seems to generate itself. Christopher Isherwood is no less condescending in *The World in the Evening* (1954), the protagonist of which flees 1941 L.A. as a consequence of a bad experience at a party "high up on the slope of the Hollywood Hills, in a ranch-style home complete with Early American maple, nautical brasswork and muslin curtains; just too cute for words. It looked as if it had been delivered, all ready equipped, from a store; and you could imagine how, if the payments weren't kept up, some men might arrive one day and take the whole place back there on a truck. . . . Most of the houses . . . I visited were like that."

Like "Golden Land," Isherwood's novel equates L.A. architecture with the set, or props, of a stage, implying both falsehood and impermanence; like Richard Gilbert, Isherwood's narrator is put off by immaculate surfaces—"I came to a halt at the edge of the pool. It was brilliantly clean; not one leaf floating on its surface, not one speck of dirt on its tiled floor"—and waxes apocalyptic: "God curse this antiseptic, heartless, hateful, neon-mirage of a city. May its swimming-pools be dried up. May all its lights go out forever. I drew a deep dizzying breath in which the perfume of star jasmine was mixed with chlorine."

As it happens, the narrator of *The World in the Evening* is, in his own words, "floundering stupidly in the mud of my own jealous misery"; he is also scathing about homosexuals, using language like "pansy bastard." Perhaps he does not speak for the author. But in representing Los Angeles by Hollywood, and its values by its domestic architecture, Isherwood, like West, O'Flaherty, Aldous Huxley, and many others, writes "perversion" in a visual code, opening an unbridgeable gap between his readers and the city.* In one of the most famous novels of Los Angeles, *The Loved One* (1948), Evelyn Waugh relishes that gap, alienating us from a city he implicitly compares, in the imperialist discourse he cultivated, to a colony: "All day the heat had been barely supportable but at evening a breeze arose in the west, blowing from the heart of the setting sun and from the ocean, which lay unseen, unheard behind the scrubby foothills. It shook the rusty fringes of palm-leaf and swelled the dry sounds of summer, the frog-voices, the grating cicadas, and the ever present pulse of music from the neighbouring native huts." These are merely the Hollywood Hills, but readers of the London edition of 1948 might well have supposed, from the accompanying drawing, that L.A. resembled Zanzibar (Fig. 34; the foothills are missing and the "unseen" ocean is clearly visible). "In that kindly light," Waugh continues, "the stained and blistered paint of the bungalow and the plot of weeds between the veranda and the dry water-hole lost their extreme shabbiness, and the two Englishmen, each in his rocking-chair, each with his whisky and soda and his outdated magazine, the counterparts of numberless fellow-countrymen exiled in the barbarous regions of the world, shared in the brief illusory rehabilitation." Waugh's chosen moment is the same as West's, a twilight that gives the illusion—by which the narrator and his readers, however, are not deceived—that the ugly foothills are "almost beautiful" and that a region scarcely fit for habitation is "rehabilitated" as a facsimile of a civilized environment. In

FIGURES 34 *(left)* AND 35 *(right).* Illustrations in *The Loved One* by Evelyn Waugh, 1948.

fact, however, *The Loved One* subsequently bypasses customary descriptions of the city in favor of a detailed inventory of the cemetery that is its central venue and symbol. A drawing from the first edition (Fig. 35) exactly captures Waugh's emphasis, presenting "Whispering Glades" as a kind of proto-Disneyland, while relegating the city of the living to its indefinite margins.

Like Tod Hackett of Yale, hopelessly pursuing the would-be starlet Faye Greener, who looks "just born, everything moist and fresh, volatile and perfumed," Waugh's outsider hero, Dennis Barlow, is attracted to a funeral cosmetician, Aimee Thanatogenos, whose name means "The Loved One of the Race of the Dead." Both women are one-dimensional foils to the ironic males; desirable but unsatisfying, they cap a series of dismissive symbols that include, in *The Loved One,* a local product called Kaiser's Stoneless Peaches, looking delicious but having the taste and texture of damp, sweet cotton. Richard Gilbert might have had this peach in mind when he extolled what must be England at the expense of L.A.: "Too many of the Los Angeles women were like meringues—attractive outside but sweetly empty within. One theory is that this is because of the boringly repetitive good weather so they never have the opportunity to enjoy the sad poetry and maturing experience of a dark overcast day."

A mature meringue is indeed hard to imagine. Sexist by today's standards, the critique labels certain shortcomings or vices of the culture as especially characteristic of women, as in Edmund Wilson's sarcastic compliment: "Los Angeles has more lovely girls serving peach freezes and appetizing sandwich specials with little pieces of sweet green pickle on the side than any other city in the world." Waugh is likewise on familiar territory in implying that women's relationship to their clothes reveals a confused order of values: "Which came first in this strange civilization, [Dennis] wondered, the foot or the shoe, the leg or the nylon stocking? Or were these uniform elegant limbs, from the stocking-top down, marketed in one cellophane envelope at the neighbourhood-store?" Like Faye Greener, Los Angeles is desirable, vain, opportunistic, and therefore contemptible—a woman, in other words, as seen by an angry or frustrated male. To this hostile rhetoric of feminization is linked an equally disparaging one of "abnormal" sexuality. Both have been taken at face value by mainstream literary criticism, as if they "proved" something about Los Angeles.

Walter Wells, for example, is probably right in linking the following images and events from *The Day of the Locust* into a pattern: Faye's swordlike legs; Homer's masturbatory manual gestures; Romola Martin (the only other woman in the Faye-besotted Homer's romantic history), described as resembling a man or a boy; a female impersonator at a bar shaped like a woman's slipper; the dwarf's lunge at Earl's testicles (here Wells argues that "sex is symbolically . . . wrenched out of order"); and Homer's interruption of the only sexual consummation in the novel (between Faye and Miguel). Such literary manipulations establish the exclusive, narrative-driven "half-world" of the novel, from which West acknowledged that he had omitted "any of the sincere, honest people who work here." His own words should caution against finding proofs of close relationship between narrative and place, as if the "moral decay" of Los Angeles were the necessary precondition for such writing.

Historian Kevin Starr appears, however, to accept such evidence when

he generalizes that "something happened in Southern California during
the 1930s. Some new vision of evil rushed in upon the American consciousness." He advances this claim with figures of speech like "the too
exotic gardens where vegetation rioted in a cancer of fecundity" and the
"flowers rotting from too much sunshine [that] pervaded the city." The
"cancer" figure begs to be corrected by Susan Sontag's devastating critique of illness as metaphor; like the image of flowers rotting from too
much sunshine (hardly the cause of rot), it moralizes the phenomena of
Los Angeles according to the norms of distant and colder climates. Glibly
equating place with behavior, rhetoric of this kind, whether of sexuality,
gender, or botany, deserves endorsement only insofar as it accomplishes
the goals of the text. It has no more authority than Isherwood's backward
glance, in *A Single Man,* from the rapacious sixties to "the tacky sleepy
slowpoke Los Angeles of the thirties," the period of several of the most
conspicuous literary assaults on L.A.'s alleged decadence.

Yet such rhetoric is still pervasive enough to shape attitudes within the
community, like that of a man interviewed for a *Los Angeles Times* article
on autumn in L.A., who complained that the good weather kept people
from staying indoors, where the stress of enforced companionship would
bond families more strongly together. If this complaint marks the comic
boundary of self-pity, its tragic dimension is asserted by the extensive literature of destruction that imagines the city as most truly itself when, layers of self-deception fallen away, it is reduced to ashes, desert, or the grave.
Starr characterizes the thirties as the epoch of "the sunshine mocking the
defeated hopes of midwesterners in sport clothes who were angry with
themselves and with Southern California because what they had come for
was not there." Surely he is recalling West's famous Hollywood crowds
whose progression from disappointment to violence is described in both
the first and the last chapters of *The Day of the Locust.* The only profit Tod
Hackett makes of his sojourn in L.A. is his (projected) painting of these
people, favorite objects of his analysis, in the act of destruction:

> Across the top, parallel with the frame, he had drawn the burning city, a
> great bonfire of architectural styles, ranging from Egyptian to Cape Cod
> colonial. Through the center, winding from left to right, was a long hill
> street and down it, spilling into the middle foreground, came the mob

carrying baseball bats and torches. For the faces of its members, he was using the innumerable sketches he had made of the people who come to California to die; the cultists of all sorts, economic as well as religious, the wave, airplane, funeral and preview watchers—all those poor devils who can only be stirred by the promise of miracles and then only to violence.

Citing this passage, Robert M. Fogelson, in *The Fragmented Metropolis: Los Angeles 1850–1930,* challenges West's assumptions, arguing that these transplanted midwesterners compensated for the loss of "community" by absorbing themselves in the rewards of family life and material possessions, forging friendships through institutional affiliations rather than neighborhoods. This analysis sounds so representative of middle-class L.A. today as to be unexceptionable. Yet West's fantasy of revenge masquerading as acute social observation completes an elaborate account of love betrayed, distinguishing clearly between the easterner who sublimates his suffering into art and the neo-Californians whose less meaningful response gives him useful material. The alleged betrayal, though projected upon a critical mass of the population, is a rationalization of personal rather than cultural failure—in Tod's case, an inability to make his mark either in love (he includes Faye in the mob) or in his career. If he is disillusioned about anything, it is about the meaningfulness of sexual desire, and this is not news, even in L.A. The novel leads one to the conclusion that it is not the lovers but the haters of Los Angeles who are the true narcissists: looking at the city, they see only themselves.

An instance is a piece of literary analysis entitled "Raymond Chandler's City of Lies," which acknowledges that art historians now understand the Art Deco architecture of the twenties and thirties as an imaginative celebration of technology and a creation of an imagery of "the future," but which nonetheless disparages such design for evading the real social problems of its era. This failing can supposedly be read in its brilliant surfaces and ornament, which amount to "contrivance" and "deception"; the author cites another critic who characterizes the extension of Art Deco stylization into the design of everyday objects as "meretricious." These interpretations broaden into claims for the "mendacity of Southern California life," "the fraudulence at the heart of the culture," and "pretense, [which in] Los Angeles . . . holds dominion over all facets of experience."

Originating in Chandler's invention of Philip Marlowe's treacherous milieu, these statements have been routed through the décor of the actual city to become conclusions based on no more evidence than themselves.

Such a circular sense of reality characterizes Maria Wyeth, the freeway cavalier of Didion's *Play It as It Lays* (1970), whose capacity for identification with space and place is a triumph of the neurotic self over objective reality. Her situation is one about which Didion elsewhere generalizes: "We tell ourselves stories in order to live. . . . We live entirely, especially if we are writers, by the imposition of a narrative line upon disparate images, by the 'ideas' with which we have learned to freeze the shifting phantasmagoria which is our actual experience." The Los Angeles of fiction and critical commentary is such a story. Because it is frequently moving, entertaining, and stylish, that story—of high ideals, disappointed expectations, cruel awakenings, and an absurd civilization—has shaped the received literary image of Los Angeles as a strange place, reached by a journey, enjoyed, railed against, and ultimately rejected. This spiritual journey is deeply satisfying to millions and has established Los Angeles as an international object lesson in human immaturity, a kind of theme park of adolescence, whose representative citizens resemble Faye Greener, "who often spent the whole day making up stories," and whose verdict is delivered by those who, like Dennis Barlow with his fare back to England paid or Tod Hackett with an idea for a painting, escape. It is a measure of Didion's clear vision, by contrast, that Maria, and not the city, disintegrates.

West's or Waugh's fictions, of course, are not thereby proved false, but the comparison suggests grounds for reevaluating these and similar stories as fables rather than as realistic narratives about Los Angeles. Their authors saw L.A. as newcomers, and some will contest the legitimacy of their points of view. For instance, surveying the entertaining, stylish, possibly even moving freaks' gallery *Daydream Houses of L.A.,* by the Anglo-American architectural critic Charles Jencks, Chris Dawson objects that "the extraordinary thing about L.A. is not simply that these houses exist, but that hundreds and thousands of them exist. This is true of almost all aspects of life here[:] . . . things . . . may seem extraordinary to the visitor, but . . . are ordinary to the locals." A kind of instant encapsulization of the familiar "ironic" perceptions of a visitor drives the brief treatment of L.A. lodged within Jay McInerney's ambivalent celebration of the wonders and terrors of New York, *Brightness Falls* (1992). Escaping from marital and corporate reversals in Manhattan, the main male character arrives in "hot, smoky" Los Angeles, whose "sun was always shining idiotically"; from the window of his limo leaving LAX he spots "a sign that said NUDE COCK-TAILS." Subsequent impressions are of "brilliant gardens and blue-green pools flourish[ing] in the rock crevices" and of a hotel that sounds a lot like the Chateau Marmont, "a literal translation of a Loire Valley castle towering above the palm trees." The supposed incongruities between, on the one hand, the earth and the vegetation, and between, on the other, the vegetation and the architecture, are not even directly pointed out: they are already coded into the literary tradition. When Françoise Sagan begins a novel with such inexact—one might say, unidiomatic—geography as "The coast road, at Santa Monica, near Hollywood," there is reason to complain that for many writers, L.A. is nothing but a "location." Her compatriot Romain Gary, writing of L.A. in 1967, glibly reiterates the orthodoxies of the moment: "Ten years ago those scrub-covered hills [i.e., of Griffith Park] were a favorite place for lovers of nature and simply lovers; today, people take a drive through this wilderness but rarely leave their cars. The crime rate is rising."

A passage chosen at random from an English novel of 1988 offers the old script with some updated scenery:

> We took more crystal Methedrine. We drove to Brentwood, to the No-Name Bar on San Vicente, a place which had only been open a few weeks and was built in imitation of the *Cheers* TV show. . . .
> "Tastes like a tyre," a man at the bar was saying, pushing away a plate that carried a barely touched hamburger. "Tell Bernice she didn't grill this burger. She leased it from Goodyear.". . . When he discovered I was English [Horace Schwartz] asked if I found Los Angeles amusing.
> "That's not quite the word," I said.
> Schwartz said, "LA's all right so long as you remember that when Chandler said it was a city with the personality of a paper cup he intended a compliment."

"Amusing" strikes a false note, exposing the author's shaky familiarity with the idiom of a Horace Schwartz. But familiarity, also, can breed contempt. A sensational verdict concludes native Angeleno Bret Easton Ellis's *Less Than Zero* (1985):

> There was a song I heard when I was in Los Angeles by a local group. The song was called "Los Angeles" and the words and images were so harsh and bitter that the song would reverberate in my mind for days. The images, I later found out, were personal and no one I knew shared them. The images I had were of people being driven mad by living in the city. Images of parents who were so hungry and unfulfilled that they ate their own children. Images of people, teenagers my own age, looking up from the asphalt and being blinded by the sun. These images stayed with me even after I left the city. Images so violent and malicious that they seemed to be my only point of reference for a long time afterwards. After I left.

To the deadpan diaries of a spoiled and brutal Christmas, this elegantly cadenced indictment adds evidence of feelings only faintly indicated before, in the repressed expression of grief for lost grandparents and for the "past" they embodied at their home in (perhaps ironically) Palm Springs. Indignant readers of *Less Than Zero* have called Ellis's teenagers to account for their failure of values but have not seemed dismayed at their lack of imagination. Yet it is their literalness of temperament (well presented in Michael Leahy's case studies of tediously self-absorbed students at Beverly Hills High School) that dooms them to seek happiness only in objects and physical acts. Fantasy and pleasure, externalized in Los Angeles as in no other great city, are absent from the consciousness of this pathetic band, who move like sophisticated androids through rituals of eroticism and status.* Their deeds are a kind of parable of the death of the heart, appropriate to L.A. particularly because of the dogged insistence of so many of its critics that the city either deliver the promised goods of paradise or acknowledge its fallen condition. That the real city must be generated in the spirit, which gives to mere phenomena a history and a meaning, seems utterly beyond them.

❧

Different stories, however, have been told. Raymond Chandler, for example, with nearly the opening words of his 1949 novel, *The Little Sister,* characteristically blends perceptivity, appreciation, enjoyment, anger, and contempt: "It was one of those clear bright summer mornings we get in the early spring in California before the high fog sets in. The rains are over. The hills are still green and in the valley across the Hollywood hills you can see snow on the high mountains. The fur stores are advertising their annual sales. The call houses that specialize in sixteen-year-old virgins are doing a land-office business. And in Beverly Hills the jacaranda trees are beginning to bloom." In *Farewell, My Lovely,* Marlowe is a passenger on a long, enforced, silent ride westward that evokes each neighborhood from Hollywood to Pacific Palisades (this journey is discussed in chap. 4). He reacts passionately to the structures, surfaces, and atmosphere of Sunset Boulevard, evoking a city adequate to the representation of complex experience: hedonism, estheticism, sensuality, greed, innocence, fantasy, and longing. Unlike West's houses, for example, fitted to their inhabitants like the architecture of fairy tales, Chandler's Sunset Boulevard sets no limit to the possibilities of experience; that it is the setting for what is happening to Marlowe is merely fortuitous. To the extent that it is a moralized landscape, it is generously so.

Chandler's Los Angeles is also "a landscape of shadows, of mists and exhalations and hidden corruption, of places like the ironically named Purissima Canyon of *Farewell, My Lovely,* where a gigolo blackmailer is beaten to death by a wealthy ex-prostitute." The passage alluded to bears out the distinction between the qualities of place and those of human behavior:

> There was loneliness and the smell of kelp and the smell of wild sage from the hills. A yellow window hung here and there, all by itself, like the last orange. Cars passed, spraying the pavement with cold white light, then growled off into the darkness again. Wisps of fog chased the stars down the sky. . . .
> Far off the purl of motors, nearer the chirp of crickets, the peculiar long drawn ee-ee-ee of tree frogs. I didn't think I was going to like those sounds any more.

Within the ellipsis, a man is murdered and Marlowe is knocked unconscious. The charms of the setting, delicately rendered, neither reinforce nor contradict the evil that occurs; what irony attaches to it arrives with human expectations and sensitivities and departs, leaving the canyon as it was.

Chandler's balanced view belies W. H. Auden's observation that his fiction surveys "the Great Wrong Place." In a kind of summing up, Marlowe, returning home after a typically difficult day,

> listened to the groundswell of the traffic on Laurel Canyon Boulevard and looked at the glare of the big angry city hanging over the shoulder of the hills through which the boulevard had been cut. Far off the banshee wail of police or fire sirens rose and fell, never for very long completely silent. . . . Out there in the night of a thousand crimes people were dying, being maimed, cut by flying glass, crushed against steering wheels or under heavy tires. People were being beaten, robbed, strangled, raped, and murdered. People were hungry, sick; bored, desperate with loneliness or remorse or fear, angry, cruel, feverish, shaken by sobs. *A city no worse than others, a city rich and vigorous and full of pride, a city lost and beaten and full of emptiness.*

Chandler's L.A. is a city of complex, often misdirected energies, but unlike the city of the satirists, his is not headed for an apocalypse. Aside from the dark events of his criminal plots, the city of his novels is an arena of desire and labor, not so distant from the city Igor Stravinsky, to the amazement of cultivated Angelenos, chose to live in. Eve Babitz (who elsewhere recalls Vladimir Nabokov's saying that he could live in Los Angeles for love of the jacarandas) tells this story about the Russian composer and L.A.:

> When I was growing up, civilized friends of my parents' and even my parents used to complain all the time about how the L.A. County Art Museum was a travesty unparalleled anywhere for dopiness. They'd really get angry every time they recalled how Stravinsky was never so much as nodded to by "the city." I used to wonder, when I was little, how a city nodded to Stravinsky. City Hall was all the way downtown, and Stravinsky lived in West Hollywood. These adults used to sigh and say, "If he lived anywhere else . . . *anywhere* else, they would have done something about him. But not Los Angeles." . . . The truth was that Stravinsky lived in L.A. because when you're in your studio, you don't have to be a finished product all the time or make formal pronouncements. Work and love—the two best things—flourish in studios. It's when you have to go outside and define everything that they often disappear.

The Los Angeles Babitz sketches in stories like "Slow Days" and "The Garden of Allah" is a place of creative process rather than finished products, vulnerable in its absence of monuments and monumental attitudes. In her account of how the film star Alla Nazimova fled her Sunset Boulevard villa in the face of fire advancing down Laurel Canyon, Babitz reinterprets the significance of L.A.'s totemic nemesis: "[Nazimova] suddenly knew that the flames could consume all she owned, she would leave for New York at once; there was no point in owning anything in Hollywood, and in this she had a curious premonition or grasp of 'place.' It's a morality tale of the unimportance of material things, though there are those who will say it's about how awful L.A. is."

Didion has defined "the city burning" as "Los Angeles's deepest image of itself," praising Nathanael West's anticipation of the Watts riots of 1965; elsewhere, however, she relates in detail the process and consequences of one of the major, unpredictable, yet inevitable conflagrations that roar across the crests of the Santa Monica Mountains until stopped by firefighters, a shift in wind, or the Pacific Ocean. Her context is a Malibu unlike the Sybaris of popular imagination, a place of labor and of shared responsibilities and anxieties.* The greatest of the anxieties materialized in the 1978 fire that ravaged twenty-five thousand acres, and with them the orchid greenhouse tended by Amado Vazquez, a place of "the most aqueous filtered light, the softest tropical air, the most silent clouds of flowers."

Products of the kind of professionalism and dedication that Didion also admires in the Malibu lifeguards, the orchids seem to symbolize the ineffable, exquisite loveliness pursued, so often to their disappointment, by romanticists of an Edenic Southern California. Destroyed by the fire, the greenhouse and its treasures are remembered as an unself-conscious symbol of the exotic appeal and vulnerability of Southern California, but because Didion assigns their glory to human dedication, intelligence, and love, they remain within the realm of the possible. With its emphasis on the dignity of labor, "Quiet Days in Malibu" is a landmark in a developing literature that appreciates Los Angeles as adequate to meaningful, heroic, and even tragic experience. Its corner of Los Angeles, the "place" to which all activities are keyed, furthermore exists *in time*, an element essentially absent from the satirical fiction that has so influenced its image, even to itself. Such a city has ceased to exist for the purpose of being the end of somebody else's journey and the beginning of their return home. L. Frank Baum, the imaginer of the fraudulent city to which Kansans travel at their peril, is fittingly interred at Forest Lawn. Unless Los Angeles is doomed to be read as a text that endlessly rewinds and repeats itself, its Oz image should be buried with him.

A Usable Past

Los Angeles is an epic—one of the greatest and
most significant migrations in the long saga of the
Aryan race.

HARRY CARR, *Los Angeles: City of Dreams*, 1935

In the Board of Supervisors' Hearing Room of the Los Angeles County Hall of Records one may study a surprising sequence of
murals—a Federal Art Project of the 1930s. "The general theme decided
upon for the murals," the official pamphlet explains, "was 'Streams of
influence that have affected California, illustrated by historical incidents
symbolizing or relating to law or matters of public record.'" Actually a
mélange of events, occasions, and objects, they are the granting of Magna
Charta, 1215; Cabrillo's landing at Los Angeles, 1542; Drake's landing
near San Francisco, 1579; the Declaration of Independence, 1776; de
Neve's founding of Los Angeles, 1781; the czar's issuance of the Russian-
American Charter, 1799; Jedediah Smith near San Gabriel, 1826; Richard
Henry Dana at San Pedro, 1835; the Treaty of Guadalupe Hidalgo, 1848;
and the Butterfield Overland Mail Stage, 1858.

Scale—the relationship of differently sized parts—has always been a

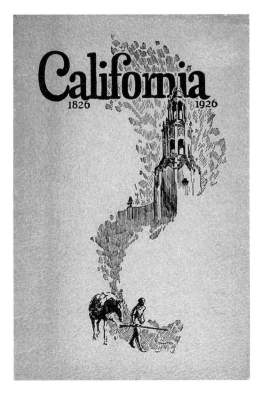

FIGURE 36. Publicity for the opening of the Carthay Circle Theatre, 1926.

problem for Los Angeles. Presumably Magna Charta and Jefferson's Declaration establish the lineage of Anglo-Saxon law and government, but, leaving aside the insult to both Spain and Mexico, both seem as beside the point as the Mayflower Compact, unless we detect a political agenda. Drake's landing suggests, unreasonably, a parity of English influence—carrying the freedoms supposedly released by the Charter—with Spanish, to be settled in favor of England's heirs (who declared independence in 1776) by the treaty of 1848. Thereby the glamour of Spain is preserved but subordinated to the manifest destiny of Anglo-Saxon government, whose provision for the rights of citizens is, in fact, extolled in the official pamphlet.

If the city of Los Angeles, in this sequence, seems overwhelmed by the burden of world history, it is L.A. itself that overwhelms in a far more characteristic type of local publicity, a brochure issued to honor the opening of the Carthay Circle Theatre in 1926 (Fig. 36). The narrative within the brochure situates the new movie house within the entire context of Cali-

EL DORADO
L A N D   O F   G O L D

A SERIES OF PICTORIAL
INTERPRETATIONS OF THE
HISTORY OF CALIFORNIA
WITH ACCOMPANYING RHYTH-
MIC STORY BY STUDENTS
OF OTIS ART INSTITUTE

THE BOOK OF OTIS
1 9 2 8

FIGURE 37. Cabrillo's ship approaching California, title page of *El Dorado: Land of Gold,* 1928.

fornia history, including the founding of Los Angeles, which is rendered in color. An illustrated survey of major events and representative episodes in the early history of the state concludes with a tribute to the history of theatre both in California and locally, a rundown of luminaries, and a mission statement about the surrounding Carthay community, whose streets and monuments memorialize men and events of California's past. Here the new theatre, like Los Angeles in the mural sequence, is on the receiving end of destiny.

Anglo mythologies of Los Angeles often presumed a fertile land prior to the Spanish settlement; Helen Hunt Jackson memorialized the Los Angeles basin of 1781 as abundant in trees and water, unlike in her own day. Yet mysteriously, the arrival of the first (non–Native American) settlers has been treated as a splendid event, executed with a European panache pop-

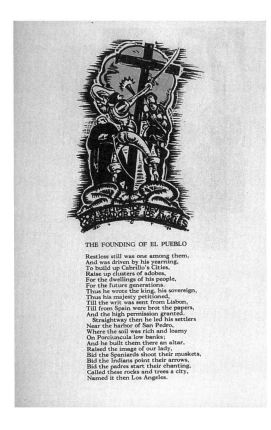

THE FOUNDING OF EL PUEBLO

Restless still was one among them,
And was driven by his yearning,
To build up Cabrillo's Cities,
Raise up clusters of adobes,
For the dwellings of his people,
For the future generations.
Thus he wrote the king, his sovereign,
Thus his majesty petitioned,
Till the writ was sent from Lisbon,
Till from Spain were brot the papers,
And the high permission granted.
  Straightway then he led his settlers
Near the harbor of San Pedro,
Where the soil was rich and loamy
On Porciuncula low banks;
And he built them there an altar,
Raised the image of our lady,
Bid the Spaniards shoot their muskets,
Bid the Indians point their arrows,
Bid the padres start their chanting,
Called these rocks and trees a city,
Named it then Los Angeles.

FIGURE 38. Representation of the founding of Los Angeles, from *El Dorado: Land of Gold*, 1928.

ular in local imagery well into the twentieth century (Figs. 37, 38)—in Fig. 38, the conqueror's stiletto heels press down upon the indigenes—and endorsed in the official ceremonies of 1931, celebrating the 150th year of the city, when a romantic scenario of the Catholic mass, other rituals, and speech makings was acted out. Jackson contributed substantially to the image of such a dramatic "Spanish" founding, writing of how "the twelve devout Spanish soldiers who founded the city named it at their leisure with a long name, musical as a chime of bells." This kind of language found its way into the semiofficial histories of the city like Charles Dwight Willard's *The Herald's History of Los Angeles* of 1901* and seemed to validate assertions like that of Louis Adamic in *The Truth about Los Angeles* (1927) that "the city's present unmistakably Christian character, its prosperity and all-round greatness, should be sought in its auspicious beginning."

Today nearly everything in Jackson's description rings false. The settlers were, in fact, overwhelmingly Indian, African, and mestizo rather than "Spanish." Her language ("devout," "founded," "city") imbues the occasion with a grandeur inconceivable in the context both of the backwater that was Alta California and the culture of the workers paid to settle it. The pueblo was not a mission, despite her sly association of its name with "bells," and in fact had no completed church until 1822. In a 1970 publication of the Archdiocese of Los Angeles, the Reverend Francis J. Weber makes the case that the Franciscans were actually hostile to the establishment of towns, that there is no evidence for Governor de Neve's presence, and that there were no requirements that a pueblo be founded in his presence, or in that of priests, or with pageantry. Finally, the much-ballyhooed long name itself, El Pueblo de Nuestra Señora La Reina de Los Angeles de Porciúncula, has been authoritatively debunked as the consequence of a series of misinterpretations and inflations of the actual name authorized in writing in 1781, "La Reina de Los Angeles."

Helen Hunt Jackson was not alone in publicizing wishful thinking as history. Major Benjamin C. Truman, a Los Angeles publicist since 1874, reported that the Spanish padres and soldiers chose the site ("the most rapturous and perfect") because of its climate and views. Such motivations seem an unlikely part of the Spanish imperial program that dictated the establishment of an agricultural community in the service of the military garrisons; Truman's language speaks to the values of his audience rather than to those of the settlers. The natural paradise he describes prolongs itself vaguely "about half a century"; suddenly, his viewpoint is retrospective, and we hear of a state of feckless unproductivity, of a "lethargic" and "somnolent" population "unconscious of the beauties and glories of the close encompassing woods and hills and the exquisite pencilings of landscape, sea, and sky." This state of affairs yields to the American period and a new population capable of appreciating the "irresistible glamour" of the place.

Jackson's 1883 account of Los Angeles contributed to the popular visual as well as narrative imagery of an "old Los Angeles" of European picturesqueness. A plate captioned "A Street in Los Angeles" (Fig. 39) evokes a city in attractive decay, like a Mediterranean town as seen by a

FIGURE 39. "A Street in Los Angeles," from *Glimpses of California and the Missions* by Helen Hunt Jackson, 1883.

British or American traveler of the time. It was her 1884 novel *Ramona*, however, that endowed all Southern California with a narrative framework for the past. Although Jackson's ruling passion was to expose the wrongs done by the government to American Indians, her enduring popularity rests on the sense of place evoked by her descriptions of the environment and social order of Mexican California. Her implicit strategy is to identify the society with the terrain, and thus to imbue the relatively stable qualities of climate, landscape, and flora with the nostalgia generated by the novel's sentimentally tragic course of events, both in the lives of the doomed lovers Ramona and Alessandro, and in the decline of their civilization.

Her reward was the internalization of her values by the very generations of Anglo immigrants who completed the transformation of a dry, bucolic countryside into an irrigated, agricultural one, and of the pueblo into a city of hustle and bustle. Paradoxically revering the culture that they had only recently displaced, devotees of *Ramona* began the Anglo habit of imagining one Los Angeles while inhabiting another. The key to this peculiar consciousness is the concept of "improvement," understood as both complementary to a past that must be preserved and yet contrary to one that must be superseded. "Nostalgia," which in its root sense means yearning not for another *time* but for another *place*, is actually another word for "homesickness"; Anglo Los Angeles was largely an effort to satisfy that yearning by building the imaginary home.

Issued by the Los Angeles County Chamber of Commerce in 1929, the pamphlet *Los Angeles County To-day* (Fig. 40) attempts on its cover to satisfy contradictory longings of this kind. A "Spanish" past, in the form of the arches of a colonial structure, both frames and introduces us to L.A. It is glorified in its architectural exaggeration, and safely in the past because it is ruined. To the left is a prospect of the bounties of reclaimed nature, and to the right a great commercial and industrial city dominated by the imposing new city hall of 1928. The mountain backdrop to both panoramas is nearly the same: each stands at the end of a vista, and we are welcomed to both by a kind of Flora, the goddess of flowers, a virgin dressed in the color of the magic fruit, the orange.

Appealing as the composition may be, it fails to make clear which Los Angeles we will experience at the end of that road, beyond that arch. The diptych structure implies equal importance of the two L.A.'s, the Arcadia and the Utopia of popular appeal, but it finesses the relationship between the two, which seem to occupy the same place at the same time. The imagery promotes the idea of "progress," but the composition denies the need to sacrifice the cultivated to the constructed. It is a "both/and" rather than an "either/or" composition, resembling the booster literature of its own and earlier times. Such unvarnished proclamations of L.A.'s desirability may have vanished or been refined into tools for marketing products and their images, but the dualistic vision of an idyllic yet dynamic city remains.

Robert G. Cowan's brief 1969 memorial, *A Backward Glance: Los Angeles, 1901–1915*, published for the Historical Society of Southern California, struggles unwittingly to resolve the contradictions set forth in the Chamber of Commerce's pretty imagery. It is the testament not of a historian but of a citizen and expresses the romantic boosterism and the bit-

FIGURE 40. Los Angeles County Chamber of Commerce promotional pamphlet, 1929.

terness of those who feel that their Anglo city of sunlight and orange trees has been taken away from them. The book is illustrated with forty photographs of commercial and residential architecture of the midwestern kind characteristic of the Los Angeles of the period discussed. Yet while eulogizing the early years of the century as an era of harmony and balance, Cowan characteristically succumbs to the temptation to glory in the city's "progress" and growth, the very factors that subverted the Arcadia for which he longs. "Los Angeles was progressing, though not without some growing pains," he formulates with an awkward ambivalence; "it was still in a most comfortable period of its history." It is difficult to reconcile the metaphor of adolescence with the "comfort" he memorializes. His catalogue of blessings is equally uncertain.

First in the order of his subjects are the topics that carry implications or direct statements of the disorder and inconvenience of 1969: smog, architecture, traffic, mail delivery, and children's behavior. Yet he destabilizes the 1901–15 period by undercutting his own arguments. "Smog was unknown," he asserts, evoking a familiar dimension of paradise lost, but in the same sentence reminding us that Cabrillo named the bay "de los fumos"—a bit of evidence often advanced to prove that L.A.'s climate is "naturally" smoggy. "The exterior appearance was not unattractive," he continues, with a characteristically ambiguous double negative, but the architecture "might be considered an unclassical hodgepodge." There remained, however, "a smattering" of gingerbread from the nineteenth century, evidence of "pride of workmanship." He is naive about the manufacture of late-nineteenth-century corbels and brackets, which were machine-turned, but his error is disquieting in that it implies a lost era of pride of workmanship that awkwardly antedates his chosen golden age. About the revival of "Spanish architecture" he is noncommittal, and on the look of contemporary L.A.—"brown derbys, hot puppies," and so on—contemptuous, yet his favored city of 1901–15 sounds far less sure of its architectural image than the later Los Angeles whose overdevelopment he deplores.

Uncertainty marks his account of the most everyday aspects of life. There were both gas and electric lighting systems, he explains, because the latter, though unreliable, was presumed to be inevitable. The furniture was "a mixture; a bit of nineteenth-century left-overs," some vaguely described designs of the period itself (called less massive and less disagreeable only than those of the previous century), and Mission Revival–style furniture that was "just coming into vogue." In a survey of a representative house, he calls attention to the indistinct function of the back parlor. Repeatedly depicting Los Angeles as in transition between a vaguely idealized past and a historically necessary future, the author muddles the conventional rhetoric of Arcadia, which operates by drawing contrasts between a catalogue of positive qualities (e.g., of climate, economy, and human relationships) and their opposites.

It would not be worth belaboring this text were it not representative of a reflexive way of thought in Southern California. Richard G. Lillard, a well-known historian, has gone so far as to compare the same era, ambivalently celebrated by Cowan, to the South before the Civil War, to Periclean Athens, and to Eden before the Fall. In language of, for 1966, astonishing sentimentality he writes: "While the men baled hay they sang together[;] . . . the young people worked cheerfully and flirted in the orchards. . . . The head of each household paid a two-dollar poll tax to vote or else worked off the fee with a day's work on the roads; a day spent working with a road gang was a happy one." Louis XIV's minister Colbert, who instituted the corvée, forced labor on the highways, would have approved. The complacent retrospective continues: "This was . . . a comfortable county world of stovewood from the canyon, water from the hillside spring, native trout from the creek, and squirrel dumplings made from chattering squirrels shot out of the wild black walnut trees."

The use of "chattering" to make the squirrels cute is a nice touch; perhaps it only unconsciously perpetuates the classical motif of the self-sacrificing animal that, like Charley Tuna, we may kill without guilt and eat without embarrassment. Yet Lillard also registers the characteristic note of instability: "It was a halfway Utopia of civilized development—post-frontier, pre-industry, pre-Hollywood, pre-automobile." His essay is in part a jeremiad on the kind of "progress" exemplified in the paving of the landscape, which prevents the earth from absorbing rainfall and replenishing wells and springs, but in part it is a tribute to the plants, railways, oil wells, and other marks of vision and industry that upset what he calls "Southern California['s] relatively motionless moment in history."

The ambiguity is a defining motif of the Anglo myth of Los Angeles, whose product and packaging may appear flatly contradictory. There is no question of deception (unless it is self-deception): the cover of the real estate brochure (Fig. 3), for example, that promises only innocent delights is meant to enhance, not obscure, the kinds of properties for sale and the afternoons to be enjoyed on their verandahs (Fig. 4). It is no surprise that only one year after Jackson's *Glimpses of California and the Missions* appeared, Jane E. Weeden published *Los Angeles: A Descriptive Poem,* the text of which is a versified city directory, inventorying services in doggerel. Nothing could more effectively counteract the extravagances of romance and reduce the whole to less than the sum of its parts.

So many and various are the colors and languages of contemporary Los Angeles that the "white man's city" of Anglo romance may seem not only racist but incredible. Little of the Mexican population, however, survived the period of the ranchos; most Yankee migrants in the late nineteenth century were of western European origin; and relatively few were born outside the United States. The myth of an Anglo golden age is grounded in the demographics of an Anglo city—which by 1930 had again altogether changed. Major Truman's histories prepare us for this golden era by denigrating the preceding one. He describes the region in the eighteenth century as a natural paradise, which remained pristine for "more than half a century" afterward. During this period it was "untouched by any spirit of progress, culture or art" and enjoyed "healthfulness of clime, equability of temperature, and a prodigality of soil." Truman never identifies what caused the bucolics of the missionary fathers to degenerate into the politics of the Mexican pueblo, nor is the war against Mexico addressed. Catholic Spain is revered for defining Southern California as a place, but its proper heirs are Protestant and white—as, in the common U.S. terminology of the early twentieth century, Latins were not. Equally important, the inheritors are movers and shakers; the enthusiastic appreciation of the landscape that Truman attributes to his own people sounds like a coded language, announcing but disguising the energies that, not satisfied with passive appreciation, will actively engage with and transform the environment.

Easterners who wish to confirm their prejudice that Los Angeles is a literary wasteland might enjoy the work of Selman Warren Stone, whose *Los Angeles Sonnets* (1953) are a jumble of noisy boosterism and romantic clichés (e.g., "Spanish Donnas, each twirling like a Queen / On nimble feet sped weary-nights away"). The author calls the cycle a history of Los Angeles and structures it on the parallel lines of myth and fiction that have shaped the popular Los Angeles understanding of the past. Moving from the prehistoric basin to the metropolis, Stone celebrates the incompatible blessings of a natural paradise and a busy commercial city. Erroneously landing Sir Francis Drake (yet again) in L.A., he implies—naively or mischievously—a connection to subsequent mercantile trade that caused Los Angeles to grow "gradually Empyrean on the Plains." Yet with a familiar lurch in perspective, he views "Los Angeles Way Back in 1899" (so one sonnet is entitled) as "a sleepy hill-town by a sluggish stream." What happened in between is not explained. Subsequent poems in the cycle are in the present tense and conclude with celebrations of the industrial city expressed in imagery of the region's natural beauties.

Such deliberate blurrings of a supposedly Arcadian past and a supposedly Utopian present—or a future on the point of being attained—sometimes seem calculated. A booster pamphlet of 1929, *Los Angeles: The Metropolis of the West*, advocates exploitation of the last frontier, the Pacific (a popular ambition at the time), and is filled with the rhetoric of progress and abundant industrial statistics; the cover, however, offers a cameo of a romantic senorita with flowers. The tensions and anxieties of the present are relieved, even nullified by a serene, replete past culture that never interferes but is always available when needed. Often the relationship is both close and patronizing, as in Harry Carr's 1935 cultural history and guide, *Los Angeles: City of Dreams*. An index of his clever blend of Anglo boosterism and promotion of the "Spanish" past is his account of how Olvera Street, a major 1930s cultural reclamation project that symbolizes touristic "Old Los Angeles," was formerly "a dirty alley, abandoned to slums and desolation. *Then we picked up our traditions.*" Through this scenery of, as he titles it, "Romance and Tamales," Carr guides a skeptical Iowan, impressing her with a few words of Spanish and his knowledge of Old California; the accompanying drawing restates his message, with the new city hall supervising the harmless amusements below (Fig. 41).

Henry Chapman Ford's folio volume *Etchings of the Franciscan Missions of California* appeared in 1883. Its oversized type and elegiac language announce the high seriousness of his enterprise, which is to record the decaying monuments of a vanished civilization:

> During a residence of several years upon the Pacific coast, I became impressed with the importance of preserving, in some pictorial form, the interesting remnants of the labors of the Franciscan Fathers, who overcame apparently insurmountable obstacles in the successful establishment of twenty-one Missions among the wild tribes scattered along the coast of Upper California. These monuments of the self-sacrificing zeal of the brotherhood are fast yielding to the corroding action of the

FIGURE 41. Drawing
of Olvera Street, from *Los
Angeles: City of Dreams,*
by Harry Carr, 1935.

elements, and, where towns have grown up about them, a spirit for
alteration has sprung up which has left but slight traces of their original
appearance.

The danger is explicitly from two directions: just as some structures are
relapsing into a state of nature, so others are being pushed into an unde-
sirable state of improvement, or "alteration." From this point of view, the
missions, in their intended landscape and condition, struck a balance that
was not only esthetic but also historical.

The subject of "Mission San Gabriel" (Fig. 42) is not a ruin but is drawn
as if it romantically were one. The power of this and similar renderings,
for decades afterward, lay not only, however, in their nostalgia; their effect was to suggest that the past was part of the landscape of Southern

FIGURE 42. "Mission San Gabriel" (1882), from *Etchings of the Franciscan Missions of California* by Henry Chapman Ford, 1883.

California and as such could be visited and, when copied, transferred to another place. The essence of this notion—the same as the faith that once impelled visitors to Southern California to retrace Ramona's steps and visit her supposed home—is that *time is contained in space*. This phenomenon, at the root of historical theme parks and sophisticated reconstructions like Williamsburg, is successful when the material past is animated and given value by cultural imagination, but misleading or even deceptive when the past is fitted to the temper of the present.* Recent experience in the Plaza suggests that the risk of misrepresentation is structural rather than accidental.

El Pueblo de Los Angeles State Historic Park, the problematic core of the pueblo, is one of the "theme parks"—as loosely defined in a popular architectural guidebook—that make up much of Southern California's public realm.* Symbol of a romantic and pious culture, its centerpiece, the Plaza Church, appears to link Los Angeles proper with the Spanish California of the missions; for much of the twentieth century it was regularly described as the "mission church." So labeled, it adorns *Los Angeles: City of Dreams* as both frontispiece and endpaper (Fig. 43). It was, however, never a mission; from the founding of the pueblo, villagers had been

FIGURE 43. Plaza Church and environs, endpapers from *Los Angeles: City of Dreams* by Harry Carr, 1935.

obliged to travel to San Gabriel for religious services, "and the priests seldom visited the pueblo, a point of controversy between the two groups." There were no attempts to build a church in Los Angeles until 1811, and the ancestor of the existing Plaza Church was dedicated only in the year of Mexico's independence.

A product of the Mexican rather than the Spanish era, the Plaza Church underwent substantial alterations in the following decades. The present mission-style belfry dates from around the turn of the twentieth century, replacing a Victorian gazebo that had in turn supplanted a single arch that extended the false facade of the pre-1860s structure (Figs. 44, 45).The new belfry has since conjured up a misleading image of Indians returning from their toil to the sound of its peals; adapted to an iconography of "Old Spain" (Fig. 46), the Plaza Church gradually assumed the image of a mission around which a town had grown. A further irony is the exact inversion of this process at San Gabriel, where not only did a town slowly crystallize, but the 1923 city hall and adjacent arcaded shops (echoing Mexican

FIGURE 44 (*top*). Plaza Church about 1900.

FIGURE 45 (*bottom*). Drawing of the Plaza before 1869.

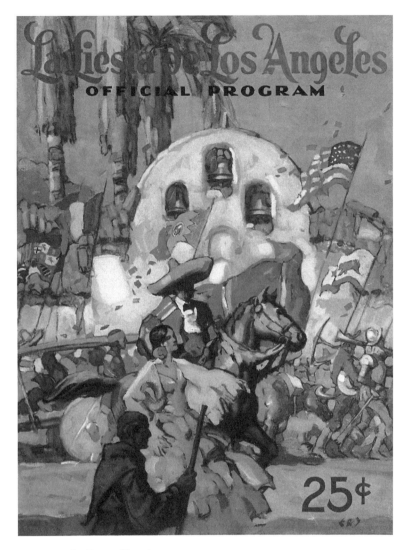

FIGURE 46. Festival brochure cover, 1931.

civic architecture) also cluster about the mission, as if to imply that the mission had always been a *pueblo* church presiding over a tiny urban ensemble (Figs. 47, 48; compare Figs. 42, 79).

Directly behind Mission San Gabriel stands the floridly romantic Mission Revival theatre completed in 1927 (and restored in 1992) for the staging of John Steven McGroarty's *Mission Play*, seen between 1912 and 1929 by about two and a half million people. Kevin Starr describes that production as a celebration of the audience's "Protestant" values of hard work and progress, anticipated by the padres' vigorous redemption of the natives from their idleness. To the extent that the playgoers of that time agreed with such an estimation of their culture, they found it provided, as Starr well says, "a usable past, a revered founding time, at once escapist and assuring, linking a parvenu society with the rich ecclesiastical cultures of Mediterranean Europe." As Starr points out, however, that past was grounded in a contradiction: "If, as McGroarty claimed, Spanish California 'was the happiest land the world has ever known,' and if the chamber of commerce approved (which it did) of McGroarty's estimation, then we have the paradox of Americans promoting their growth in Southern California via a mythic perception of a time and place that had been destroyed by the arrival of Americans."

Revisionist scholarship and cultural history today have tipped the balance of the Hispanic past from Spain to Mexico,* but they have not suppressed the desire to reinvent a replete rather than a marginal culture. The gradual manufacture of a synthetic "pueblo" has been carefully surveyed by Roger Hatheway. Visitors to the Plaza today may be sophisticated enough to enjoy shopping Olvera Street without taking it literally, but the Mediterranean look of the adjacent branch of Bank of America is so suggestive of sympathetic adaptation that they may be surprised to learn that this building originally had neither arches nor tiles. It was built about 1898 as the New Standard Concentrator Company and later housed a Chinese restaurant and a joke and novelty shop.

Serious political difficulties would arise today were Mexican Americans, rather than Anglos, to be deprived of a recoverable Old Los Angeles. Nevertheless, comparisons with Anglo myths of a Spanish city mysteriously destined to be inhabited by midwestern Protestants are telling. Ironically, the actual history of what is now El Pueblo de Los Angeles State

FIGURE 47. San Gabriel Mission after earthquake damage
(photographed in 1991) and (at left) the 1923 city hall.

Historic Park is multiethnic, as Hatheway makes clear; Chinese, African American, French, and Italian residents and property owners dominated the area for much of the nineteenth and twentieth centuries. Nobody wishes to excite cultural animosities around charming Olvera Street, but a claim by several of those ethnic groups for visible representation of some sort in the outdoor history book of the pueblo would be consistent with the efforts of generations of Mexican Americans to reclaim their own local heritage.

Beyond the borders of the pueblo, the ranchos, primary beneficiaries of the secularization acts of 1834–36, became, after 1884, the basis of an elaborate mythology. Their vanishing has been deeply lamented—both their society, in *Ramona* and its subsequent cult, and, more recently, their arid-climate ecology. Those complaints, however, merge confusingly with regret for the loss of the American agriculture-based civilization that displaced the ranchos, and even of the landscape displaced by the ranchos themselves. "Long since gone," writes Lillard, "are the antelope, deer, elk, coyotes, rabbits, cougars, grizzlies, condors, and a winged biomass of ducks and geese of the year 1781, when Felipe de Neve founded Los Angeles, and of many decades that followed. Gone are the grassy cattle-range

FIGURE 48. San Gabriel City Hall and adjacent 1927 commercial buildings.

lands, the big fields where dry farming brought in bulging crops of grain and beans, pioneering orchards famous for citrus, olives, and figs, and the truck gardens for strawberries or green vegetables, which were much of the low-elevation scene from 1881 until the era of World War II." Yet which of these several landscapes—wild, ranched, or cultivated—does the author regret? The second was erased by the third as early as the late 1880s, yet here they are collapsed into a single "past" from which we are irrevocably divided. In fact the two postwilderness ecologies are often imagined as one. In a passionate condemnation of development, Hildegarde Flanner, writing in the late 1950s, stresses the continuity of a tradition of "appreciation of the earth," and the *addition* of "sumptuous and orderly" orange groves to the "idyllic and natural charm of valley and foothill"; that "union," she asserts, is the essence of Southern California.

It was not exactly a union, however, that was envisioned by the creators of the citrus orchards. The English-speaking settlers of the nineteenth century were contemptuous of the indigenous population's failure to cultivate intensively; in his annual message for 1856, the governor of California lamented the new state's untapped potential.* Others dismissed the population as incapable of taking up Nature's invitation "'to the noblest and richest rewards of honorable toil.'" If the land was Arcadian, it was nevertheless incomplete, "requiring protection [and] needing the transforming hand of man to embellish, realize, and improve" it. A passion for development was fueled by an enthusiastic response (as Truman gives evidence) to the natural and mythic beauties of the region, with its echoes of the biblical paradise, and newcomers rejoiced in the esthetic as much as in the commercial potential of the soil. Edwin Bryant complained, in *What I Saw in California,* about the lack not only of commercial but of ornamental planting. Before 1884 there was no competing *Ramona* mythology of an achieved, replete order of gracious haciendas; rather, the terrain was figured as an underdeveloped natural paradise. As Streatfield says, this Arcadia "inspired utopian dreams," as of course it still does.

Citrus orchards, first developed commercially on a large scale in the 1870s, were the substance and symbol of the new civilization. Though linked with an old, romantic culture ("You pluck an orange," wrote an encomiast in 1878, "from a tree that was venerable when Charles the Fourth was king of Spain"), they testified mainly to the virtue and irresistibility of improvements. Seedling oranges had arrived with the Spanish in the previous century, along with grapes, olives, figs, and wheat, but it was the 1870s and 1880s that saw the introduction of navel and Valencia oranges, the Lisbon and the Eureka lemon, and (in 1890) the seedless grapefruit. In 1876 Magnolia Avenue in Riverside (Fig. 49) was laid out as an almost ceremonial boulevard through the orange groves, as if the orchards were the blocks of a city. In such a place, wrote John Codman in *The Round Trip* (1879), citizens "sit on the verandahs of their pretty cottages . . . inhaling the pure air or equable climate, reading novels, or elaborate works of philosophy according to their mental activity, from day to day, and waiting from year to year for their oranges to grow." The essential configuration of their environment appears less operatic in a photograph than on a citrus label, but no less tranquil (Fig. 50).

Had this system remained stable, perhaps only a few people, contemplating the thoughts of Jean-Jacques Rousseau amid the lemon groves, would have regretted pushing to the margin the people, wild animals, and entire ecological system of the older Los Angeles basin and adjacent valleys. Their system has in turn been destroyed during a century of dispersed

FIGURE 49. Magnolia Avenue, Riverside, from *Art Work on Southern California* by Lou V. Chapin, 1900.

growth brought about by the same values that created it. Immigrants to Los Angeles, with their small-town values and distrust of big cities, were the target population for the residential suburb; their distribution can be credited to an esthetic impulse as well, that of fitting the population to the envisioned climate of life in an idealized garden. The epoch of the orchards is also the epoch of the new towns (72,350 acres platted in 1887–89 alone) that eventually overwhelmed and uprooted what Joan Didion calls "the talismanic fruit." Writing in 1890, Theodore Strong Van Dyke speaks for those who saw the land boom of the previous decade as a violation not of a precivilized Eden but of an achieved order of relationships between men and the land: "Little it mattered [to speculators] where the land lay. North, south, east, west, in a hole or on a hill, it was all the same to a man who never saw it, never wanted to see it, and never expected to go near

FIGURE 50.   Orange groves, Riverside County (undated
photograph).

it, but did expect to sell it to some other ass in thirty days for twice what
he paid for it." Van Dyke's complaint must have rung hollow in Mexican
ears; he speaks to a particular and aging generation of Anglos. Development perpetuated the dynamic that planted the orchards; automobile suburbs have been no more destructive of the orange-grove and philosophy-
on-the-porch configuration than were the citrus farms of the cattle ranches
they dispossessed. Yet Van Dyke in 1890 and Flanner almost seventy years
later give voice to a continuing consciousness of values that, if not lost,
have at least been misplaced.

Anglos began to assume the burden of guilt for the destruction of paradise when they wept over Jackson's novel, whose dashing rancheros and
vaqueros seemed to populate an Old California altogether unlike the one
dismissed by earlier American observers. Similar sentiments are cultivated
by a very white audience at the annual Ramona Pageant in Hemet even
today. There is no paradox here. The myth that establishes Arcadia also
accounts for its destruction; it is only the latecomers and aliens who can

memorialize it. Their testimony to the value of the vanished culture is their penance for supplanting it. In any case, guilt has been displaced by the transformation of Old California into a province not of Mexico but of Spain. Helen Hunt Jackson is less responsible for this than are her admirers. In *Ramona*, the heroine's childhood home is described as Mexican, though with a Spanish heritage: "The Senora Moreno's house was one of the best specimens to be found in California of the representative house of the half-barbaric, half-elegant, wholly generous and free-handed life led there by Mexican men and women of degree in the early part of this century, under the rule of the Spanish and Mexican viceroys, when the laws of the Indies were still the law of the land, and its old name, 'New Spain,' was an ever-present link and stimulus to the warmest memories and deepest patriotisms of its people."

So tremendous was the novel's impact that to the second edition, only two years afterward, the publisher appended a description of "Ramona's Home: A Visit to the Camulos Ranch, and to Scenes Described by 'H. H.'" Two years later the publicist Charles Lummis issued a volume of photographs of the same estate in Ventura County, which Jackson had in fact briefly visited. The 1886 appendix not only treats the novel as historical record, pointing to various rooms of the house, for example, as where a particular character slept, but also appropriates the language of the novel to describe the existing house. Lummis's volume uses photographs for similar ends, but adds poetry celebrating the Camulos rancho as preserving "the heart of mother Spain."* There are no allusions to Mexico. A double process is at work here, of reading the landscape as if it were fiction and fiction as if it were the landscape—and that landscape is becoming European.

Lost though that world might have been, it was recoverable through the cultivation of the orange, marketed even (Fig. 51) from the Camulos estate itself. The ironies here are rich, not only because *Ramona* happens to be a fiction (but which many either believed or desperately wished to believe was fact) but also because the civilization eulogized in *Ramona* depended on wheat and cattle, not oranges. The del Valle family who owned the Camulos rancho had in fact pioneered citrus farming after the collapse of the cattle industry in the droughts of the 1860s; they were in

FIGURE 51. Citrus label from the Camulos rancho, the supposed "home of Ramona."

a sense proto-Yankees, one of whom earned a *Los Angeles Times* eulogy on his death shortly before World War II. The citrus label, while appealing to nostalgia, actually documents a successful adaptation to the new order; thus converge the mythologies of two desired Arcadian landscapes, one full of cattle and the other of orchards.

Because there has been an implicit agreement between several otherwise disagreeing groups that the Yankee influx irrevocably altered a rural society, it is worth recognizing a dissenting opinion: that by 1822, if not before, the pueblo was urbanizing. Howard J. Nelson cites the completion of the Plaza church (1822), the pueblo's elevation to the rank of *ciudad* (1835) and its being named capital of the territory (although the government was not moved to Los Angeles until 1845), and the listing of craftsmen in the censuses of 1836 and 1844, thus challenging the view (as in Fogelson 1967) that until 1846 Los Angeles supported merely a subsistence economy of farmworkers and ranchers. From Nelson's perspective, American rule accelerated, but did not initiate, a process already under way, which the rancho system, contrary to conventional opinion, had not seriously inhibited. Nelson's early L.A. was, as contemporary scholarship affirms, composed of many ethnic groups; to see them as citizens rather than as savages, peons, herdsmen, cowboys, and—finally—victims is to celebrate a continuing city rather than to bewail a sequence of obliterated Arcadias. This point of view is very appealing today. The small population and physical bulk of 1840s Los Angeles, however, whatever the ethnic ratios or building types, and the slightness of the economy, whatever its structure, weaken the argument. It is, nonetheless, a contribution to the redefinition of "primitive Los Angeles," a process that might be called the Search for a Usable Past.

Q

The conflation of images that produced the Home of Ramona citrus label was fulfilled in the architecture by which Southern California was substantially refashioned as an imaginary province of Spain. "The intellectual justification for this revival," David Gebhard observes, "was admittedly a bit thin, but it would be difficult to deny that the visual results were often impressive." In a confused appeal for a "distinctive architecture in Southern California," the Allied Architects Association of Los Angeles in 1925 endorsed the following propositions: that the region is Mediterranean both ecologically and culturally; that its architecture and landscaping should perpetuate the "collective memory" of Spain, Italy, and the south of France; that, however, the "seductive influence" of those regions should merely influence, not dictate, architectural designs; that Southern California is a land of romance; but that its founding was "sordid," achieved not by Spanish aristocrats but by "Indians, half breeds, and negroes, conscripts and undesirables"—behind whom, however, lay the glamour and grandeur of Spain, Italy, and so forth.

It is to the credit of the author of this statement, the architect Harwood

Hewitt, that he acknowledges the identities of the founders of the pueblo, now the object of revisionist history that takes pride in its Mexican (not Spanish) and mixed-race origins. A panorama of padres, dons, soldiers, and the governor, amid imperial banners and images of the Virgin, was far more to the taste of the time in which Hewitt wrote and was perpetuated in murals and children's textbooks for decades afterward. But Hewitt's appeal is characteristic of an Anglo desire to enjoy the benefits of "Mediterranean" culture without being tainted by its alleged decadence and dreaded dark complexions. Recognizing that the Mediterranean past is not the source of his own culture, Hewitt acknowledges that it must be conjured up, like, as he puts it, the "castles in Spain" of dreams, thereby to "give back to the people of Southern California that of which they have been deprived; a distinctive architecture that is theirs and only theirs."

How they can be given back what they never possessed is understandable if we allow that what is required is not history but imagination. Hewitt's editorial appears in the *Bulletin* of the Allied Architects Association of Los Angeles, which was published between 1924 and 1926. Its issues were illustrated largely with romantic sketches of "Spanish" Los Angeles but also with a De Mille movie set. For an era enamored of the spectacular temporary architecture of expositions, the architecture of the film set is both plausible and satisfactory. The tradition that Hewitt's appeal helps establish is familiar to critics of Los Angeles; it is that of the invented city, the film set become reality, and its logic is the suspended one of the dream.

The Spanish Colonial Revival of 1915 was one of a sequence of distinct but related Hispanic and Mediterranean movements in California architecture beginning in the late nineteenth century and still going on. What Hewitt somewhat tortuously calls for—in effect, an invented culture—had been unabashedly provided at the 1915 Panama-California Exposition in San Diego. Buildings representing California—for example, the San Joaquin Valley Building or the Southern California Counties Building— were full-dress models of what the architecture of these regions *ought to have been,* and consequently patterns for what it ought to become. A contemporary observed that it was "an attempt to embody the romance of old Spanish civilization, with its mixture of the spirit of adventure and the spirit of devotion, *to build such a city as would have fulfilled the visions of Fray Junipero Serra.*" Bruce Porter, introducing *Stately Homes of California* (1915), preposterously asserts that the contemporary gardens of rich Californians were "but a resumption—a return to the earliest precedents furnished by southern Europe and the transplanted memories of the missionaries." The past thus is created by an architecture and landscaping of the present that pretends to "revive" what never (in California) existed; what is significant is not the victory of any particular style but the mechanism of transmission and the order of influence and of events.

An isolated structure, a train station, decently landscaped and carefully framed by the photographer (Fig. 52) sums up the kind of public realm that was hoped for;* a long overlapping sequence (Figs. 53–63) dispassionately records how it took hold along the west side of La Brea Avenue between Fourth and Ninth Streets about 1930, and Mid-City Cut Rate Drug Store (Fig. 64), in exaggerated close-up, announces the decline. Various causes could be adduced for the decay of the experiment in Mediterraneanism, and all are correct at some point or another. Small businesses require signage and publicity in a way that large ones (like the railroad), civic structures, and private houses do not. Those signs are also conspicuously in English (which perhaps seemed reassuring at the train station) and are frequently out of scale with the facades and in competition with them and with each other. Law and custom in America argue against the kind of planning and control that could prevent gaps, or intrusive Tudor cottages, in the neo-Spanish street facade. Broad, flat, and seemingly interminable, La Brea Avenue itself trivializes the scale and ornament of the buildings; in cooperation with the signage, the roadbed defines the real space and implies the real activities of the avenue, reducing the fragments of Old Spain to ruins before their time.

Some of these urban sequences, like the Chapman Market on Sixth Street near MacArthur Park, are now being enthusiastically restored. It takes an act of faith, however, to live in an imaginary city; successful as Los Angelenos have been in accomplishing this in residential neighborhoods, they have not kept that faith along the commercial streets. The will to a romantic Spanish city was rarely, in Los Angeles, truly retrograde; there were few efforts to import the values that stood behind such architecture. It is better

FIGURE 52. East Los Angeles Union Pacific Railway Station by Gilbert S. Underwood, 1928.

FIGURES 53–58. West side of La Brea Avenue between Fourth and Ninth Streets (undated photographs).

FIGURES 59–63. West side
of La Brea Avenue between
Fourth and Ninth Streets
(undated photographs).

FIGURE 64. Spanish Colonial Revival drugstore smothered in
advertising, 1940s.

understood as a Utopian gesture toward the creation of a replete and integrated setting for the business of daily life, like what has been partially achieved in the streets of Santa Barbara, or, within its limits, at Balboa Park in San Diego. In Los Angeles, it was in competition with other such visions, and one Utopia does not tolerate another.

In the shifting ideologies of architecture, the pattern of a golden age followed by a fall from grace is the key to interpreting more than one style. Esther McCoy lambastes the Panama-California Exposition for corrupting a supposedly native architectural tradition with the "sudden self-consciousness" of the highly pictorial Spanish Colonial Revival. In setting a native against an imported style, she reinforces the mythology that a primal error has led Californians astray; hers is the architectural equivalent of the obsession with the Owens Valley water diversion. "Up to 1915," she claims, "California was remarkably free of borrowed architectural forms." Where once was "indigenous work . . . independent in spirit, noted for its freedom and form, its symmetry, and the flexible plan which reflected the needs of the user," there appeared a regional equivalent of the much demonized Columbian Exposition of 1893, said by McCoy, in the moralizing manner of the period, to have "interrupted the flowering of modern work in Chicago."

McCoy's complaint is not directed merely at appearances; she deploys the judgmental categories of modernism to a particularly Californian end, that of putting the case for nature over culture. A new architecture of the region was thwarted in its progress of "maturing naturally," and something not of the soil was planted in its place. Her contribution to the quarrel for California's soul is an argument for the transmission of an essence from what is unaffectedly American and western, via the high-minded Craftsman style, to the great Los Angeles modernists, Schindler and Neutra. In overstating the originality of California architecture prior to 1915—at the very least, the Victorian look of downtown L.A. (Fig. 65) might have been acknowledged—McCoy selectively defines a genuine as opposed to a factitious California. By comparison, Hewitt sounds naive, but both are struggling to shape the future by controlling the past.

Theory and criticism have, in fact, risen to the challenge posed by history to myth. An instance is the architecture of Wallace Neff, the most im-

FIGURE 65. The Victorian look of downtown Los Angeles: drawing from *Pen Sketches of Los Angeles*, 1896.

itated California architect of the middle and late 1920s.* Long disparaged as "theatrical," Neff's work is today admired for that very quality. For David Gebhard, "theatrical" describes "the finished building's cultivated lack of reality [and] the atmosphere of the silent film," fusing "the frequently played game between conveying a sense of the reality of the moment, or of the past, and the sense of a dreamlike quality of the improbable and unreal. In the twenties and thirties this architectural game was looked upon as an open, much relished sport by architects (and also of course by their clients) who skillfully manipulated a wide variety of traditional images."

The Thomson House in Beverly Hills, Gebhard says, is "Andalusian" in the sense that Carcassonne is medieval French—as one might prefer it, rather than as it was. What the owners, a scriptwriter and an actor, sought, writes Alson Clark, "was unusual, something that was impressive and yet thumbed its nose at convention in a nice way—imaginative, good-natured, whimsical grandeur, not mock impressiveness." A fitting emblem is the matched coats of arms flanking the window above the portal, which Clark describes heraldically as "a roll of film rampant over a horse's head . . . emblazoned with a horseshoe for the good luck needed in Hollywood." These sympathetic readings in part reflect the lightening of the high modernist burden and the lifting of the obligation to disap-

FIGURE 66. Cover of
El Dorado: Land of Gold,
1928.

prove of rich people's tastes in building, but something pertinent to L.A. is at work also: the process by which something threatening to the integrity of the culture has been accepted and revalued as essential to that culture. In part, that threat was Southern California's most popular residential style, deprecated as middle class and false from the 1940s on, but more recently defended, for example by Charles Moore, as "a Southland archetype . . . the image of our transformed semi-desert, climatically Mediterranean landscape, the architecture of our innocence. It is our primal idea of home." In other words, Spanish Colonial and Mexican Revival architecture are legitimate because they restore and renew the heritages not of those countries but of California itself.

The threat was also Hollywood and the illusionistic architecture of the movie set, which are now widely believed to embody values worth preserving. The successful accommodation of past to present in Los Angeles has come about, as Ford's San Gabriel etching suggests, by making the past accessible in the neighborhood—by what might be called the spatialization

FIGURE 67. Opening of the Vermont Avenue Market, 1931.

of time. Spread by the triumph of the mission style, which multiplied Old California in step with the burgeoning of the New (Fig. 66), the recoverable past was legitimized by the movies, whose often conspicuous sets—notably for D. W. Griffith's *Intolerance,* a Babylon in full view after 1916 near the intersection of Hollywood and Sunset Boulevards—competed successfully with the monuments of local architects.* In a city where the opening of a market was handled like a movie premiere (Fig. 67), it was inevitable that the distinction between stage and permanent architecture should break down. Lloyd Wright (aka Frank Lloyd Wright Jr.), for example, who worked both independently and with his father in Los Angeles from 1911 through the early twenties, and who continued to practice in L.A. until his death, used theatrical techniques such as "stucco-covered wood stud walls which appear to be solid concrete" and other illusionistic techniques, as in the Harry Carr House (1925), "where he stenciled on geometric patterns reminiscent of pre-cast block because the client could not afford the real thing." His Sowden House of 1926 (Fig. 1) looks "even more primitive than pre-Columbian; it is a cave, although we are at the same time fully aware that it is a stage-set cave[;] . . . the central interior court

FIGURE 68. Selig Zoo, Lincoln Park, Los Angeles (undated photograph).

with its pairs of Mayan-like stele, rows of piers and pyramid entrances are what one might expect to encounter in a Hollywood science fiction film of the 30s." The inner court was in any case designed to allow theatrical productions and film screenings in an atmosphere like that of the great movie houses. The circle was completed when the actual sets of films, especially those vaguely located in "Old California," became indistinguishable from the kind of architecture found on the streets of L.A. itself.

It will seem less peculiar to think of history as a sequence of places rather than periods of time if we recall that that is how it is, or used to be, taught to schoolchildren, whose studies of ancient history typically carry them from Egypt to Babylon to Greece to Rome. As a sequence of places, these cultures exist simultaneously as a gallery of recoverable pasts. Rapid growth, the yearning for a past, and the examples of the film set brought about in Los Angeles a landscape of atemporal historicism, one generally accepted and enjoyed by a public eager to possess the past on convenient terms. A corner of Lincoln Park (Fig. 68), with its "mission" and its subtropical vegetation, suggests that such landscapes can crop up almost anywhere, even at the zoo. It is appropriate that the theme park, which spatializes historical periods as a sequence of locations

(deeply indebted to the techniques of stage-set landscaping and architecture), is rooted in L.A.

For at least a half century it has been commonplace to deplore the de-
generation of "travel" into "tourism." "Sights" that have become classified
like objects in a glass case and travels that are ritualized into tours are set
against a standard of the "unspoiled." In this mapping of the experiential terrain, the integrity of a place, its phenomena, folk, and characteristic activities, can tolerate only so much intrusion by the curious before being "spoiled." The French Quarter in New Orleans is one of the threatened
sites, and the cable car rides in San Francisco one of the threatened activities; the overwhelming presence of *other* "foreigners" and the small numbers of the natives challenge the integrity of the experience. They may
seem like theme parks and rides in theme parks, where only the set and
the visitor exist. There are no more natives.

This allegedly deplorable state of affairs, however, can hardly be said
to have arisen in L.A., for the well-documented reason that the tourist industry preceded the sights, and the rides preceded the destinations. This
is not the paradox that it appears to be, for Los Angeles has similarly invented itself in other ways. The first and most influential of many promotional books, Charles Nordhoff's *California: For Health, Pleasure, and Residence, a Book for Travelers and Settlers* (1872) was commissioned in advance
of the wave of migration that it was intended to stimulate. Rail lines entered undeveloped areas of the region on the same principle, creating the
communities by first ensuring the transportation, and the Port of Los Angeles was willed into existence before the boundaries of Los Angeles even
touched it, and before it was dredged to accommodate large vessels. Especially from about 1900 to 1920, the interurban lines carrying tourists on
organized expeditions to Mount Lowe above Pasadena, through the orange groves to Riverside, and to Santa Monica for a day at the beach made
the experience of these sites possible to begin with—indeed, defined them
as beautiful things to see or pleasant things to do. The Red Cars did not
simply make the mountains, ocean, and orange groves accessible; they
linked them as events in a process, a mapping of a tourist's day (Fig. 69).

Certain destinations were even invented to justify the journey, like the
Ostrich Farm in South Pasadena and the Mission Inn at Riverside, itself

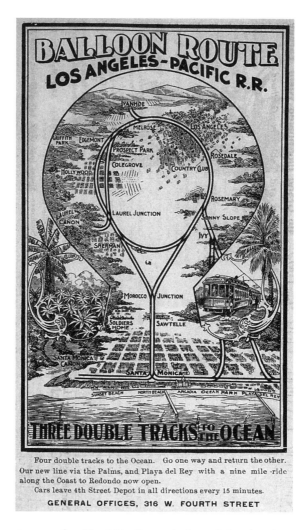

FIGURE 69. Tourist trolley route through Los Angeles County, from *La Fiesta de Los Angeles* (brochure), 1903.

an epitome of Southern California romanticism.* Venice Beach, though not created as a terminus, grew in tandem with the rail line that fed it. Tourism around Los Angeles consisted mostly of rides—up mountains, through orchards, along the oceanfront, and—at Catalina—over subtropical waters. Before the days of studio tours, there were two sorts of experiences to be savored en route: natural (including cultivated) wonders, and a free-floating romantic "Spanish" past, minus its population. Some sites were actually used as film sets: Busch Gardens (1903), seventy-five landscaped acres between Orange Grove Avenue and the Arroyo Seco in Pasadena, appeared in many movies before it was subdivided in the 1940s. The selling of the region to newcomers (both settlers and tourists), the preponderance of natural over manufactured attractions, and the multiplication of artifacts evoking a mythic past across a vast, heretofore nearly unsettled landscape, justify backdating at least to 1900 the metaphors of L.A. as "theme park" and set of rides.

Visitors frequently say that in Los Angeles they sense the passage of time only faintly. Usually this is attributed to the absence of the four classical seasons. The weather in Los Angeles, however, is unpredictable; as Joan Didion has pointed out, seasonal differences probably do less to define the rhythms of daily life than sudden, often unpredicted interruptions. The dreaded Santa Ana winds are the best known of these, but there are rare violent tropical storms and abrupt rises and falls in temperature and humidity, as well as startling variations across the city at any given time. This is nonlinear weather.

As a built environment, Los Angeles is similarly nonlinear, not only because it is so decentralized but also because its architecture, built so rapidly in overlapping waves of historical, innovative, and idiosyncratic styles, does not record the evolution of its culture in time. Architecturally, Los Angeles has been described by Barbara Goldstein as a historical pastiche where the appropriation rather than the invention of styles has negated any sense that architecture "develops" or "progresses" along the lines of a biological metaphor of growth, maturity, and decline. "Academic historicism," Goldstein argues, "would be invisible in Los Angeles," because the force of a scholarly quotation (a carefully imitated Palladian villa, for example) depends on the sense of the otherness and distance of the quoted source. Lacking a perceptible linear continuity with the past, the evocative, allusive structures (some naive, some ironic, some even mocking) that make up whole neighborhoods of L.A. align past styles in the field of the present. Although the period styles don't fool us—nobody believes that a Tudor cottage in Hollywood dates from the sixteenth century—they nevertheless, by blurring the concept of period, inhibit or neutralize rebellion; all innovation in L.A. is an accretion or juxtaposition rather than a negation.

Because of its perpetual state of innovation, Los Angeles is often, but misleadingly, called a city of "the future," a period subjected to frequent and embarrassing revision. L.A. is better understood as existing in a perpetual present, having interrupted the culturally induced sense of linear progression in time and appropriated the past to present uses. It has preempted the past. The lesson of its eclecticism is that the past is easily retrievable; indeed, the present is the assemblage of its parts. The Getty Museum in Malibu, for instance, *presents* the past with a bravura that has discomfited both the high-minded and the trendy, partly because it reconstitutes an ancient villa as if it were new, and partly because its presentations of immaculate objects are didactic, or, in Didion's word, "unrelenting."* Denying visitors the artificial pleasures of the patina of elapsed time, the Getty resembles other ensembles where there is a like accessibility to an imagined, pristine past, and where time may also be spatialized into equally accessible period zones, like Frontierland or New Orleans Square at Disneyland.

The ambiguity of "periods" in Los Angeles architecture is heightened by the juxtaposition of classics of the International Style with examples of the various Hispanic revivals, often of about the same date. In the work of Irving Gill, those styles even appear synthesized, for qualities that modernist theory took to be incompatible—powerful historical precedent and cultural allusion, and the imagery of white, machine-finished surfaces (Fig. 70)—are here united as early as the second decade of the twentieth century. As an assemblage of styles defying periodization, Los Angeles may claim to exist in an eternal present, but Gill has a special right to be recognized as the architect of an undated and undating present time.

Writing in *The Craftsman* in 1916, he advocated building a house that

FIGURE 70. Horatio West Court by Irving Gill, Santa Monica, 1921. Photograph © Marvin Rand, 1999.

is "simple, plain, and substantial as a boulder" and then allowing natural processes to soften and erode its surfaces, and vines and flowers both to brighten and to shadow it. He favored practical designs that would minimize housework and upkeep, and concrete because of its industrial and technological associations and because he thought it echoed the earth beneath. In the Dodge House, generally regarded as his masterpiece, he sought to elevate concrete to the dignity of stone, rather as Thomas Jefferson, in whom idealism and practical ingenuity were similarly joined, raised brick and wood to the dignity of marble. Interested (like Jefferson) in building for a society, he designed for the model industrial town of Torrance (Fig. 114). He is described without contradiction as both artful and childlike. Interesting works by architects who later moved in quite different directions, like Myron Hunt's Fowler House of 1916, buttress Esther McCoy's argument that a synthesis of traditional and innovative styles might have developed in L.A. upon the base established by Gill.

Although his work bulks small on the cityscape—a handful of extant houses and apartment complexes in various states of preservation and change, fragments of Torrance, and the persistent memories and photographs of what has been demolished—Gill is the moral touchstone of Los Angeles architecture. His work and its enduring mystique suggest several definitions appropriate not only to the built environment but also to the sense of time in Los Angeles and the sense of its relationship to place. One is that the past perpetuates itself, mutating through legends and architectural forms and rarely relinquishing an advantage. Another is that the present is synthetic, an accommodation of different "pasts" into a workable arrangement. Finally, the past is the necessary counterweight to the future in the architecture—literal and metaphorical—of the city of the present; the traditional, romantic, and kitschy elements of Los Angeles culture are as much a raid upon the storehouse of previous decades and centuries as they are an invention of an imagery of the future. As a sometime L.A. resident of the 1930s and 1940s, William Faulkner, observed, "The past is never dead. It's not even past."

4   The Shapes of L.A.

Los Angeles when viewed from the air, appears to
be a vast grid-like carpet that has been carelessly
laid down, leaving rumpled corners where the
hills and mountains surround the central plain.

SITE ENVIRONMENTAL DESIGN,
UNBUILT PERSHING SQUARE
PROPOSAL, 1986

The physical shapelessness of Los Angeles is
reflected in the moral anarchy of its people.

RICHARD GILBERT,
City of the Angels, 1964

❦

L.A. is today routinely described as a "postmodern" city. As
the architectural historian Christine Boyer has written, "Here there is no
opposition between the center of the city and its periphery, no distinction
between the built and natural environment to mark one's passage. . . . [Los
Angeles] is a non-place existing in constant flux and successive interfaces."
This flouting of hierarchy is not, however, a phenomenon of recent
decades; it is written into the evolution of the city as a sequence of nego-
tiations among competing archetypes. Los Angeles is an unstable synthesis of several conceptual models, each of which claims to give the city
its essential character. The fluid environment that Boyer describes is a consequence of the interpenetration of these models, each of which has its

FIGURE 71. Collier residence, South Pasadena, about 1895.

own internal hierarchy, but no one of which can dictate the shape of the twentieth-century city. Cases can be made for different categories, but the most consistent and coherent seem to be the following: *wilderness, countryside, park, village, acropolis,* and *road.*

These terms identify obvious phenomena of Los Angeles; they are also names for stages through which Los Angeles has passed, which continue to exist and which are frequently summoned up as models for a better L.A. to come. Because the city extends so far and folds back upon itself in so many layers, one or two are likely to be invoked, to the exclusion of others, when people try to make sense of "Los Angeles" as a unity—for example, in debates on the limits of growth or on the use of water.

A note on gardens: Although they are everywhere, gardens make up only a narrow conceptual model for Los Angeles. Even more in arid Southern California than elsewhere, gardens were not discovered but planted, by the same labor that shaped their context of streets and structures. There are exceptions: Fig. 18 (the Glen Rosa section of Pasadena, ca. 1880) appears to document a pathed and civilized town of giant plants instead of buildings, as many new arrivals of the late nineteenth century may have, at some dreaming level, expected to find. Their gardens (e.g., Fig. 71 as compared to Fig. 18) were, and still largely are, only a local instance of a larger design. The garden as the overriding model for Los Angeles comes into play only at extremes of the scale—either as vast orchards or as isolated flora, especially the emblematic palm. Regret for a lost city of orchards has been examined in chapter 3; the same desire and anguish has been transferred to the palm tree, discussed below. Gardens, a component of larger systems, are implicit throughout.

ℚ WILDERNESS

The deserts, mountains, and salt sea surrounding and penetrating Los Angeles belie the emollient climate that, most of the time, across much of the terrain, persuades native and visitor alike that Southern California is some sort of land of heart's desire. Patches of arid soil can be watered and elegantly landscaped, savage gorges can be planted and settled to resemble Tuscany, and the local ocean usually behaves as peacefully as its name suggests. But in combination with the wild, nearly unpredictable swings in wind, temperature, and humidity, and the inscrutable logic of earthquakes, L.A.'s natural envelope presses inescapably upon awareness like the imagined environment of another planet.

Wilderness in Southern California is entwined with the legendary landscape called the West. The West can be variously understood as a direction, an ecology, or a history; the purist Walter Prescott Webb limited the term to "the arid and semi-arid lands between the 100th meridian and the coastal ranges," so leaving Los Angeles in some undefined zone beyond. In 1858, Los Angeles's isolation, as much from Northern California as from the rest of the country, was announced on the map to anyone contemplating the risky journey (Fig. 72; see also Figs. 31, 32) across a terrain with no obvious trail. The West was a "flat surface leading to riches"; the line of the horizon ambiguously promised those riches, and Southern California might have seemed like either the last stretch of lands to be crossed or something lying on their far side. Defined as the land of low rainfall, the West of course includes Los Angeles, which, as everybody knows,

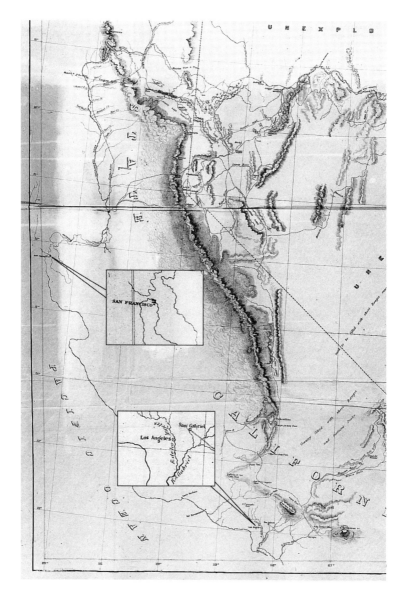

FIGURE 72. Detail of figure 31, showing Los Angeles at the end of the
overland route to Southern California.

hauls its water from afar. This importation, which is logically compara-ble to bringing fuel to heat northern cities, but is rarely so defended, arouses embarrassment and even guilt over the compromising of a dry wilderness landscape. Such compromises built "the West" as a modern civilization, and in this regard at least, L.A. shares the West's ambivalent sense of its identity.*

Behind the ambivalence lies a problem of ontology. Is the West essen-tially a frontier pointing to something beyond, whether across the Pacific, or across the stars, or toward a new technology or culture; or is it an achieved, stable system like that of the East or Europe? These questions may seem unanswerable, as they expose, but cannot resolve, psycholog-ical tensions between the anxieties that come with desire and the disap-pointments that limit its realization, or between the competing claims of a state of becoming and a state of being. It is normal to want the benefits of both. The argument is not as abstract as it sounds: debates between developers and preservationists express this deep division and perpet-uate the quarrel between change, felt as a creative act that releases hid-den powers (gold, for example, or water) from the earth and that sum-mons cities out of the void, and an almost mystical attachment to the land, an attitude both reinforced by and in conflict with the veneration of pri-vate property.

The West encompasses its contradictions when it is recognized as *a civ-ilization in the wilderness,* as opposed to one in a tamed and orderly nature. Los Angeles is its epitome, manifesting the wilderness not as a lost past but as an accessible present, woven into the texture of the built environ-ment and aggressively making itself known in phenomena of landscape and weather. How wrenching the struggle has been at all levels, political as well as ecological, to assimilate the land to the uses of city and suburb is evident when we compare L.A. with similarly proportioned London, which has taken so much longer, and been resisted in so many ways, in its absorption of the ancient county of Middlesex. Admiration as well as frus-tration and violence characterize Los Angeles's treatment of its natural envelope, paralleling the citizens' characteristic will both to dwell in the common Arcadia and to build private Utopias.

Two works of art (chosen from many) speak to the pressure and pres-

FIGURE 73. Desert garden, Huntington Library, San Marino.

ence of the wilderness in greater L.A.—the desert garden at the Huntington Library in San Marino (Fig. 73) and David Hockney's *Pearblossom Hwy., 11–18th April, 1986* (Fig. 74), which the artist collaged from photographs taken in the northern reaches of L.A. County. Both are desert landscapes telescoped and intensified, one by unnaturally close planting and the other by illusionistic foreshortenings; each makes quickly and intensely available the essential yet, because of the vast distances, dispersed and elusive constituents of the background to Southern California. Each testifies to a human presence that gives order but that cannot exercise complete control: the savage, intimidating plants belie the elegance of the "garden" and its walks, just as signage and litter stand (or lie) in problematic relationship to the inhospitable rock and sand beyond.

How is civilization accommodated in such an environment? A surprising visitor in the 1870s, Ludwig Salvator, archduke of Austria, prefaced the published account of his visit with a frontispiece captioned "Aus der Huerta von Los Angeles," or "from the garden of Los Angeles," using a Spanish (rather than German) word for orchard or irrigated land that implies cultivation (Fig. 75). As the plate shows, however, the terrain is indistinguishable from "unimproved" land, an effect for which some landscape architects still strive, especially since L.A.'s growth has caused dis-

FIGURE 74. *Pearblossom Hwy., 11–18th April, 1986* (second version) by David Hockney, 1986. Photographic collage, 71½ x 107". © David Hockney. The J. Paul Getty Museum, Los Angeles.

tant desert towns, well beyond the reach of the seaside ecology, to be redefined as part of the metropolis. The shift in attitude that has brought us to appreciate the desert as a wilderness to be celebrated and enjoyed rather than as a wasteland to be shunned made itself felt at the beginning of the twentieth century by writers like John C. Van Dyke (*The Desert*, 1901) and the transcendentalist Mary Austin (*The Land of Little Rain*, 1903). Modest affirmations of the principle may be seen in plantings all over L.A. (Fig. 76); they are not merely "desert gardens" but affirmations that the desert is itself a garden, and that Los Angeles is both. The local foothill stone architecture makes the implicit claim that people have a place in the California wilderness on compatible terms; "El Alisal" of the journalist and booster Charles Fletcher Lummis (to whose circle Austin belonged) and

FIGURE 75. "Aus der Huerta
von Los Angeles," frontispiece
to *Eine Blume aus dem Goldenen
Lande: oder, Los Angeles* by
Ludwig Salvator, archduke of
Austria, 1878.

the less visited Pitzer House in Claremont are examples. Stylistically, a turning point was reached in Schindler's King's Road House of 1921–22, expressing the imagery of the desert camp in the language of the new European esthetics and lending its authority to a local tradition of sophisticated primitivism.

Some have found the conditions and values of wilderness life in the supposedly privileged enclaves of the canyons, characterized by rugged terrain, distance from city services, the ancient chaparral ecosystem with its abundant, though threatened, wildlife, and the perils of fire and mud slides. Although a multimillion-dollar house hanging precipitously over a crevasse, its ornamental plants vandalized by deer, foxes, and snakes, may seem the stuff of a *New Yorker* satire, the way of life Richard Lillard ascribed in 1981 to some 16 percent of the population has been extended by distant foothill and mountain development—with occasionally catastrophic consequences. In the local hierarchy of taste, high marks are awarded to those who reconcile wide vistas and striking architectural design to a tricky canyon site, whereas excessive grading, destruction of the

FIGURE 76. *Hollywood Garden, 1966* by David Hockney.
Acrylic on canvas, 72 x 72". © David Hockney.

chaparral system, and even insensitive siting (the "pushy" effect of houses
on stilts that appear to strain for the view) are generally deplored—except
by developers and their clients. The basis of judgment, often explicit, is
the degree to which the wilderness characteristics of the site have been
accepted, with certain implications of the strenuous life and the sacrifice
of bourgeois amenities like a pool or a garage.

Indeed, a rarely acknowledged strain of high-mindedness in Southern
California culture has assisted the translation of craftsman values into
newer idioms, among them arid, low-maintenance gardens, materials that
are natural-looking (like adobe) or severely industrial, and pavilion-like
structures that admit the outdoors. On both flat and canyon sites, such
designs make, with varying degrees of success, the claim of perpetuating rather than eradicating the wildness in the earth. They are widely
known through beautiful photographs in glossy publications and speak,

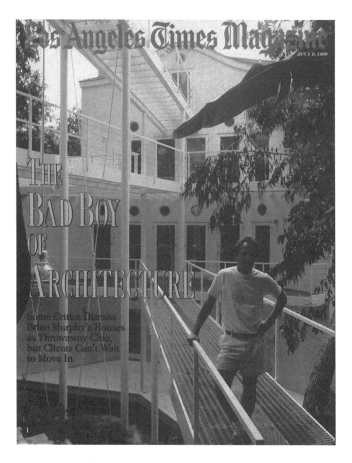

FIGURE 77. Architect Brian Murphy and one of his designs.
Photograph Tim Street-Porter. Copyright 1989, Los Angeles
Times.

besides, to the culture's admiration for the apparent emergence of the
sleek from the rugged—a process exemplified on an individual scale in
exercise-machine workouts. Canyon houses like those of the architect Brian
Murphy, for example (Fig. 77), project an image of technological daring in
the service of, rather than in conflict with, the improbably vertical sites;
this photograph, used on the cover of the Sunday *Los Angeles Times Magazine*, has been seen by millions. Delight in such triumphs of laid-back lux-

ury may be a form of self-congratulation, which certain artists would prefer to correct.

Sam Shepard's play *True West* (first produced in 1980) takes place inside a house somewhere on the margin of Los Angeles, possibly in Palmdale. It is the drama of a struggle between two brothers. One, a threatening figure, suddenly, from the desert, enters a suburban home. Mysterious and manipulative, he upstages his settled, screenwriter brother, from whom he has long been estranged, by persuading a producer on a Los Angeles golf course to accept his own rather than his brother's screenplay. Self-fashioning and adaptable, he is a survivor on both terrains, the wilderness where he has been living and the watered lawns that symbolize victory in the Hollywood rat race. One impression left by the play's announced symbolic structure is that the golf course is the desert watered— that one dangerously competitive landscape has supplanted another. Figuratively situated between the two, the suburban house, a local icon of the balance achieved between nature and development, proves a fragile and unstable shelter, easily usurped by one who understands the rules of the bigger games played on either side of its precarious civility.

The essentially "western" character of L.A. is revealed in a famous sequence of images, Edward Ruscha's black-and-white photographs collectively titled *Every Building on the Sunset Strip* (1966) (Fig. 78). Published between covers as a literal strip unfolding to more than twenty-five feet in length, Ruscha's architectural record, positioning one side of the street against the other across a void of white space, mildly mocks the site itself by degrading the artery that unifies (if anything does) the flanking facades. *Every Building* has been much praised for its alleged exposure of the shallowness thought to inhere in the buildings, signs, and occasional gas-guzzling cars, and, with less predisposition by the critics to discover their values in the image, for calling attention (by means of overlapping frames) to disjunctions and incoherencies in the visual experience of the Strip. However, "all I was after," Ruscha says, "was that store-front plane. It's like a Western town in a way. A store-front plane of a Western town is just paper and everything behind it is nothing." Behind the fragile facades of western storefronts stretch indefinable vacancies of landscape, suggesting a city as ephemeral as litter. It is not surprising that Shepard's wilder-

FIGURE 78. Detail from *Every Building on the Sunset Strip* by Edward Ruscha, 1966.

ness, both desired and dreaded, derides the political and moral pretensions of the city, but it may surprise that Ruscha's makes so light of them.

A common metaphor for the primal state of a landscape is "virgin territory," a loaded, dangerous expression implying that the land either is
waiting to get married or is vulnerable to rape. Many who are rightly
horrified by rape strongly endorse marriage. Los Angeles's ambivalent
handling of its wilderness heritage reflects a number of overlapping impulses to move both "forward" and "back," as if uncertain of the ethical
status of its treatment of the land as found. Acts of transformation—
unironically, of *civilization,* of the making of a city-state—have supplanted
the terrain with a series of, in the eighteenth-century language of estate
management, "improvements." Many such improvements seemed like the
biblically sanctioned plantation of gardens in the wasteland, and even today, in memory and imagination, they have displaced the earlier landscape with their claims to be the real virgin territory, the real paradise lost.
Appeals for the preservation or restoration of a landscape unaltered by

civilization may clash, therefore, with nostalgia for some displacing phase of that civilization. Vast orchards and seemingly infinite neighborhoods of modest houses in substantial gardens are the two most successful displacers of the wilderness model, and their incompatibility with each other, because the orchards were often leveled to make room for the neighborhoods, complicates the search for a baseline Los Angeles.

Los Angeles comes to terms with the wilderness by symbolically asserting its presence while denying its power. One vehicle for this exercise in cultural fantasy is the palm tree. Some twenty-five thousand of them were planted in honor of the 1932 Olympic games, and the palm has become virtually synonymous with the city. Introducing it into L.A. (only one species, *Washingtonia filifera,* is native to California, actually to Palm Springs) was of course not altogether a myth- and symbol-freighted activity; merchants are said to have favored them because their foliage didn't block the signs on their shops. But the palm's function in Los Angeles is the exact opposite of that of the nurturing, profitable orange tree, which it has altogether supplanted in advertising and display; the palm is conspicuously uncivilized, a desert plant that gives no meaningful fruit (date palms, another species, don't line Hollywood Boulevard) or shade. Even its oasis symbolism is usually nullified by spaced, linear planting. Tough but fragile-looking, it is valued esthetically, as a kind of alter ego to that segment of the population that admires feral elegance and as an affirmation of a desired wildness in the culture of the city. To assert that "Los Angeles *is* the palm tree" is also to assert that Los Angeles is the desert.

Ruscha, again, is clever about the deep background to the L.A. streetscape: his small volume of apparently arbitrarily chosen images, *A Few Palm Trees* (1971), treats its subjects as scientifically classifiable objects (Fig. 33). He informs the reader that each tree is photographed from the west, as if to establish an equivalency of perspective; each is presented without visual context but on the facing page is identified by its address. Either as plates in a text or, fantastically, as citizens, the trees cease to be wild. Arguably, the L.A. palm tree has mutated through endless stylizations in graphics and other media to the point that it is perceived less as a plant than as an artifact. A city that takes pleasure in the wildness of its artifacts also cultivates the artifice of its wilderness.

FIGURE 79. *San Gabriel Mission* by Ferdinand Deppe, 1832.

❦   COUNTRYSIDE

The Camino Real that linked the Spanish settlements of early California has survived as an idealized memory of a landscape dotted with significant structures. That significance is, for most non-Catholic admirers, only superficially spiritual; these structures' enduring power is architectural. This is a consequence not of the famous "Mission style," although its importance cannot be overstated, but of their presence as middle-distance structures adjusted to a landscape that they neither overwhelm nor disappear into. This relationship was apparent well before the American period, as an 1832 canvas by an itinerant German makes clear (Fig. 79).* Los Angeles at one conceptual level is a system of dispersed structures. Many find it most characteristically itself where low-density housing stretches indefinitely through its greater and lesser valleys (Fig. 80). Persisting through Los Angeles history is the rhetoric, enshrined in

FIGURE 80. Detail of a bird's-eye view of Los Angeles, 1909.

its own planning documents as well as in the abuse of detractors, of an anti-city deliberately or unconsciously rejecting the densities of street and housing that elsewhere sharply distinguish town from country. The mission and cityscape here pictured are images of what the anti-city seeks to accomplish: first, the fashioning of small, self-sufficient systems within a huge but definable and related context; and second, the dispersal of those systems as evenly as possible across that context.

"Countryside" differs from wilderness in being thoroughly mastered to civilized use—or, of course, abuse. In a region that has little "country" in the amenable sense of, for example, the Shenandoah Valley or the Kentish downs, Los Angeles is as much an invented countryside as an invented city. Like the Wilderness, this Los Angeles is pervasive but intermittent, never present in its entirety at one time; its sporadic development has been overwhelmed by pressures of population in some districts even as, or even before, it has reshaped the land in another. The vast Wolfskill orchard just to the south of the pueblo, for example, was paved over long before the watering, after 1913, of the San Fernando Valley. There has never been a completely rural L.A., postwilderness but preindustrial, of the kind imagined by Pacoast Brand Fruit (Fig. 24).

And it is not, in fact, on the citrus and other farms that we find the countryside that still demands to be implemented, or protests eradication, but rather in a series of constructions that mediate between an idealized countryside life and the business of the modern city. These structures and systems of architecture and landscape descend from the missions, in their found environments, and include great houses, certain residential areas, projects for large housing developments, resort hotels, and at least one stadium. Within a self-sufficient architectural context, each claims, explicitly or implicitly, to empower a moderately large number of people with certain prerogatives of urban life, and this self-referring context, whether a single structure, an integrated group of related structures, or a recognizable system of related buildings, is framed, enhanced, and justified by its natural setting.

One of the most frequent and disappointing sights in the richer districts of Los Angeles is an overscaled house on a measly lot. There exist dignified urban streets symbolic of wealth and power, in the Hancock Park area for example, but the cheek-by-jowl display of much of the better-known Beverly Hills flatlands has come to typify how the rich build. Land values are very high; it is unrealistic to maintain large grounds; anyway, from the crests of the highly desirable hills and ranges the illusion of a wider domain, to Catalina Island on a clear day, can be had by the very rich without the bother of rolled lawns. Around Pasadena especially (Fig. 81), this strategy was mastered a long time ago.

Before the higher reaches of L.A. were colonized, however, villas of the rich were relatively accessible from the city street. The essence of the ideology of the villa since ancient times has been the structuring of nature around a house built primarily for relaxation and the cultivation of the physical and spiritual pleasures of existence; one variant of that ideology has been the notion that the villa is a community of people and a model of a replete, self-sustaining way of life. The two imperatives—life in an idyllic garden and life in a community of manageable dimensions—give significance to several of the great structures on the L.A. landscape. Architectural style is of less consequence than the uses to which these es-

FIGURE 81. View over the Arroyo Seco, 1885.

tates have been put, and although the masterpieces of Charles and Henry Greene are not commonly mentioned in the same breath as Myron Hunt and Elmer Grey's ponderous Huntington mansion, they are alike in being models of the good life as locally understood.

Several large properties have survived primarily as civic institutions. Of these, Greene and Greene's 1908 Gamble House is the most revered, as it seems to incorporate the ethics of the Craftsman movement with the romance of expansive California villa life—in this case, expanding over the Arroyo Seco. Reyner Banham, L.A.'s toughest-minded enthusiast, describes it mystically,* and visitors approach it like pilgrims. Luxurious as it is, the house is a Platonic prototype of the democratic Craftsman style and appears intimately related to thousands of far more modest dwellings. It exemplifies the suasive power of a great house in a substantial landscape (careful landscaping and the vista compensate for the lack of extensive grounds) to sum up the "real" Los Angeles of imagination and desire.

The 207 acres of the Huntington estate in San Marino are open to the public as a library, art gallery, and botanical garden, according to the intentions of the railway magnate who shaped the estate from the beginning to its present uses. Sited to draw upon the dignity of the San Gabriel range backdrop, the mansion (Fig. 82) commands a vast, hazy panorama of undistinguished suburbs to the south. Its contemporary counterpart is the J. Paul Getty Museum (1972–73) in Malibu, a reconstruction of a buried

FIGURE 82. Henry E. Huntington residence by Myron Hunt
and Elmer Grey, San Marino, 1911.

villa and gardens at Herculaneum, built to house an art collection. Each
property sustains the image of a natural environment that both validates
and defers to a great house. The Huntington and the Getty are emblematic of a Los Angeles deeply desired by many, one that should dispense a
cascade of natural wonders without abridgment by weather or season. It
is a measure of Los Angeles's characteristic populism that these two vast
enclaves of apparent privilege (whose locations mark the drift of wealth
from the Pasadena area to the ocean) are both popular, accessible, and (until recently, in the case of the Huntington) free.

   Substantial estates like Myron Hunt's unbuilt Lewis Bradbury Villa
(1917) for a sloping site in Duarte, Gordon Kaufmann's 1925–28 Greystone
(Beverly Hills's largest house) for Edward L. Doheny, and Wallace Neff's
unbuilt 1928 design (his most elaborate) for Doheny's son in Beverly Hills
are more representative of the Los Angeles of private wealth. Distant towns
that are now fiscal and spiritual suburbs of Los Angeles—Palm Springs,
most famously—play host to large, well-protected estates of a kind now
rarely found in Los Angeles except on the crests above West L.A. and Malibu. One remarkable (unbuilt) project utilizing a characteristically lofty
L.A. site was Schindler's 1927 "translucent house" for Aline Barnsdall

FIGURE 83. Theodore A. Willard House by Robert B. Stacy-Judd, Beverly Hills, 1929.

above the upper coast of Palos Verdes. Extensive as these properties are, or were intended to be—the Bradbury project recalls a Roman villa—they are scaled back from the truly baronial pretensions of the Huntington mansion. In drawings, especially, their effect often depends upon an implied extension of the property into the air or over the Pacific Ocean.

Certain areas of Pasadena and neighboring towns especially preserve the vestiges of the extensive grounds that once surrounded such houses as Greene and Greene's Blacker House (1907). Here still, intermittently, lies a settled landscape denser in architecture than an exurban zone of great estates, but more spacious than a street of expensive houses, like, for example, La Mesa Drive in Santa Monica. The next step is an accommodation of the great house to the grid of the city block; a 1929 rendering of the T. A. Willard House, Beverly Hills (Fig. 83), by the Mayan-influenced architect Robert B. Stacy-Judd, will bring to mind countless L.A. houses trying to give the impression of plenty of front yard. Sequences of large houses in San Marino, especially those by Wallace Neff and in his style, stretch the city block, as an organizing device for a residential neighborhood, to its limit. At the level of the grand suburb rather than the country estate, these districts perpetuate the vision, however qualified, of a city of demesnes.

FIGURE 84 *(above)*.
Doheny Ranch Resort
project by Frank Lloyd
Wright, Beverly Hills,
1923, perspective
drawing.

FIGURE 85 *(left)*.
Trousdale Estates
development, Beverly
Hills, after 1955.

Frank Lloyd Wright created designs for a chunk of the Doheny estate
in Beverly Hills, perhaps (there is little documentation) as part of a speculative venture. The area is now known as Trousdale Estates. Busy in the
early 1920s on several local projects, Wright had already called for houses
to be "beautiful in California in the way that California herself is beautiful," asserting that what he would call "organic architecture" developed
rather than violated the inherent properties of the site. The almost Chinese poetry of his "wild, sharp ridges fuzzy with chaparral" (Fig. 84)
should be contrasted with the flattened, terraced hills as they have actually been developed (Fig. 85). Wright's unexecuted proposals of 1923 trans-
late the idealism of Arcadian development into his Mayan-influenced
textile-block medium as well as into the typology of a landscape of villas. Individual structures, though massive and domineering (Fig. 86), are

FIGURE 86. Doheny Ranch Resort project by Frank Lloyd Wright, Beverly Hills, 1923, perspective drawing of House B (detail).

fitted into the contours of the site, and anticipate the 1924 Ennis House above East Hollywood (Fig. 120).

The drawings propose neither a megastructure nor a sequence of roughly equivalent buildings, but rather a decentralized, though palatial, complex unified by ramps, terraces, and hanging gardens; they read equally well as an extraordinarily landscaped winding road on which the amenities of architecture have been lavished. Wright's linear organization implies indefinite extension and an absence of hierarchy; characteristically, his vision of landscape brought to life through architecture is as urbane as it is antiurban, somewhat like the epochal hillside construction at Praeneste in the first century B.C., both mimicking and transcending its site. This is countryside on an imperial scale. It utilizes the unique sites of the upper reaches and crests of L.A.'s rugged hill ranges, but to a purpose more consistent with the public-spirited accessibility of the Huntington and the Getty (both the Malibu villa and the new center above Brentwood). Unlike almost any other of Los Angeles's projected or realized elite zones, Wright's designs affirm continuity and communication between structures rather than what actually characterizes much of recent multimillion-dollar construction: hostile separation or awkward juxtaposition. In his painterly vision, villas crown and unify a landscape, and might have succeeded in giving the Santa Monica range the civic dignity and communal presence that their unbuilt state seemed to call for.

For much of this century the Huntington Hotel (Fig. 87, as remodeled

FIGURE 87. Huntington Hotel as remodeled by Myron Hunt,
Pasadena, 1913.

by Myron Hunt in 1913) in Pasadena has given visitors the illusion that
they were part of its neighborhood of impressive estates, among them the
Blacker House only a couple of (very long, curving) blocks away. It was
one of a collection of castlelike hostelries dating in spirit from the turn of
the century, when the conceptual model of "health resort" dictated many
easterners' image of Los Angeles, and when a middle and upper-middle
class of recreation as well as health seekers responded to the seductive
publicity of the Southern Pacific's subsidized *Sunset* magazine. The
Greater Pasadena of oranges, mountain expeditions, and a kind of expatriate eastern culture was the favored venue. Another hotel, now serving
as a federal courthouse and offices, was the Vista del Arroyo (Figs. 88, 89),
romantically poised above the Colorado Street Bridge within a few hundred yards of the Gamble House. It is a measure of how narrowly specific,
even fixated, was the imagery of subtropical repose, that the Maryland
Hotel's Italianate garden pergola of 1903 (Fig. 90), designed by Myron
Hunt in the course of his landscaping work there, was reproduced on post-
cards as a popular icon of Mediterranean California.

Even as Los Angeles infilled about them, the grand hotels like the Raymond (Fig. 91) asserted their visual control of great spaces. Carefully
framed photography suggests an aristocratic environment of chateau and
gardens, even where an actual city lies in view (Fig. 92). Distances and
emptiness were an early part of their structure and their scheme: on the

FIGURE 88 *(top)*. Vista del Arroyo Hotel by Marston and Van Pelt and George Wiemeyer, Pasadena, 1920; tower, 1930.

FIGURE 89 *(bottom)*. Gardens of the Vista del Arroyo Hotel.

FIGURE 90 *(top).* Pergola (1903) by Myron Hunt, Maryland Hotel, Pasadena.

FIGURE 91 *(bottom).* View south over the San Gabriel Valley from the Raymond Hotel, Pasadena, in 1905.

FIGURE 92. View toward Pasadena with the Hotel Green in the center, about 1907.

"Grand Round" of a day's excursion, carriage drives circled east and north of Pasadena, stopping, for example, at the Sierra Madre Villa, a resort favored by invalids, for its famous lavish lunch. Where such hotels could not command a wild or a cultivated landscape, they resorted to the classic L.A. maneuver, the appropriation of air and space; such is the key to the architectural presence of the Vista del Arroyo, and such would have been the effect, thanks to the Pacific Ocean, of Myron Hunt's proposed hotel (1919) at the terminus of Wilshire Boulevard in Santa Monica (Fig. 93). Soaring from the beach and spanning the Pacific Coast Highway, the hotel is an exclamation point anchoring the end of L.A.'s most aspiring corridor. Here it confidently restates the imagery of a city of baronial demesnes—great piles in a great landscape—on the newly chic oceanfront. Elsewhere Hunt saw his and H. C. Chambers's design for an Andalusian hilltop village materialize as the Flintridge Hotel (1927) (Fig. 94), one of a number of commissions that apply the imagery of a comparatively di-

FIGURE 93. Hotel project, terminus of Wilshire Boulevard, by Myron Hunt, Santa Monica, 1919.

versified, complex community to the purposes of one more homogeneous and more narrowly defined—that is, a hotel masquerading as a village. This kind of adaptation characterizes many recent, sophisticated L.A. projects, like shopping centers, campuses, and condominium complexes.

By their configuration of architectural grandeur within a substantial, even limitless, natural setting, the resort hotels perpetuated the dream of an innocent enjoyment of wealth and status. It is this dream that connects the typologically diverse structures of the L.A. "countryside," the structures that make up a city of "villas in a landscape." To the extent that Los Angeles has been shaped by visions of paradise, it has sought to provide the paradisal social fantasy of a democracy of the elite. Everybody in paradise is a winner. Public services disguised as citadels of privilege attempt to gratify both impulses, toward exaltation and transcendence and toward democracy and accessibility. Not only estate museums on the model of the Huntington but also Wright's comprehensive design for the Santa Monica hills deploy a dual imagery of elite withdrawal and expansive invitation to resolve the ambivalence. Resort hotels similarly market to an

FIGURE 94. Flintridge Biltmore Hotel project for Frank P. Flint, by Myron Hunt and Harold C. Chambers, Flintridge, 1926–27.

anonymous public the illusion of privilege, consisting in a withdrawal from the business of life for a leisurely contemplation of a landscape from the heights of one of its dominating structures.

The experience, as of all hotel life, is by nature ephemeral, and understood to be so by all parties to the transaction; a certain anxiety arises from the perception that with time the experience will dissipate, because money runs out and because guests get bored. For citizens as well as for tourists, remaining in paradise is difficult, but the problem is one of space rather than time and is mediated through variously naive and sophisticated alignments of house and grounds. In deploying the visible imagery of a gated private estate to the ends of an accessible civic garden, the Huntington set a pattern of devolution that has permanently blurred the distinction in L.A. between the city as a collection of private properties and the city as the communal garden of mythic desire. In its upper-middle-class residential architecture, an ambivalent relationship between interior and exterior, often analyzed as the architectural response to the benign climate, also signals the unresolved tension between the house's private function as shelter and its civic duty of extending the urban garden. To possess both one's own manageable little garden and, at the same time, the totality of Los Angeles, is the paradox of local desire.

Vestiges of a model of an ideal L.A. of associated dwellings sited in a benign and expansive landscape appear in housing developments of a more modest kind than found on the sweeping drives of Oak Knoll Avenue in Pasadena. For example, Ain, Johnson, and Day's drawing (Fig. 95)

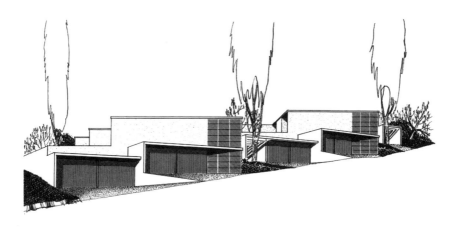

FIGURE 95 *(top).* Avenel Housing by Gregory Ain (with Joseph Johnson and Alfred Day), Silver Lake (drawing), 1946–47.

FIGURE 96 *(bottom).* Channel Heights Housing by Richard Neutra, San Pedro, 1942. Photograph Julius Shulman, Hon. AIA.

FIGURE 97. The Rose Bowl as projected by Myron Hunt
and Harold C. Chambers, 1922.

endows party-wall houses on a city street with the presence of a great villa
dramatically sited and backdropped, and Richard Neutra's much praised
San Pedro development (Fig. 96) achieves at least the suggestion of
grandeur with modest houses distributed across a gently sloping site. But
these practical responses to middle- and working-class housing needs are
faint echoes. The true successor to the earlier models of the villa in a landscape is Myron Hunt's Rose Bowl (1922) in the Arroyo Seco, which, before remodeling, spilled a track out of its open south end (Fig. 97). The
Rose Bowl is, of course, the most democratically accessible of structures,
but in Hunt's design it was also as sensitive an improvement upon its site

as anything conceived by Wright. Inverting the customary strategy of, for instance, lofty resort hotels, Hunt deposited a flattened citadel that reminds us of the greater surrounding natural bowl, and whose open end acknowledges the mouth of the arroyo itself. The Rose Bowl not only draws great crowds to one of Los Angeles's most distinctive natural, and quasi-rural (more so, of course, in 1922), settings; it nestles them within it. Perhaps, before the watercourse in the arroyo was concreted or the stadium closed off at the end, there was no better place, not even the porches of the distant, overseeing Gamble House or its Craftsman progeny dotting the slopes, to imagine the idealized city of great structures in a vast and nurturing garden.

⊙   P A R K

> Strangers, wooed to our city by the great salubrity of our climate, and the well-founded reports of our wondrous resources, look in vain for the public parks, gardens, and promenades beautified and adorned by fountains, trees and flowers, that add so much to the health and beauty of other cities.
>
> E D I T O R I A L , *Los Angeles Daily News,* 23 JANUARY 1869

Los Angeles is uncomfortable with its parks, which, whatever their amenities, are unsystematized and sporadic, no match for the found abundance of ocean, beach, mountain, and desert. The important ones range from often-revised Pershing Square, a five-acre downtown city block set aside in 1866, to the barely manageable wilderness of Griffith Park, the bulk of whose 4,064 acres (an area larger than Beverly Hills) was the unwelcome gift of a convicted felon.* Griffith's size and public services (the observatory, Greek Theatre, barbecue pits) recall New York's Central Park, but despite its appearance of centrality on a map, it is relatively inaccessible. Pershing, however, is Los Angeles's symbolic headache, too conspicuous to be ignored but too small to withstand the pressures or conceal the depredations of traffic, trash, and the ungenteel. Only its location makes it important, but that importance is reflected in the self-conscious evolution of its design.

Pershing Square has been a civic symbol, however unwittingly, since it was fenced and planted in 1870. Early views reveal a small town common (Fig. 98, p. 146), and in a map of the 1880s it bears one of its early names, "Lower Plaza," as if it were a variation on the heart of the traditional pueblo. There is, however, nothing Mexican about the surrounding architecture. By 1900 (Fig. 99, p. 146), the mature planting, bandstand, and modest amenities of what was by now known as Central Park appear to fulfill the implied role of an Anglo alternative to the Plaza.

In 1910 Griffith J. Griffith strongly urged the development of his neglected donation, which had been denied a $125,000 appropriation for roads to and within it, and protested what he saw as undue and excessively costly proposed "improvements" to the rival Central Park. One hundred sixty thousand dollars had been appropriated for new structures and pavement, with the loss of a quantity of mature trees. Whatever his motivations, Griffith's complaint foreshadows later disputes, over this and other city parks, between the advocates of nature and rest and the advocates of social amenities. The amenities envisioned in the World War I era were middle class and aimed at accommodating the genteel tranquillity of the park, reminiscent of the decorative and botanically instructive city gardens of a Riviera town, to the needs of office workers rather than nannies and the retired. In the twenties and thirties, the now-renamed Pershing Square retained its curving paths and lush vegetation, as the tropical paradise in miniature required by the high expectations of citizens.

Dominated by the 1923 Biltmore Hotel, the entire ensemble (Fig. 100, p. 146) appears to have achieved the maximum balance between vegetation and architecture, and would eventually complement the structured poetry of the 1939 Mission Revival Union Station, with its romantic planting and its visual extension through the Plaza to the 1928 city hall. As the latter sequence introduced and naturalized the arriving visitor, so the square, which by the twenties occupied the heart of the commercial district, epitomized for office workers, in a grid of masonry and concrete, a more authentic Los Angeles of luxuriant natural beauty. The success of Pershing Square in these decades was due not only to its planting and design but also to its transmission of a threatened heritage.

Pershing Square was often praised in those years for its botany and other amenities, but Myron H. Broomell, whose *The City Built on Sand* (1948) is a meditation on futility enlivened by abuse of L.A., remarks not on the planting but on the personnel: "Old men and females, landladies and cranks, / Bums, saints, and zanies" soon destined to transfer either to Skid Row or to the city's terminal park, Forest Lawn. His observation marks a mutation of the imagination: Pershing Square is changing to the condition of today's downtown parks, a refuge for the marginal and a lair for the predatory. The threat, in other words, had materialized, and the park's imagery of a garden of repose came to appear inadequate or pathetic in the face of new cultural pressures. A redesign was inevitable.

To discourage vagrants above and encourage parking below, the 1950–51 remodelers transformed this urban garden (however down at the heels) into a kind of concrete lid, relegating palm trees to planters (Fig. 101, p. 147). As David Gebhard and Robert Winter remark in *Los Angeles: An Architectural Guide,* "The idea of a multilayered parking structure under a park is an attractive one. Seemingly it is the best of both worlds, a park and a place for autos." As the meeting point of the nature-driven Arcadian and the technology-driven Utopian visions of Los Angeles, it was the right symbol at the right moment. Gebhard and Winter note, however, what with hindsight seems so obvious, that the entering and exiting vehicles compress, clutter, and pollute the perimeter of a park, compromising and even spoiling it for pedestrians. In his 1967 series *Thirtyfour Parking Lots in Los Angeles,* Edward Ruscha captioned his aerial photograph of the square *Pershing Square underground lot, 5th & Hill,* thus implicitly erasing the park and redefining the site as merely the roof of the garage beneath. Even the perverse satisfaction of "reading" this remodeling as an inevitable acknowledgment of the tyranny of the automobile is diluted by the compromises in the design, which recalls the downtown of any ordinary middle-sized city hiding its embarrassing garage under the vestige of a green space. The loss of faith in L.A. as a fusion of Arcadia and Utopia is summed up in respectable L.A.'s avoidance of Pershing Square, indeed of downtown generally, in the 1960s and 1970s, when Reyner Banham dismissed downtown as irrelevant.

A competition was held in 1986 for the redesign of the park, with the explicit requirement that the underground garage be retained and the im-

plicit one that the design express a metaphor. Perhaps the most literal realization of the latter requirement, at least among the finalists, was a project that ramped a massive symbolic freeway at treetop level across the
park. The winner was, however, the SITE Environmental Design group
(Fig. 102, p. 147), whose more sophisticated interpretation of the specifi-
cation generated a project "meant to compress virtually all of Los Angeles
experience into a 'metaphorical magic carpet' with the paving grid representing the flatland street system and the rolling edges symbolizing the
area's hills and mountains." Such publicized verbal and visual figures
reflect the city's intense consciousness of the instruments by which it represents itself, evident also in the subsequent competition for the Walt Disney Concert Hall. SITE won the Pershing Square commission, said jury
chairman Charles Moore, "because the design represented a new idea capable of changing the face of Los Angeles." In the end, the commission
was withdrawn from SITE and the square was developed as a hopeful
symbol of Mexican-Anglo cultural interdependence, thus implicitly conceding the end of Anglo hegemony.

The park in the 1960s, however, was not without admirers. "Sleazy, a
bit dusty, very masculine," L.A.'s downtown and its park appealed to
David Hockney; "the resonance of [this] otherwise bland image . . . can
only be understood if one knows that the location is the centre of the ho-
mosexual activity" described in John Rechy's *City of Night* (1963); "Hockney has depicted the Square, which is actually very drab and grey, as a
virtual forest of palm trees in response to the poetic description found on
the first page of Rechy's book: 'Remember Pershing Square and the apa-
thetic palmtrees' (Fig. 103, p. 148)." Hockney himself has said that the
painting is faithful to "L.A. in the flatlands: long straight roads, right an-
gles, cubes"; although it is too slight a work to bear the full weight of Los
Angeles symbolism, *Building, Pershing Square* nevertheless sums up a
generic Los Angeles of the mind. Hockney's imagery, playing the sensuous palms against the impersonal architecture, is elemental and characteristic of many zones of L.A., but by his choice of place and title he adds recognition of the site as a sexual marketplace. Although they are not what the
city fathers have in mind, these are components of a landscape of desire.

No city block, however conspicuous and however well designed,

FIGURE 98 *(above).*
Central Park (later Pershing
Square) about 1880.

FIGURE 99 *(right).*
Central Park, from *Art
Work on Southern California*
by Lou V. Chapin, 1900.

FIGURE 100 *(below).*
Pershing Square in 1927.

FIGURE 101 *(top).* Pershing Square about 1951.

FIGURE 102 *(bottom).* Pershing Square project by SITE Environmental Design, 1986.

FIGURE 103. *Building, Pershing Square, Los Angeles* by David Hockney, 1964. Acrylic on canvas, 58 x 58". © David Hockney.

could have such capability unless it persuaded people to accept it as an, even *the,* epitome of the city, the space where the city's essential character is represented. The shift from the bold conceptual metaphors of the 1986 competition to the didacticism of the 1993 park may owe more to politics than to phenomenology and esthetics, but arguably the burden of symbolic self-consciousness had simply become too great. Noting that metaphor "can be a double-edged sword," one critic observed of the SITE project that "by making a uniform and non-hierarchical pattern the plan seems to symbolize the sprawl and lack of a center that are stereotypically associated, whether fairly or not, with Los Angeles." There is an even greater difficulty in looking to an urban park as the symbol of Los Ange-

FIGURE 104. St. James Park, Los Angeles, from *Art Work on Southern California* by Lou V. Chapin, 1900.

les. Set apart as protected zones for nature and recreation, parks imply that what is outside their bounds lacks those amenities. The park is a compensation for the failures of the paved environment. In most cities, this might seem obvious, but the subconsciousness of Los Angeles resists the limitation, as at least one interpretation of the city shows.

In 1900 a volume of handsome photographs called *Art Work on Southern California,* with a text by Lou V. Chapin, was published in a boxed set of twelve fascicles. Both the title and the presentation assert something beyond mere information or advertising, although the text's discreet propaganda extends to reassurances about the availability of good help. Insofar as it addresses Los Angeles, the work is an exquisite, highly selective interpretation of the city as a sequence of parks. This conceptual model differs from the imagined "countryside" in its urbanity, present to a greater or lesser degree in amenities like pavements, curbs, lamps, ornamental plantings, or merely a width and straightness of corridor announcing the city rather than the countryside.

St. James Park (Fig. 104), for example, is actually not a "park" but a lavishly planted residential enclave. Chapin's camera dissolves distinctions

FIGURE 105. Adams Street, Los Angeles, from *Art Work on Southern California* by Lou V. Chapin, 1900.

between what is formally a "park" and what is not, focusing on what is common to St. James Park, wealthy, conventional Adams Street (Fig. 105), Hollenbeck Park (Fig. 106), and Palm Drive (Fig. 107). Parks were indeed set aside during the periods of late-nineteenth-century expansion, Echo and Elysian in particular, but Chapin's pictures suggest that it didn't make much difference in a city already designed like a park. The sequence of images in Chapin's fascicles records an unassertive development from unimproved nature (ocean, mountains, and desert are all represented) by way of apparently unremarkable but essential mechanisms (pictures of irrigation canals [Fig. 11] and flumes, for instance) to such Arcadian neighborhoods as West Adams Street and St. James Park. It is an elegantly simple history of L.A., and the product is not only lush but clean and nearly empty, as if waiting for someone's arrival.

Booster literature of the period often took the form of photograph albums, but most (for example, *In and about Los Angeles,* of 1906, which stresses downtown and its business opportunities), unlike Chapin's sophisticated production, used boastful and feverish rhetoric to underscore images of growth and profit. Chapin's essay, distributed through the fascicles, is soothing and polite, and his views of the areas where money is

FIGURE 106 (*above*).
Hollenbeck Park, Los
Angeles, from *Art Work
on Southern California* by
Lou V. Chapin, 1900.

FIGURE 107 (*left*).
Palm Drive, Los Angeles,
from *Art Work on Southern
California* by Lou V. Chapin,
1900.

made, Broadway and Spring Street for instance, picture neat, impressive new buildings on tranquil, uncrowded streets. These images, like those of the residential areas, cannot be assembled into any larger configuration, much less into an overview of the entire city. It is impossible to "read" a relationship between the commercial and residential districts, just as it is difficult to group the Arcadian districts into a controlling urban scheme. "Downtown," as Chapin captures it, is what we would call an "industrial park," a zoned area for productivity. It is one of a series of autonomous parks.

Although it defines an important way of seeing Los Angeles, the "park" model has little to do with what the word usually identifies. As the third conceptual stage in Los Angeles's modern development, the "park" supplants the "countryside"—with its unique structures sited in expansive landscapes—by a more urbane imagery of a planted, pathed, lighted, groomed, *accessorized* city. Pasadena attempted to fashion itself as such a place from the 1880s through the 1920s, salvaging its natural heritage of live oaks by planting them extensively along the streets and symbolically at city hall. An aggressive program of planting in the city's many parks was, in the long run, overshadowed by the competition for status that saw oaks, palms, cypresses, and other species flourish on private properties. What is amazing is not that a city of trees and flowers failed to displace one of frame and brick, but the extent to which it did.

No such city flourishes today; the closest instance is a Los Angeles neighborhood, the large hilltop enclave of Bel Air. It comes as close as possible to furnishing that abundance of gardens and planted roadways that, by contextualizing a community in a park, makes parks redundant. As an entirety, Bel Air is effectively invisible; its outstanding buildings are mostly swathed and veiled in planting that submerges the twisting roads and prevents grand effects of landscape. Beneath it, in West L.A., Mid-Wilshire, and far beyond, lies a vast Los Angeles of bungalows stationed in gardens, looking suburban but in fact stretching across the girth of the city; on reduced scales and budgets they imperfectly extend this notional park. The lack of flat parkland in Los Angeles, and even the meagerness of such amenities as planted medians, may be due as much to the perception that the need was being satisfied on private lands as to simple

greed or lack of civic spirit. Residents of an openwork city of low structures, distributed relatively evenly across a well-planted landscape, had
little interest in the ideas of compensation and recuperation implicit in the
urban park. At the beginning of the twenty-first century, however, this
openwork city appears so threatened by multifamily dwellings in modest
neighborhoods and by the "mansionizing" phenomenon in opulent ones
as to discredit the vision evoked by Chapin's seductive photography.

⊙ VILLAGE

An old plan of a youthful-sounding town, Redondo Beach
(Fig. 108), looks like a Utopianist's dream—a symmetrical organism whose
transparent clarity is relieved by calculated variety. This unexecuted design is one of many efforts to master stretches of L.A., both politically independent cities and neighborhoods of Los Angeles proper, by giving
them a shape. With the subdivision of the ranchos, the need for "definition" in its root sense becomes apparent; an 1887 map, otherwise exuding
the confidence of a midwestern river-city, discloses the shapelessness of
the Los Angeles flatland in the almost neurotic palisades of young trees
that define each empty block (Fig. 109). Here in embryo is a dialogue between the Arcadia of undifferentiated and the Utopia of appropriated
space, one typically resolved in the sequence of urban enclaves that constitute the conceptual model of the village. These include many, but not
all, of the independent cities that make up nearly half the area of Los Angeles County,* many distinctive neighborhoods within the city of Los Angeles itself, and certain kinds of communities of related structures.

The concept of the "village" describes a place that is both an epitome
and a center. It is found wherever the desire to identify with the city as a
whole can be reconciled to the need to define and control one's negotia-
tions with that immense entity. To live in one of the villages within L.A.
is to be centered within L.A., even if that center is in peripheral Malibu.
There are dozens of variations on the observation that Los Angeles is many
suburbs in search of a city, but the search for this identity in fact moves
in the opposite direction. As a name, a landscape, and a concept, "L.A."
overrides its constituent towns and districts, which, to a mobile popula-

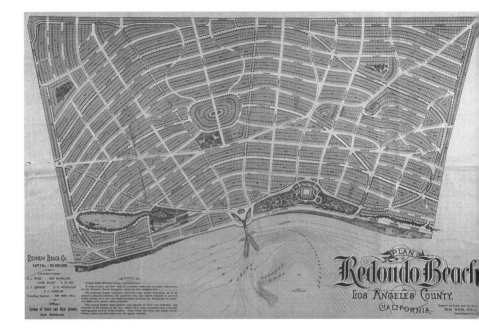

FIGURE 108. Calculated order and calculated variety at Redondo Beach, 1887.

tion, are, more often than not, found rather than given communities, elected rather than native acres. Of course the choice may be reluctant, a matter of pocketbook compromise, but the impetus to "locate," to settle where site and community are idiosyncratically expressive and nurturing, is negotiated in every real estate office.

The act of self-delimitation is clearest when locating in a politically exclusive or a topographically aloof zone, like South Pasadena or Topanga Canyon. These are places that, according to different definitions, promise the best of Los Angeles and provide controls for its use and enjoyment. Often there is a hierarchy of topography even within a politically privileged area, such as the famous residential ascent in Beverly Hills from the relatively modest houses and apartments below Santa Monica Boulevard, to the flat zone of conspicuous mansions between Santa Monica and Sunset Boulevards, to the more secluded properties in the hills north of Sunset. Even the flow of the flatlands of the city of Los Angeles is inter-

FIGURE 109. Perspective of Los Angeles, from *Views of Los Angeles and Vicinity, Cal.,* about 1887.

rupted by statutory and purely perceptual differentiations that set certain areas apart; some, like Hancock Park, have no particular focus but extend more or less uniformly to edges well defined by boulevards; others, like Larchmont, have an unmistakable center but ambiguous borders; still others, like Carthay, have a history and a symbolism despite the erosion of their characteristic architecture and the preempting of their streets by through traffic. Insofar as both independent cities and neighborhoods constitute imagined communities, with the aura and perhaps the mechanisms (like severe parking restrictions) of exclusivity, they are villages, places of shared privileges and obligations.

The real estate pages of the *Los Angeles Times* are full of success stories about men and women who, by buying a house, have identified themselves with a part of the city—with creative Whitley Heights, eclectic Silverlake, innovative Olive Hill, or courageous Watts. It is not just the property, but the challenges and rewards of the immediate community, that constitute the success. Their testimony, however, is double-edged: stressing the rewards of discovery and "moving in," the coverage reinforces the dissatisfaction that might lead others to appraise their options and move out. In pages devoted to selling property, this is not surprising; restlessness drives the market as well as the story. Because they are keys to unlocking the rewards of the greater city rather than ends in themselves, urban villages inspire only provisional loyalties. A character in Evelyn Waugh's *The Loved One* describes his relocations over the decades from the Hollywood Hills to Bel Air to Pacific Palisades, as if manifest destiny had segued into real estate chic.

Urban villages are likely to be resented because they are exclusive—that is, they exclude. *The New Yorker*'s late architecture critic Brendan Gill expresses some representative attitudes toward the enclave that symbolizes privilege to the entire world: "Beverly Hills was—and is—as pretty and artificial as if it had been made out of spun sugar. It has no hospitals, because nobody is ever supposed to be sick there. It has no cemeteries, because nobody is ever supposed to die there. The building in Beverly Hills for which people feel the greatest reverence is not a church but a hotel." The structure that symbolizes New York probably isn't a church either, but an office building. Nor is it reasonable to imply that by burying their dead elsewhere its citizens evade the realities of existence; who today is buried in Manhattan? The underlying flaw in Gill's reasoning, however, is the assumption that people withdraw to Beverly Hills, or to any such enclave, to live apart from Los Angeles. Living in an L.A. enclave is a strategy for profiting from the city as a whole on better than average, or the best possible, terms, and should not be confused with escaping to Ojai or Santa Barbara.

That confusion is understandable, however, in the light of a role L.A. has shared with certain other cities that occupy a privileged off-center position. Oscar Wilde, of all people, described Los Angeles as "a sort of Naples," and Gill compares it to Pompeii, at least insofar as both face natural catastrophes. Both analogies evoke "that unmistakable sensation of being in a provincial capital that is so cosmopolitan, and at the same time so far away, that the world itself has become its province." The toy cities in Ronald Firbank's novels have something of this liberated quality, the feeling of urbanity without responsibility. The last place to look for this in L.A. is in the Civic Center downtown; the urban village that tries to communicate it the most is West Hollywood, especially as imaged in the cover David Hockney created for the town's signature magazine (Fig. 110). Here, ideally, the éclat of high architecture—Cesar Pelli's Pacific Design Center—coexists easily with bungalows.

Not all urban villages, however, have so succeeded in reconciling the

FIGURE 110. *Hancock St., West Hollywood, I* by David Hockney, 1989 (art used on the cover of *West Hollywood Magazine*). Oil on canvas, 16½ x 10½". © David Hockney.

FIGURE 111. Westwood Village, 1939.

imagery of both small community and big city. Sometimes "L.A." overwhelms them; a 1939 image of Westwood Village contains clues as to why (Fig. 111). In some ways the prototypically self-conscious L.A. "village," Westwood appears to sit cozily at the foot of UCLA. The threat lies exactly where the camera stands, in the unlimited access into the "village" from an increasingly busy urban corridor, "a windy canyon," as Mike Davis puts it, "between bizarrely configured office towers." It is interesting to compare the explicit invitations of this and other similarly framed publicity photos, such as that for Rolling Hills Estates in Palos Verdes in 1937 (Fig. 112). Their apparent fragility notwithstanding, the Virginian or Kentucky-like wooden fences and gates of Rolling Hills define a politically privileged zone, an independent city that can close those gates when the land is settled. A local historian enthuses that the Palos Verdes Peninsula, although within commuting distance of downtown, "has preserved to a remarkable extent the carefree enjoyment of the simple things which once made all of California a pastoral paradise." The message would seem to be that not only are those two ancient antagonists, private property and

FIGURE 112. Entrance to Rolling Hills Estates, Palos Verdes, about 1937.

pastoral existence, compatible today; they are interdependent. Westwood of the sprightly turrets has no such corporate privilege. Can it, asks the *Los Angeles Times*, "be restored to its former glory, or is it doomed to re-main a 33-acre clutch of movie theaters, pizza parlors and yogurt dis-pensaries, lost in the shadows of the new high-rise office buildings along Wilshire Boulevard?"

Irving Gill's coherent design for the center of Torrance (1912) failed de-spite the advantages of that city's political independence. A model seven-hundred-acre industrial town laid out by the Olmsted brothers (sons of the creator of New York's Central Park), Torrance was intended to have a railway station, a civic center, shops, and housing for the employees of Pacific Electric, Union Tool, and the Llewelyn Iron Works. Its character-less site (Fig. 113) could illustrate both the opportunities and the absence of cues for the "early" planners and architects throughout Los Angeles, charged with conjuring a coherent urban form, almost overnight, out of such an emptiness. It was a significant commission for Gill, whom Esther

FIGURE 113. Site of Torrance before 1911.

McCoy praises as the first West Coast architect to concern himself with company towns, barracks for laborers, and other types of industrial-age housing. Yet Gill's designs have a symbolic power that goes well beyond those intentions. His mission imagery is rightly praised as "the source of a set of design principles which represented a search for fundamental truths," but particularly at Torrance, because they were to define a community, Gill's structures were an idealized reconstruction of the pueblo. At the same time, what by his imagery appears as a vessel of the past constituted, in its radical utilitarianism, a laboratory for practical modern life.

Gill is both the poet of white walls set off by flowering vines and the advocate of "a Californian ideal of the sanitary, labor saving house" who fought dust with plain surfaces and central vacuum outlets in the walls.

Gill's concrete cottages, however, met stiff resistance, and most of his plan was either unbuilt, altered, razed, or used for contrary purposes. For example, the intended entrance to the city, the railway station (Fig. 114), was, until its 1990s conversion into a chic restaurant, used only for freight. Today the ghostly monuments and members of Gill's Torrance drowse in the underutilized spaces of a central city whose energies now flow along the adjacent boulevards. In part the failure lies in Gill's Utopianism, which at Torrance seems to have consisted in a design too uncompromising and self-referring for a town whose psychological and economic dependence upon the surrounding city is high.

Gill's courtyard housing projects have been more successful, at least in their influence, and point toward a more workable negotiation of boundary tensions. His 1910 Lewis Courts in Sierra Madre, now smothered in vegetation, is a village of workmen's houses set in gardens and linked by loggias that form nearly continuous walls on two sides and the suggestion of walls on the others. His better-known, much praised Horatio West Court (1921) in Santa Monica was another low-cost project of four-room units (Fig. 70). At the scale of courtyard housing, the urban village has had a startling success, but (as the present value of housing in Gill's surviving projects demonstrates) not for a blue-collar clientele. The success lies in the resolution of the problematic relationship between the enclave and its urban context.

Manageable, replicable, adjustable to a great range of incomes, and comfortable within the urban grid, the Los Angeles courtyard housing block reconciles the impulse to maximize liberty and choice with the need for an extended and shaped environment. These are bourgeois rather than working-class values. Their fulfillment expresses what Stefanos Polyzoides and his colleagues call the "ideal of instant place": "The original desert ecology of the Los Angeles basin was the cause of the inhospitality, landscape homogeneity, and placelessness of the region. In analogical terms, the urban structure of Los Angeles was also developed as a desert covering vast and undifferentiated private-urban-use expanses interrupted only

FIGURE 114. The symbolic gate to Torrance: the train station by Irving Gill, 1912. Photograph © Marvin Rand, 1999.

FIGURE 115. La Vista Terrace (undated photograph).

by occasional places of commercial or public activity strung along linear movement routes. The ideal of place in Los Angeles is achieved by the exclusion of the surrounding context and by the definition of a protected interior realm that nurtures and safeguards private or limited shared values."

Using the metaphor of an oasis, Polyzoides, Sherwood, and Tice find courtyard housing appropriate to the fragile "frontier" environment of urban L.A. It counters the anxieties brought about by the formlessness of a landscape of single-family houses, providing "both concrete and symbolic references to the idea of a shared life motivated by concerns higher than the pursuit of mere survival." Most characteristically for opportunistic, capitalist L.A., courtyard housing annuls the "egalitarian" ideals and esthetics dominant in post–World War I architectural ideology and manifested in uniform, repeated dwelling units. As an early example suggests (Fig. 115), the status of "village" is confirmed by the priority of the ensemble over the particular dwelling: courtyard housing "emphasizes urban continuity and focuses on the development of urban space as a positive element. Buildings are formed as objects that define complex hierarchies of open-air public places at different scales. The shape and content of these spaces is fixed before issues of individual dwellings are resolved." Those spaces are L.A.'s continuation, at a semiprivate scale, of "the public realm of streets and squares" of traditional cities; here, it may be argued, "a sense of community is achieved through variety and the possibility that disparate architectural elements, when combined, can generate a common public realm."

For many thousands of middle-class citizens, especially in the flat, vaguely defined regions of the city, courtyard housing afforded a degree of exclusivity otherwise found only where terrain or cost presented insuperable barriers. The surviving examples are imbued with the supposed glamour of the twenties, but their architectural descendant, the L.A. stuccoed box, has its own aura as "the symbol, for good or ill, of one of the golden ages of Los Angeles, the 1950s."* Its function, like that of courtyard housing, was to provide both suitable imagery for a romantic Southern California lifestyle and adequate mediation between the public and private realms: "It is difficult to know whether to classify the stucco box as a 1940s garden apartment denuded of much of its garden or as a miniature tenement that has gained a garnish of landscaping. The imagery is that of the resort, redolent with air of escapism which might ingenuously refer to the tropics. . . . This notion of being on vacation all year round was symbolized by the landscaping, the lighting, the graphics, and the outdoor access to all the units."

The fact that their ratio of lot coverage equaled or excelled that of earlier tenements in Los Angeles seems, as John Chase and John Beach note, to have been rendered invisible. Both systems of housing are compromises with the vaunted image of a city of detached private homes but deserve, as in the sympathetic analyses just cited, to be recognized as efforts toward the creation of manageable small communities as well as deviations from the ideal of the homestead. Perhaps their latest incarnations are the image-conscious nests of suburban condominiums that shoehorn seven or eight homes into an acre of carefully landscaped gates, walks, arches, fountains, pools, floral borders and other zones intended to create the im-

pression of the public areas of a village. Springing up typically in growing places like Irvine and the Simi Valley, these projects constitute what
developers call "increased densification," with the added rhetoric (in the
words of the architect Barry Berkus) of a near-mythic prototype: "in fact,
density can increase the desirability of a community by creating a friendly
village atmosphere, not unlike in a Mediterranean country."

Easier to recognize as villages, however, are college campuses, which
before World War II were likely to be indebted to the University of Virginia, Thomas Jefferson's "academical village" of 1819. The California Institute of Technology, in Pasadena, an example of such a layout, is a synopsis of evolving conceptions of "what was Californian about California."
The succession of architects—Elmer Grey, Myron Hunt, Bertram Grosvenor Goodhue, and Gordon Kaufmann—and their proposed and executed designs register the flowering and fading of sequential images of
Los Angeles. The look of "a rural hacienda" governed Grey and Hunt's
initial drawings, which spoke to the provincial romanticism of the culture:
"They initiated a strategy that considered campus buildings to be gener-
alized lofts, stable and specific in their facades but general and change-
able in their interior plans. They also suggested that buildings should be
stylistically related to each other and that the elements of that style should
be appropriate to the culture of California. Finally, they proposed an overall organizational scheme that—through courtyards, arcades, large walls
with small openings, spare ornament and rich landscapes—generated a
campus from out of the context of a Pasadena that was somewhere between the frontier and civilization."

Goodhue's proposed 1923 design could hardly be more different. His
formal, gorgeous European imagery, the offspring of his work at the San
Diego exposition of 1915, declares that Caltech is not a farm but an enclave of high urbanity in an otherwise less self-conscious architectural context. Urbanity is reflected in Goodhue's plan, as well, which tightens his
predecessors' proposed layout. In his aerial perspective (Fig. 116), of which
black-and-white reproduction can give only an approximate sense, the
blue dome of the imperious central structure is tied by color to the mountain backdrop, to the water parterres, and even to the thick leafage of the
trees; it thereby pulls the natural environment into the system of the cam-

FIGURE 116. Perspective of proposed California Institute of Technology campus by Bertram Grosvenor Goodhue, Pasadena, 1923.

pus, a zone of white-and-red structures between the layers of green and blue. Thus Goodhue has it both ways, demarcating his campus while rendering it as the epitome of its surroundings.

Departing from Goodhue's grander idiom, his 1928 successor Gordon Kaufmann introduced the eclectic, complex, yet relaxed and hedonistic imagery practiced in the great private houses of the time, especially around Pasadena, and recognizable as the "California style." Both men, like Hunt and Grey before them, were translating their thinking about Southern California into designs that would make that thought a reality. Kaufmann's wider variety of building types—villa, palace, and farm for his athenaeum (Fig. 117) and monastery, hacienda, and apartment house for his dormitories—suggests that Goodhue's designs are naive, the product of too exclusive a vision. Perhaps the most interesting aspect of Kaufmann's work, and what most clearly distinguishes it from Goodhue's, is its distance from its models; it is said that his work depicts a subject, which

FIGURE 117. Athenaeum by Gordon Kaufmann, California Institute of Technology, 1930.

is of course the romance of the Mediterranean; to depict, however, is not to import. Kaufmann's vision goes beyond Goodhue's, in his implicit recognition that Mediterranean California is an act of the mind, and a choice, not a historical imposition or a necessity.

A college, of course, is a place of temporary residence, for only some of the students and for a specified short time. Even the faculty may very narrowly ration their time on campus. Although the architecture of institutions like Caltech may allude to the Jeffersonian model, which incorporates professors' residences into the ranges of students' rooms, the reality is otherwise, the modern academical village being a daytime workplace with varying degrees of after-hours activities, like sports and concerts, that simulate the complete life of a town but on a cyclical rather than an evolving basis. Frank Gehry's strikingly designed neo-Italian-hilltop "village" of Loyola Law School (Fig. 118) is frankly urban and defensive behind its fences, except that its inhabitants lock themselves out rather than inside at close of day. The conceptual model of the village governs these as well

FIGURE 118. Loyola University
Law School by Frank Gehry, Los
Angeles, 1984.

as other kinds of development in Los Angeles, even, or especially, where
residence is temporary and the full implications of the concept of a
defined community need not be faced.

Several projects for clustered communities tailored to needs of business
rather than dwelling include shopping and civic centers. Often they are
revisions as well as innovations, acknowledging existing buildings that
serve the same or similar purposes, recycling them or perpetuating their
nondescript imagery in eye-catching ways. Reflecting a high level of education and cultural self-consciousness, they allude elaborately to revered,
especially Italian, precedents of organization and enclosure. The Morphosis group's 1982 project for the Hermosa Beach Commercial Center,
"drawn from a model of the arcaded Italian town," incorporated path-
ways, courtyards, and a "civic amphitheatre gallery" into the existing fabric of commercial buildings and streets, a shopping arcade, and bungalows;
the added parking would have been subterranean, so sustaining—for the
patrons who typically arrive and depart by private car—the image of a
pedestrian-centered community. The courts of Charles Moore's Beverly

FIGURE 119. Beverly Hills Civic
Center by Charles Moore/Urban
Innovations and others, 1981–92.

Hills Civic Center (Fig. 119) are as assertive as Morphosis's proposed galleries and plazas would have been discreet, evoking another urban village model, the miniature city-within-the-city, like the network of the Imperial Fora in Rome, or like eighteenth-century Bath, which gestures to
its medieval cathedral somewhat as the new work at Beverly Hills acknowledges the existing Spanish Colonial Revival city hall of 1932, a
landmark of past grandeur and, on the L.A. time line, a structure of equiv-
alently venerable antiquity.

Another realized project, also indebted to Italian sources, is Frank
Gehry's Edgemar complex, set well back from the beach in Santa Monica.
In its architect's words, it is "a miniature historic small town, a kind of
dolls' house San Gimignano," yet as unlike the Hermosa and Beverly Hills
designs as they are unlike each other. Homeliness transmuted into high
drama is part of Gehry's sense of a local esthetic of the idiosyncratically
commonplace and the usefully trashy—qualities apparent in the dramatic
use of industrial materials and even in the name. "Edgemar," which was
maintained from the dairy that used to occupy the site, operates at another

level of L.A. culture, that of the hybrid English/Spanish place-name in the wrong place, like "Vista Gardens," denounced in Alison Lurie's *The Nowhere City* for having no vista of any gardens to begin with (compare the West L.A. neighborhood of Mar Vista, whose Spanish words are deformed into English syntax). When they become "ironic" and "allusive," as at Gehry's Edgemar, these manglings confirm the closing of the long chapter of the Anglo appropriation of a Spanish-speaking culture.

Such sophisticated venues for working and shopping seem to be efforts, in the characteristic L.A. way, to have things both ways. They offer the fabric and design of scaled, intimate, and varied experience but on the user's terms, with, as it is said of some human relationships, no commitment. The theme park is the extreme example of this urban phenomenon, exemplified in the manufactured and staged experience of carefully defined, integral environments at—of course—Disneyland. The Anaheim wonderland has been much admired for its paradoxically retrograde urbanity; here the free spirits of Freewayland ride docilely on public transportation, for example, and stroll through the nine-tenths-scale streets of small towns. In a wider sense, however, Disneyland is an attempt to give visitors an unusually comprehensive sense of place by naturalizing and localizing them in coherent, meaningful environments. Some of these are villages in the obvious sense—the French Quarter, Main Street—but others are villages of the mind, inaccessible, desired places. The task of Disneyland is to give the customer access, control, and proprietorship over them and their powerful metaphors.

These zones follow (or did so, before recent revisions) a kind of logical order, from Adventureland to Tomorrowland. In Adventureland, the ambiguities of space and place are eliminated by the elimination of time; this is a pretemporal zone (wild, unredeemed, "natural") where "place" is the entire earth itself. At Frontierland, time enters the equation but is spatialized by being identified with a place, although that place is/was portable, always on the edge of advancing U.S. occupation of the West. The fulfillment of Frontierland is Main Street, a deliberately ambivalent evocation both of change, because it appeals to nostalgia for what has vanished, and of permanence, because its imagery is felt to shelter enduring values of close community, fruitful labor, and innocent pleasure. Fantasyland intervenes between Main Street and Tomorrowland, effectively blotting out the "present" and easing the transition to the final zone, where, as at the beginning, the anxieties of time are neutralized by being collapsed into a future that is a place. As Louis Marin observes, that place is America; it is also Southern California.

Disneyland's vast scale is a heroic effort to represent an idealized past America as the fulcrum of universal time and space, and from it to convey the pretending travelers into the future of their collective dreams. Tourists are not merely shown reproductions of those places and times, but are centered in them; as the focus, the reason for the existence of each zone, visitors sense that it was waiting for them. It is to this sense of a controllable and therefore meaningful environment that the concept of the village speaks. Disneyland's architecture and transportation systems make interestingly oblique comments about L.A. and can even be thought of as epitomizing it, but its larger meaning is its metaphysical definition of the urban village as the mental state of being meaningfully centered in, and in control of, one's environment.

The triple identity of Tomorrowland as the Future, America, and Southern California embodies the desire to grasp L.A. as a phenomenal unity; at a strenuously maintained level of perception, L.A. is a single, coherent place. Cesar Pelli observes that in designing for a Southern California site the architect must be cued by an eternal condition of blue skies and a flat, backdropped, palm-dotted, freeway-crisscrossed landscape of ephemeral structures: "What is there now," he says, "is somehow temporary and replaceable. The real Los Angeles exists only in the future." Every project, therefore, speaks not only to its immediate context but also to the whole city, a Tomorrowland of urban design experienced as a coherent and integrated system.

There is, of course, in Glendale, another Tomorrowland, in its way an urban village. Hubert Eaton, who wrested control of it from the Tropico Company, developers of a failed subdivision, had the inspired business sense to combine the services of a mortuary with those of a graveyard. Providing a full range of funeral services in a setting of natural and artistic beauty, Eaton seemed to restore something lost and to fulfill something promised: "Forest Lawn, after all, had been built to provide the illusion of a village-made supportive environment, an environment which urbanization had fragmented and destroyed. Eaton seemed to have had an instinctive sense of the unmet needs of the uprooted Midwestern small town folk he served[:] . . . he had only to probe his own perceptions to sense the alienation and isolation endemic to the city."

Although it is full of imitations of European art and architecture, Forest Lawn was characterized by Evelyn Waugh as "the *only* thing in California that is not a copy of something else." His satire on Los Angeles, *The Loved One* (1948), centers on the great burial ground, emphasizing the seriousness of purpose and attention to detail that distinguish this town of the dead from, as it appears in the novel, the unconvincing city of the living. Although Eaton's customers presumably accepted at face value what Waugh enjoyed with irony, both recognize and endorse Forest Lawn as an intimate, professional, hierarchical, and romantic system of relationships, one that with some success has, in its gardens and structures, defined a formal relationship between human beings, art, and nature, and that in its bureaux and laboratories has harnessed the labor of the living to the honor of the dead. Marketed even to the young as the ultimate address, it reassures thousands of people that their search for a continuing city is not in vain.

⊙ ACROPOLIS

The great misfortune of London, to the eye[,] . . . is the want of elevation. There is no architectural impression without a certain degree of height, and the London street-vista has none of that sort of pride.
HENRY JAMES

Perceived as a part not of the West but of the Southwest, Los Angeles belongs to an imaginative realm that, while hospitable to provincial Spanish building types like the mission and the hacienda, yearns for more authoritative forms. Charles F. Lummis had urged the construction of cheap, practical mud adobes, but Frank Lloyd Wright and his son Lloyd Wright in their projects and buildings aimed at a Southwest of high monumentality. Designing as if Los Angeles were a desert, they conceived houses having the reserved power of temples exposed to a blinding sun yet shuttered from prying eyes. This imagery attempts to transport the grandeur of pre-Columbian Mesoamerican architecture into Los Angeles, but also evokes Native American sky-cities in New Mexico and appears remote from the midwestern populism of the senior Wright's generously dispersed prairie projects. The sites are usually high, sloping, even difficult, and although the textile and concrete blocks (Fig. 120) used for many are replicable, the finished products are unique.

Frank Lloyd Wright's sojourns in Los Angeles alternated with his visits to Japan, where he was working primarily on the Imperial Hotel. Despite the vast differences between the cultures, it is not difficult to sense a connection between the designs he felt appropriate to a still guarded, aristocratic, and highly self-dramatizing culture and the priestly mysteries of his L.A. work. He seems to have visualized Los Angeles as a sort of base in need of a cap, and just as a desert acquires form by contrast with a mesa, so the city he contemptuously dismissed as a repository of prosperous layabouts would come into focus as the setting for his most conspicuous houses. His concrete blocks, especially, speak of a created rather than found terrain: "We would take that despised outcast of the building industry— the concrete block—out from underfoot or from the gutter—find hitherto unsuspected soul in it—make it live as a thing of beauty—textured like the trees. Yes, the building would be made of blocks as a kind of tree itself standing at home among the other trees in its native land." His idea is to create, even to force, an organic module out of a landscape lacking organic building materials (that is, trees). Plastic and stylized, they multiply rapidly into the masses of the Ennis House (Fig. 120) and the Doheny Ranch Resort (Figs. 84, 86), which appear not to grow out of their sites, like plants, but to complete them, like battlements or bridges. In fact, Wright wanted to shake off the omnipresent Californian envelope of vegetation, of which he complained in his 1932 *Autobiography:* "California . . . smothers the whole in eucalyptus and mimosa arms as she gently kisses all with roses. Thus are buried the mistakes of a decorative picturizing architect, whose art and decoration had entirely taken the place of architecture there."

As I suggested at the beginning of this chapter, it is difficult to see L.A. as a unity without suppressing part of the evidence; in calling for an architecture that would be "beautiful in California in the way that California herself is beautiful," Wright was participating in that familiar gambit

FIGURE 120. Ennis House by Frank Lloyd Wright, Los Angeles, 1924. Photograph Julius Shulman, Hon. AIA.

FIGURE 121. East Hollywood viewed from Olive Hill, 1895.

of reduction and expansion by which *amateurs* of California, in the literal sense of the word, *lovers*, refine the found landscape into the image of their desire. Wright's desert vision of a southwestern L.A. suppresses the compromising properties of flora or inscribes their patterns in the masonry, and thereby asserts the authority of structure over landscape. This is the essence of the conceptual model of the acropolis.

In L.A.'s climate of self-fashioning aristocracy, Wright connected with a patron, the oil heiress and social radical Aline Barnsdall, who commissioned a complex of structures on Olive Hill, a prominent feature of East Hollywood (Fig. 121). Usually referred to by the names of its main structure, the 1920 "Barnsdall" or (after the repeated design motif) "Hollyhock"

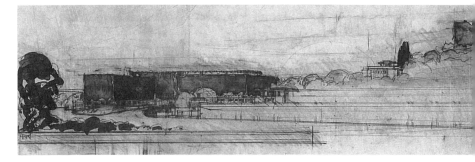

FIGURE 122. Barnsdall Park project by Frank Lloyd Wright, Olive Hill, Los Angeles, 1917–21, drawing of perspective from the north (detail).

House, the East Hollywood complex was in fact a projected community of structures and people reminiscent, in their ambition, of a Renaissance prince (Fig. 122). Barnsdall wanted this ungridded thirty-six-acre superblock, recently planted in olive trees, to be an artists' community centering on her principal residence (one of three). Wright's overall perspective from the north—what is today a disorderly stretch of Hollywood Boulevard—puts the main structure, here merely blocked in, into its intended relationship with the unachieved original program, which included a theatre, artists' residences, apartment house, cinema, cottages, and shops.

Wright ridiculed the "homely midwest invasion" that had obscured a landscape of drama and extremes, "the poetic thing this land was." L.A., the "edge city" of popular metaphor, was sited, in language to which Wright responded, "on a crust of earth at the edge of a sea that ended a world." Such imagined history and topology called for an intensely felt design. Vincent Scully finds a source at the Mayan metropolis Yaxchilán, on the border of Mexico and Guatemala, arguing that out of such a "cultural condensation" Wright sought "to form a new unity" and, by adapting such forms and motifs, to assert a genius of place more elaborate than what American Indians or Spaniards had bequeathed. Wright and Barnsdall were clearly creating more than a cluster of luxurious villas or a useful system of cultural services; the dominating site and equally imposing

constructions in the round justify both Scully's reading of the designs as a recapitulation of the hill itself and further metaphorical equations of the entire complex with Hollywood and even the entire L.A. basin. The ceremonial, templelike qualities of the main house, with its processional freestanding hollyhocks and terraces suggesting ancient observatories, seem to confer dignity upon the city at its feet; the overall configuration, of a site and structure that link earth and sky, invites characterizations like "mythic."

If such language sounds embarrassing today, perhaps it is because sensibilities have been so thoroughly secularized as to require a different vocabulary. The exalted domesticity photographed in the Koenig Case Study House #22 (Fig. 21) should be compared, however, as an L.A. icon in the line of descent from Miss Barnsdall's theatrical high city. In his biography of the senior Wright, Brendan Gill says that the Hollyhock House "imposed itself upon the naked crown of Olive Hill with a tyrannous blatancy, seeming to crush the land beneath it"; he may be responding to the imperiousness of elevated architecture, which symbolizes that "culture of cities," to use Lewis Mumford's term, that is the antagonist of Arcadia's egalitarianism. Wright, of course, acknowledged no such metaphors, grandly but benignly observing the winter landscape receding to a merger of (as he saw them) blue mountains with blue sky and remarking that he had expressed "in the silhouette of the Olive Hill house a sense of the breadth and romance of the region."

Yet Olive Hill also shuns the city below. Here, as with all his subsequent concrete block houses, Wright rejected L.A.'s characteristic and readily available flat sites in favor of pronounced heights and slopes; however much in its formal properties the Barnsdall complex may epitomize Los Angeles, it does not echo its characteristic topography. Nor has it succeeded in embodying the values of aristocratic patronage. L.A. is full of rich and powerful men and women, but they have no status as aristocrats. The aristocracy of L.A. is made up not of oil heiresses but of the glamorous and the publicized; how they appropriate the mythologies of caste and blood is well dramatized in the film *Sunset Boulevard,* whose heroine, merely a passé film star, lives in Gothic seclusion, sustained—as if she were an exiled noblewoman—by European symbols of prestige: a grand servant and an even grander automobile. The abridgment and abandonment of Olive Hill, which Barnsdall soon deeded to a (yet again) reluctant city, say something not only about her accumulating disagreements with Wright but also about her uncertain position as a personal patron in a business rapidly incorporating and mythologizing; the mythologies of show business in Los Angeles had passed beyond her. Nevertheless, Olive Hill is a landmark in Hollywood for several reasons. Situated where the streetcars turned from Vermont Avenue onto Hollywood Boulevard, Olive Hill, had it ever fulfilled its purposes, might have been a kind of gate or entrance marker. The main house itself, its interior court an open-air theatre, epitomizes the complex's dedication to show business. As such, it is an important recognition of Los Angeles's transformation into the world's entertainment capital. All the senior Wright's dramatically situated Los Angeles houses speak to a new sense of the power of images; divested of their priestly and egoistic personas, they anticipate his son's Sowden House of 1926 (Fig. 1), which is "pure Hollywood."

"In 1925," Lloyd Wright said in 1966, "I was young and the city was young. The pueblo had been situated on the river, the commercial center was there, and Bunker Hill lay in the center of the district. I chose that as the acropolis for the city area, not then thinking in terms of the total area, only that it was the pueblo." He is describing his competition entry for the Los Angeles Civic Center of 1925 (Fig. 123; Pershing Square appears in the lower right of the drawing), and in the accepted ideology of four

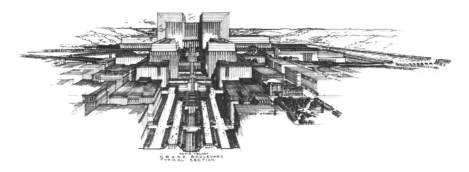

FIGURE 123. Los Angeles Civic Center project by Lloyd Wright, 1925.

and five decades later, apologizing for the apparent naïveté of overrating "downtown." Today, with Bunker Hill and the rest of downtown thick with skyscrapers, the topographical logic and sensuous appeal of his unified design may be greater than it was even in the 1920s. Synthesizing a stepped-temple complex with the vertical lines of the American skyscraper, the younger Wright also wedded a Beaux Arts cruciform plan to a complex layering of transportation, buildings, and gardens; "the provision for multiple 'speedways', rapid transit, roadways for slow moving vehicles and airplane landing fields, are part and parcel of the futurist ideas of the teens and 20s." Lloyd Wright was reported at the time as calling it a "unified organic structure" joining transportation systems at the local, transcontinental, and transoceanic levels.

Bunker Hill was a prosperous Victorian residential district, not a center of civic or business activity; after the propertied classes departed, it survived as a conspicuous and uncomfortable symbol of urban decay. A pre-urban-renewal photograph (Fig. 124) of a sloping site on West Temple Street shows us what earnest planners saw about 1950: a suspect environment of opportunistic, outmoded, and failed designs, more appropriate to a decayed eastern or southern city than to Los Angeles. Fettered by low shops, the palm-flanked 1887 manse bears witness to the early victory of the horizontal and the ordinary over the vertical and the grandiose; after 1970 it was moved and eventually demolished.

This image exposes the Bunker Hill of 1930s and 1940s imagination,

FIGURE 124. The Rochester, 1887, 1012 West Temple Street, Los Angeles.

the raffish venue of John Fante's novels of struggle and pathos, especially *Ask the Dust* (1939), and, as Edward Dimendberg has pointed out, of film noir treatments of unsavory L.A. Overlapping civic rhetorics about sanitation, crime, overcrowding, and immigration found common ground on Bunker Hill. Its problems, however, though real, were unremarkable; the Pico-Union area, for example, with a similar social history, seems rarely to have troubled the civic conscience. The difference is that Bunker Hill was dangerously conspicuous; visibility only aggravated anxieties about what irregularities and vices it might be sheltering. L.A.'s approach to it is consistent with general patterns of urban renewal in the 1950s and 1960s, but the concentration of interest, and the ferocity of the changes made, suggest profound discomfort with the sheer salience of the site.

Partially leveled, or, as the design critic for the *Los Angeles Times* put it, "lobotomized," Bunker Hill still rises above the commercial zones to its south and east, but the effect is largely negated by the march of corporate towers down Grand Avenue. The buildings that now overpower the site do not group well together; in their absence, one might imagine that the dainty kremlin that is the Museum of Contemporary Art could have more effectively crowned the rise. An effort to assert the authority of Bunker Hill has been made by an elaborate outdoor staircase sweeping past the First Interstate World Center (the Library Tower) toward Bertram Goodhue's 1926 Central Library across Fifth Street. Because the Library Tower is the tallest building in L.A. and the Central Library the architectural gem of the area, the stairs, popularly called the "Spanish Steps" by analogy with those in Rome, have the symbolic as well as the functional intention of joining the forest of corporate towers to the civic and retail zones at their base. The center of energy, however, is not on the hill but at its foot.

The conceptual model of the acropolis has not worked well in L.A., in part because the terrain's elevations in the round are unimportant compared to its flat surfaces and curtain-wall backdrops. But the acropolis is an ambitious mechanism for organization and control; designs of this kind emerge as a response to, and effort to master, unchecked horizontal growth. Lloyd Wright's notion that his hierarchy of systems (trains, cars, airplanes) would localize the world in his Capitol only exaggerates the more practical effect of localizing the city there. What was essentially metaphoric at the father's Olive Hill is literal on the son's envisioned, if not on today's actual, Bunker Hill: a "high city" can cause its surroundings to be read as a "low city." In 1925 Wallace Neff drew a design for a hill in Pasadena, an effort contemporary with Wright's Civic Center; it also asserts hierarchy, in Neff's case that of a ramped and girdled Mediterranean hill-village, with its base, middle, and crown. Both unrealized projects evoke an intermittently apparent Los Angeles, one pathetically missing in the Civic Center as actually built, but indirectly and ironically invoked by Cesar Pelli's dazzling complex of furniture showrooms called the Pacific Design Center. The first of these, built in 1975, is the humped mass in David Hockney's signature painting (Fig. 110); the achieved group of several bold structures recalls the great ceremonial erections of an ancient city as the buildings gather protectively around a simulacrum of a public square.

Nothing in 1980s Los Angeles more successfully promoted an image of civic authority than this configuration of plaza and domineering,

unique buildings, and nothing in reality was less so. In part this was because the showrooms were originally wholesale and closed to the public;
in part it was a factor of the site, which, low and sloping, neither flatland
nor hill, implies transition rather than arrival. That suggestion is probably appropriate for what is really a glamorous entrepôt. A third reason is
the setting close up against, but not as a part of, the backdropping hills;
Pelli's bulky, spaceshiplike structures dominate the toylike environment
of West Hollywood, but they in turn are dominated by the Santa Monica
Mountains, to which in fact they lend proportion. In this way the Pacific
Design Center functions effectively on the scale of L.A. as a whole, but
not as its acropolis, a dignity to which it does not pretend. That honor
could have been claimed only by the mountains themselves, at least until the opening in December 1997 of Richard Meier's enormous Getty Center (Fig. 125), the first achieved construction that succeeds in redefining
them as a base supporting a crown of architecture.

Often compared to a Tuscan hill town, the Getty might be better analo-
gized to a palatial citadel of the kind found in such Asian cities as Jodh-
pur: a complex of authority and services not to be confused with the mundane city at its feet. It will be several years, at least, before L.A. settles down
to being the base of which the Getty is the crown: the sour aftertaste of so
much hostile preopening publicity, accusing the institution of elitism and
deploring its fortresslike effect as viewed from the San Diego freeway below, must be reconciled to the startling *overuse* of the complex by thousands who flock there as if to a theme park—for although entrances can
be strictly controlled, the length of time people stay, once up there, has
proved to be greater than anticipated, with a consequent much-joked-
about pressure on the rest rooms. The spatial and visual experiences the
Getty offers, however, have convinced many that it is the worthy successor of earlier points of vantage over earlier, flatter, L.A.'s; perhaps its spiritual predecessor is the Griffith Park Observatory, which both offers a major perspective and looks like the kind of place that is supposed to do so.
From the coulisses between the Getty's dramatically angled masonry
slabs, L.A.'s dispersed clusters of tall buildings make sense as a sequence,
perhaps for the first time.

The Getty's chief rival for visual control of the Los Angeles basin remains the Hollywood Sign, the signature mental image of the city. In Ed-

FIGURE 125. Getty Center by Richard Meier, Los Angeles, 1997.

ward Ruscha's fantasized version of 1968 (Fig. 126), the sign, rather than projecting from the face of the ridge (Fig. 127), rides its crest. This is where it "psychologically ought to be," as big and conspicuous as it is in imagination. Once the name of a residential development ("Hollywoodland"— the last four letters were removed) and subsequently a kind of label for Hollywood below, the sign is now an object of pilgrimage in its own right. Local residents are used to tourists standing in the middle of Beachwood Canyon Drive to photograph it, or, more oddly, asking directions to it in the twisting roads of the hills, as if it were important to get close to an ob-

FIGURE 126 *(top)*. *Hollywood* by Edward Ruscha, 1968. Silk screen, 17½ x 44½".

FIGURE 127 *(bottom)*. A 1998 shot of the Hollywood Sign and environs.

ject intended to be noticed from a distance. Constituted only of air, light, barren earth, and the name of a desire, it has come to represent not a subdivision nor even an industry but an idea, and for that reason people want to touch it, as if to touch the essence of L.A. The agenda of every conceptual model is to represent itself as the essential city, and, although as topography and architecture the acropolis has had an uneven record, it has succeeded here, in a purely semiotic victory.

Conceding the limitations of his 1925 Civic Center project, Lloyd Wright in 1966 said, "With the increasing speed, a concept of more breadth was needed. The little ditch that had made the pueblo was no longer the dominant element in the area, either geographically or otherwise. It became apparent to me that the great star of this city was not *estancias;* they were not the focal point, but the Pacific Ocean front from Point Dume to Orange County. It became obvious that we should develop that, and go back through the various mountain ranges and coordinate all our traffic and parkways in accord with the natural topography. This," he concluded, "I have done," referring to his regional urban plan of 1962, which proposed rings of freeways around the center and perimeter of the city, intersecting north-south and east-west corridors. The anchor of his project was the waterfront, graced by an offshore causeway that created a lagoon. Wright seems to have felt that this feature was the justification of what otherwise could be thought of as a huge backup system. "I have coordinated highways and waterways to create marinas, great floating cities," he continued, "a magnificent forefront for the city."

What Wright confidently projected was more than a transportation network; like other planners of L.A.'s roads, he imposed a mythology of movement upon the basin. In his case it was simple and directional: good roads meant better access to the essential city, the paradise of pleasure and leisure that he visualized as the beach, rather like the received image of Rio de Janeiro. Roadways, in this way of thinking, are keys that unlock the terrain's hidden gifts. Because they could be quickly and dramatically landscaped, streets and roads figured prominently in early L.A. publicity; Magnolia Avenue (Fig. 49) and Palm Drive (Fig. 107), among many others, are both more monumental and more inviting than most of the architecture of the period. Perhaps they subliminally reinforced the "quest" mythology promoted by the region; where there are roads there must be destinations, even destinations as fanciful as El Dorado.

A project promoted by Harry Chandler of the *Los Angeles Times* and noisily boosted in Sherley Hunter's 1923 *Why Los Angeles Will Become the World's Greatest City* proposed an enormous 230-foot-wide boulevard be-

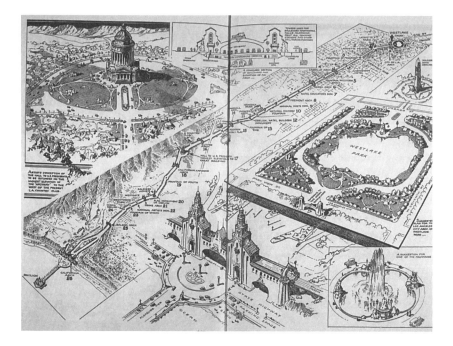

FIGURE 128. Thoroughfare project for Los Angeles by Aurele Vermeulen (land-scape architect), 1923.

ginning at Westlake (now MacArthur) Park and following the routes of Wilshire and San Vicente Boulevards into the Santa Monica Canyon and so to the ocean (Fig. 128). It is natural today to ridicule its transparent effort to pass off a gigantic speculative moneymaking venture as an act of homage to the soldiers, artists, presidents, and other worthies honored by its structures and fountains. Hindsight situates this nearly forgotten scheme in the line of the political and judicial struggles to transform residentially zoned Wilshire into the commercial prodigy of the late twenties and thirties; developer A. W. Ross actually began putting together what would be called the "Miracle Mile," between Fairfax and La Brea Avenues, as early as 1924.

But however retrograde its exposition imagery (not only San Diego 1915, but also Chicago 1893), however windy its celebration of the godfathers of California, and however misplaced its pretensions to glorify, for instance, poets, the imaginary boulevard overlay a route followed by American Indians, Spaniards, Mexicans, and Anglos for centuries. It renders in three dimensions a mental image of the city's movement toward its future. Stripped of its stucco, much of the project has in one form or another taken shape; even the subway proposed in the multilayered transportation section at the top of the drawing is back in favor beneath Wilshire Boulevard today, although the equestrian lane has found no advocate. The pueblo lands are virtually out of the picture, represented only by the stretch from Westlake to Lafayette Park; a "West L.A." is taking shape in the form of a linear city, and as if the edge of the continent were not enough, the exposition architecture marches along a pier into the Pacific.

In Hunter's excited prose, the scheme is the germ of an expanding system of transportation that would eventually both embrace and define concentric zones to the north, east, and south:

A great *unfolding* of a dream, spread out over a back country *reaching* into Nevada, the San Joaquin Valley, Utah to Salt Lake City, Arizona, and portions of New Mexico and Colorado—down to San Diego and into Mexico. Today the community of Los Angeles has a *fifty-mile* radius, bristling with the *start* of industrial development—this radius is *amply* cared for by a network of electric lines: hardly more than *tomorrow* this radius will *extend* to *one hundred miles*. . . . When the hundred-mile radius is *filled* to a *comfortable* convenience . . . [it] will take on *another* fifty miles or so, that the *circle* will, *constantly*, remain a metropolitan district reaching almost to San Diego and up to the San Jacinto mountains—*another* network of motor roads, electric lines, air-navigtion landing fields, ware-houses—and *always* a *mingling* of agriculture and fruit-growing *with* industrial establishments and everyone *enjoying* the year-round outdoor climate and healthfulness.

Joan Didion has characterized Harry Chandler's ambitions for Los Angeles as visionary to the extent that where conventional opinion saw in Los Angeles an unmanaged sprawl, Chandler envisioned, or schemed for, "a new kind of city, which would seem to have no finite limits, a literal cloud on the land that would eventually touch the Tehachapi range to the north and the Mexican border to the south, the San Bernardino Mountains to the east and the Pacific to the west; not just a city, finally, but its own nation—the Southland." Much as walls are thought to define the ancient city, by marking off its space as *not*-country, so "roads" are the key to this projected Los Angeles, annexing space to the limits imposed by geography.

Among the responses to the anxieties induced by new and rapid kinds of transportation is the effort to subordinate them to architecture, for example by running rail lines directly through buildings at all sorts of levels. This concept was popular in visionary drawings of the late nineteenth and early twentieth centuries, often in conjunction with futuristic essays or science fiction. The effect is to assert the primacy of the building, in part because the transportation lines are lifted from the earth and move on a wholly artificial roadbed, in part because the buildings appear to emit and absorb them. In this manner, in the 1923 project, trains are hoisted aloft and channeled through the gigantic California Arch. The boulevard arches, exaggerated in size, have a similar controlling function, seemingly framing the flow of cars, establishing the scale for the flanking frontage roads, sheltering and defining the other systems of movement (rail, foot, and horse), and stapling together the halves of the city split by the great artery. Their towers are also designated as police, road-maintenance, and first-aid stations; telephone booths; and public toilets.

What is, in the end, illusory and even absurd about these arches is not their rapidly dating Spanish/fairgrounds symbolism, but rather their pretensions to exercise this degree of authority. They speak to the half of regional sensibility that demands a replete, appropriate imagery, one that does not expand but that closes and completes the stage set of a desired Los Angeles. Expositions and, later, theme parks satisfy such desires, and, in the drawing, the meeting of the boulevard and the Pacific Coast Highway looks like an intersection in such a fairground or park. The roadbed itself, represented in the publicity brochure as a means for the realization of the civic amenities symbolized by and contained in these superstructures, is in fact the only viable part of the system. One of the many schemes for unifying Los Angeles's railway termini (Fig. 129) is an analogous instance of the conceptual subordination of the place to the means of getting through it. Fourth, Sixth, and Seventh Streets have become, in the drawing, mere overpasses, and the Los Angeles River recalls a canal in

FIGURE 129. Noerenberg plan for a passenger railroad terminal for Los Angeles, about 1926.

the formal gardens of a baroque country house. The station itself looks like a pair of ventilators upon the carapace of iron and concrete.

A similar uncertainty about priorities destabilizes the attractive park-way schemes of the 1920s and 1930s. They were first conceived as adjuncts to plans for unsnarling downtown traffic, which by 1924, with some four hundred thousand vehicles registered in the county, was sufficiently damaging to business to justify the creation of a traffic commission and the production of a report focusing on downtown. Some of the proposed solutions were bold, to say the least, like a no-nonsense diagonal boule-vard thrusting First Street northwest across Hollywood to the Cahuenga Pass. Lamenting the fact that Los Angeles had the nation's most congested streets, the report nevertheless reinforces the mythology of motion, as-serting that "there is no day in the year [in Los Angeles] when it is im-possible or even uncomfortable to ride in an open car."

"Parkways," a secondary concern of the report, are proposed as routes for passenger vehicles only, "made exceptionally agreeable . . . for plea-sure travel by every possible means, but especially by the feeling of openness that comes only with plenty of width and by an ample enframement of trees, shrubs, and other plantations." Unlike thoroughfares, roads of this kind would, in the commission's imagination, actually assume the functions of more traditional public spaces; they would be "simply elongated parks in which people circulate for the pleasure they find in them." As David Brodsly observes, this "vocabulary and imagery continued to haunt city planning for the subsequent two decades."

In 1925 the Allied Architects Association's proposal for the Civic Center—the same competition for which Lloyd Wright submitted his striking designs—called for the reconstruction of Bunker Hill both as a city park and as the fulcrum of a system of Arcadian motorways "through this park, connecting with Mulholland Drive through the Hollywood Hills, and reaching the beaches and the countryside in ease." In the following year, an official identified as the Efficiency Director of the city's Department of Water and Power, complaining of increasing congestion both in housing and in traffic and arguing for an automobile-based decentralized metropolis, describes the streets of downtown as "badly handicapped by 'Bunker Hill.'" Clearly, for him, the road has become the conceptual model for the city, its *parti* in architectural language. Perhaps the sense that the parkway could actually displace the merely functional street, and thereby transform "traffic" into some kind of Arcadian activity, influenced a suggestively titled 1927 article in *The New Republic*, "Los Angeles: The City That Is Bacchanalian—in a Nice Way": "I saw huge boulevards, sixty paces wide, unfurl in smooth ribbons through the welter of sandstone and steel. Parks rolled out like green rugs. . . . At every street intersection one roadway dipped beneath the other. The city turned rapidly into paradise—retaining its motor cars."

In 1930, the Citizens' Committee on Parks, Playgrounds, and Beaches published proposals by the Olmsted brothers and their associates that placed parkways at the center of transportation consciousness:

> One of the most urgent park needs of the Los Angeles Region [is] the need for a system of interconnected pleasureway parks, regional in scope.
>
> Such a system should be so distributed that no home will be more than a few miles from some part of it; and should be so designed that,

having reached any part of it, one may drive within the system for pleasure, and *with* pleasure, for many miles under thoroughly agreeable conditions and in pleasant surroundings. Free from interruption of ordinary urban and suburban conditions, driving there may be either wholly for the pleasure of such driving or, more generally, it may be over the pleasantest if not always the shortest route to some other recreational objective.

The plan ambitiously reshapes riverbeds and canyons into parkways, and plants a causeway between Pacific Palisades and Playa del Rey; the cost, spread over four to five decades, is projected at $143,850,000.

Taken at its word, the proposal constitutes a radical definition of what a city should be and what its citizens have the right to expect—in effect, universal neighborhood access to a kind of "automobile park," a linear city of movement through an endless ribbon of green. Unlike a Utopian plan, the one for Redondo Beach for instance (Fig. 108), this one appears to discover what was implicit in the landscape, as if coaxing the underlying pattern of the region out of the awkward impositions of streets and blocks. The stated objective is, after all, Arcadian: *pleasure* is reiterated not only as the most important experience of driving (the emphasis in the quotation is original), but also as its goal ("some other recreational objective"). Yet those vaguely envisioned destinations seem less important, as the proposal is worded, than the trips themselves, which have the important effect of making the city of the imagination roughly coterminous with the city (or county) of maps and boundaries. Red Car day-trippers had made elaborate circuits of the region, but with the exception of the passage through the (by 1930, disappearing) citrus groves, their trips were, at least in principle, means to ends. Parkways envision an experiential city whose rewards, to the driver in the private car, are manifest in all corners.

In *The City in History* (1961), Lewis Mumford sets down the arresting statistic that about one-third of the region, and *two-thirds* (Mumford's emphasis) of "central" Los Angeles, is occupied by roadways and their supporting apparatuses. He speaks for the substantial body of opinion that sees Los Angeles as the prime culprit among cities that have surrendered their constitution to the automobile: "Los Angeles has now [1961] become an undifferentiated mass of houses, walled off into sectors by many-laned expressways, with ramps and viaducts that create special bottlenecks of their own. These expressways move but a small fraction of the traffic per hour once carried by public transportation, at a much lower rate of speed, in an environment befouled by smog, itself produced by the lethal exhausts of the technologically backward motor cars."

Scott L. Bottles has authoritatively debunked the legend, asserted by Mumford as if it were indisputable, and still widely accepted within and beyond Los Angeles, that a beloved and efficient network of streetcars was destroyed by a conspiracy of internal-combustion engine manufacturers. Arguing that ideology and esthetics in the twenties combined to generate a "Greater Los Angeles" of dispersed, automobile-served communities, Bottles documents popular and Progressivist anger against the privately owned streetcar lines and explains the belief, shared by planners and ordinary citizens, that Los Angeles was an ideal urban environment because it was decentralized. Angelenos preferred suburban dispersal even when plenty of land near downtown remained undeveloped.

Reinforcing these attitudes may be what journalist Jan Morris describes as the "comradeship" of L.A., "a common sense of release or opportunity, tinged with a spice of holiday." The pursuit of happiness in Los Angeles often appears to be a highly professional activity; the surfing beaches, for example, are "no place for dilettantes." The 1930 plan projects a similar double image of the pleasure principle and the technological imperative. There is something faintly comic about the notion of an enormous engineering project that, in its own words, facilitates driving longer distances than necessary purely for the fun of it, but that sense of the ridiculous is not habitual in L.A. (Berthold Brecht is said to have complained that "scarcely anywhere have I found life more difficult than here in this show place of 'easy going'".) Behind Bottles's analysis lies an unspoken local equation of sociopolitical with hedonistic goals, and the bitterness often expressed about the freeways today speaks for the thwarting of the latter as much as of the former.

As Raymond Chandler's Philip Marlowe drives in and around L.A., his contradictory responses to the city sometimes harmonize in the flow of the sequence of images; sometimes, when the sequence becomes a maddening circuit around nothing, they do not. *Farewell, My Lovely* (1940) presents through Marlowe's eye a virtual survey of Sunset Boulevard from "the bright mile or two of the Strip," where he remarks dispassionately on the commerce in flesh and luxuries, to the idyll of Beverly Hills, "all colors of the spectrum and crystal clear in an evening without fog," then "past shadowed mansions" and along the curves of the road until he reaches "the sudden cool dusk and the drift of wind from the sea." There is much more: Marlowe's sharp eye scans and judges, but ultimately all his reactions merge into the cinematic flow of an unfolding story; unwittingly, he even anticipates the delicate and improbable orange grove at Charles Moore's Rodes House (1979) in Brentwood, which would lie along this route. The lyricism is nicely out of synch with the situation, as Marlowe is a somewhat reluctant passenger in a sinister automobile, en route to a dangerous destination.

In another passage, from *The Little Sister* (1949), he moves of his own accord, turning east on Sunset, then north, then west, navigating Ventura Boulevard and its packs of hot-rodders and sedans driven by fatigued citizens en route to their evenings of "the sports page, the blatting of the radio, the whining of their spoiled children, and the gabble of their silly wives." The ride embraces some of the most characteristic of L.A. automotive structures and infrastructures, among them drive-in restaurants with "chipper hard-eyed car-hops," and massive trucks that rumble north down the Sepulveda Pass, making noises like caged beasts. From Encino to Malibu he broods cynically on vanity and easy sex while "a breeze, unbroken from the ocean, danced casually across the night." The characterless Pacific seems, as it did to Edmund Wilson, empty of affect. Finally, "I smelled Los Angeles before I got to it. It smelled stale and old like a living room that had been closed too long. But the colored lights fooled you. The lights were wonderful. There ought to be a monument to the man who invented neon lights. Fifteen stories high, solid marble. There's a boy who really made something out of nothing."

What is convincingly L.A. about the second drive in particular is Marlowe's free-ranging attention; traffic is a minor distraction from the passing panorama. Both passages, however, present L.A. as viewed through the windows of a moving automobile, an experience that is not only the best way to see the city but also the key to its structure. The quality of Marlowe's judgments is another matter; Chandler allows him, in the second passage, a repeated self-correction ("you're not human tonight") against facile condemnations, and in the former, Marlowe's pleasure in the disclosures of the route is tempered by satirical characterizations of the egos and libidos behind the facades. Both capacities, delight and disgust, should be recalled when the rhetoric of the freeways displaces that of the surface streets.

The disgust is reflexive, despite impressive defenses of the utility and beauty of the freeways by Reyner Banham, David Brodsly, and others. As evidence of hostility to them, however, Brodsly's eloquent *L.A. Freeway: An Appreciative Essay* cites lines from Malvina Reynolds's 1966 song "The Cement Octopus":

> There's a cement octopus that sits in Sacramento, I think,
> Gets red tape to eat, gasoline taxes to drink,
> And it grows by day and it grows by night,
> And it rolls over everything in sight,
> Oh stand by me and protect that tree
> From the freeway misery.

About this lyric, Brodsly observes, "The predominance of serpentine imagery, augmented by related images such as octopus tentacles or aberrations of the natural world, suggests the freeway's power to represent the modern equivalent of primordial evil." Peter Plagens's angry attacks on Banham's upbeat analysis include "Los Angeles: The Ecology of Evil" (1972) and the sardonically titled "The LA Connection: Pushing Freeways" (1973), articles that treat freeways as metonyms for L.A. and L.A. as a metonym for capitalism. Definitions like "Los Angeles is a huge, shallow toilet bowl" or a journalist's loaded metaphors that link L.A. freeways with "every other once-virginal city that has been penetrated by the interstate highway system" may have only the subjective validity of the song quoted above or of the two allusions to drug addiction in the title of Plagens's 1973 article. Those predisposed to agree will feel vindicated.

Yet the freeway was, in Brodsly's words, "the logical next step in making the Los Angeles dream a reality." To some extent the reasons are pragmatic: many different interest groups once agreed that freeways would solve their problems by promoting both growth, decentralization, and (because of the relatively consistent quality of access) stable land values. "The freeways," argues Scott Bottles, "were essential to their vision of a modern, uncrowded metropolis composed of single-family dwellings and pastoral beauty." They have evolved, however, into the outstanding tools and symbols of a metropolis that no longer agrees on those three goals, and as such are repeatedly invoked to account for the successes and failures of the city as a whole. Claes Oldenburg's "happening" *Autobodys,* performed in Los Angeles in 1963 and consisting of an appearance of carefully chosen cars on a parking lot illuminated by car headlights and watched by spectators in automobiles, "emphasized Los Angeles's dependence on the car and the sterility of its freeway culture." The freeways' folkloric status is sustained by constant radio warnings of major slowdowns and accidents and memorable spillages like glue (July 31, 1989), nacho cheese and lard (June 24, 1991), and goats (February 18, 1996). It was as if the triumph of the private car over the hindrances of streetcars and pedestrians coincided with the end of the dream of a landscape of lush mobility, the vision of the parkway (Fig. 130). "Time spent on [the freeways]," asserts a 1966 *New Yorker* piece, "can be counted as time lost."

Of course, there is plenty of evidence for their efficiency and their advantages over public transportation, and a simple comparison, made with care by Banham, of the virtual overlay of the freeways along the routes of the Pacific Electric rail lines, disposes of the argument (as made, for example, by Richard Gilbert) that the freeways cut into pieces a previously unified central city. "Planning" in Los Angeles has been synonymous with "transportation" not only in the freeway era but since the first rails were laid. As Frank Dimster observes, even surface streets dictate perceptions of the spatial pattern of the city: "The architectural composition lining the streets is secondary and in fact often hidden by vegetation. Thus, the identity of an area is given by the dominant street use and not by dominant buildings." All "roads," iron or asphalt, make up, from this perspective, not only the most recent conceptual model of Los Angeles but also the only one that has effectively been perfected, in the

FIGURE 130. Arroyo Seco Parkway, 1940.

Aristotelian sense of the word: freeways are (as far as we can imagine) the final stage.

The battle between their lovers and haters is a matter of psychology and even esthetics more than of calculations of time saved or money lost. Banham is no less subjective than the author of the *New Yorker* article just quoted in generalizing from "[his] own observations of Angeleno drivers at close range" that "the freeway is not a limbo of existential *angst* but the place where they spend the two calmest and most rewarding hours of their daily lives." Banham also suggests, however, that the concentration necessary for a complete appreciation of the experience may induce "a state of heightened awareness that some locals find mystical." This higher key of argument governs Joan Didion's definition of "the freeway experience" as "the only secular communion Los Angeles has." The act of partaking of an adored body, which is what "communion" implies, will seem less extravagant a sentiment on the part of a woman who has also testified to her youthful love for New York: "I do not mean 'love' in any colloquial way, I mean that I was in love with the city, the way you love the first person who ever touches you and never love anyone quite that way again."

To be in touch with Los Angeles in this sense, of identifying oneself with its most elemental and primary rhythms, is the achievement of Maria Wyeth, in Didion's novel *Play It as It Lays* (1970):

Once she was on the freeway and had maneuvered her way to a fast lane she turned on the radio at high volume and she drove. She drove the San Diego to the Harbor, the Harbor up to the Hollywood, the Hollywood to the Golden State, the Santa Monica, the Santa Ana, the Pasadena, the Ventura. She drove it as a riverman runs a river, every day more attuned to its currents, its deceptions, and just as a riverman feels the pull of the rapids in the lull between sleeping and waking, so Maria lay at night in the still of Beverly Hills and saw the great signs soar overhead at seventy miles an hour, *Normandie ¼ Vermont ¾ Harbor Fwy 1*. Again and again she returned to an intricate stretch just south of the interchange where successful passage from the Hollywood onto the Harbor required a diagonal move across four lanes of traffic. On the afternoon she finally did it without once braking or once losing the beat on the radio she was exhilarated, and that night slept dreamlessly.

Maria personifies that total identification with the freeways that Didion calls "actual participation, [which] requires a total surrender, a concentration so intense as to seem a kind of narcosis." The simultaneous experience of fluidity and stability, the two apparently incompatible conditions pursued by early advocates of the freeways as the formula for a successful L.A., are internalized in Maria's temperament and detached from considerations of property and utility. The freeways, in other words, have become an end in themselves, paralleling the ocean, the mountains, and the desert as a kind of proving ground for another quasi-athletic, quasi-experiential cult. "Actual participants," Didion says, "think only about where they are." There is no still center to this technological and spiritual Utopia of the freeway; in Maria's head there is, however, a destination that is also a return: the desert of her childhood—a Nevada hamlet now obliterated beneath a missile firing range—and the desert of her marriage, for her estranged husband, a director, is out there on location where the freeways finally exhaust themselves.

5   Inventing Arcadia

Les vrais paradis sont les paradis qu'on a perdus.
MARCEL PROUST

Q

       A farmer, a plow, a horse, and a view of the hills (Fig. 131): the image is of a preurban Los Angeles but on an English model by way of the happier corners of Appalachia, where the solitary yeoman and his decent homestead complete the picture of a laborer's idyll. These, however, are the *Hollywood* Hills, and the year is 1900, well after the date of the aggressive 1887 perspective put forth by H. H. Wilcox (Fig. 27). The maneuver by which more than a decade of property development has seemingly been annulled has something to do with the scope and marketing strategy of the publication, *Art Work on Southern California*, from which the image is taken, but it also exemplifies the continuing process in L.A. of laying claim to the past in the very act of devising the present.

     In the characteristic iconography of L.A., a natural paradise coexists with developers' ambitions or is even impervious to them. Its poles are

FIGURE 131. Scene near Hollywood, from *Art Work on Southern California* by Lou V. Chapin, 1900.

pretty close: photographs of a winter rose garden (Fig. 132) or of an effortlessly urbane street (Fig. 133) seem to document an achieved harmony between culture and nature. Even the instruments of power may appear benign (Fig. 134). In a stern rejection of such fantasies, the cover of Mike Davis's *City of Quartz* chooses, of all possible images for the presentation of L.A., the Metropolitan Detention Center downtown, without flowers. The anger that informs this book perpetuates a tradition of disillusion and disgust explicable in the light of the region's pretensions to a perfection probably attainable only in memory or imagination. "The only true paradise," Proust warns, "is paradise lost."

The early work of David Hockney and of Edward Ruscha constitutes a body of representation of Los Angeles that transcends the mechanical

FIGURE 132 *(top).* Winter scene in Pasadena (undated photograph).

FIGURE 133 *(bottom).* Street scene in Los Angeles, early 1920s.

FIGURE 134. Hollywood Police Station, 1600 block of Cahuenga Boulevard, about 1910.

alternation between enthusiasm and disgust. Unlike as they are, the two artists defined the moment at which what was salvageable in the romance of an idyllic Southern California could be revivified at a level of full consciousness. Their work is highly aware of contradictions but is free of the sarcasm that in journalistic attacks on L.A. has customarily been misdefined as "irony." Both were provincials and outsiders (Yorkshire; Oklahoma), and both responded to the city as a physique rather than as a narrative. Each is inclusive, acknowledging an environment of concrete as well as of earth, air, and water. With the passage of decades each artist has moved to more internalized and conceptualized ways of representing reality, but in their 1960s and 1970s work both succeeded in generating highly accessible imagery of a place seemingly not subject to the erosions of time.

An avenue of entry into Arcadia is by way of homosexuality, which in classical pastoral literature, where the components of Arcadian idealism are set forth, is exemplary because it is free from the contingencies of wealth, work, and status.* Hockney's fresh response to a scene of which everybody else was thoroughly tired, Pershing Square (Fig. 103), stands imaginatively, and approximately chronologically, at the beginning of his canvases and drawings of a replete and highly eroticized environment. No doubt some of the hostility to Hockney's work is expressive of hostility to these ancient structures of esthetics and erotics; beauty (not wisdom or power or honor or wealth) is the greatest pastoral value. Peter Plagens's claim, for example, that Hockney's swimming pool pictures (e.g., Fig. 135) disclose "the vacancy at the heart of physical pleasure" is indistinguishable from the language of arguments against nonprocreative sex.

In other areas as well, hostility to Los Angeles coincides not with L.A.'s failures but with its successes; the antagonism is not to smog, so to speak, but to sunlight. The received attitude is exemplified by Robert Hughes in a 1972 *Time* article: "Part of the attraction that Hockney's work exerts is its mixture of unusual *guile* and apparent naïveté. He is a painter of frozen pleasures, held in *ironic* parentheses as though behind glass—the *artificial* but absorbingly *hedonistic* blue of Los Angeles swimming pools, the *plastic* palms, the *flat glitter* of light on a shower stall or a street facade. It is all painted *deadpan*" (emphasis added). The use of "irony" as the tool for resolving all contradictions situates the analysis firmly in the literary culture of its age. Where the image conflicts with the perceiver's assumptions, its surfaces are presumed to be facades concealing the truth, which yields itself up to the critic who wears no rose-tinted spectacles. The italicized terms refer to the formal properties of a Hockney canvas, but in Hughes's prose they do not describe the image; they drive it. Brought to life as metaphors—*flat* meaning lacking depth, *glitter* meaning lacking both restraint and inner light, *plastic* meaning lacking substantive and structural integrity, and so forth—they become judgmental terms. The obligation to "interpret" works of art, denounced by Susan Sontag as long ago as 1964 ("In place of a hermeneutics we need an erotics of art"), converts Hockney's imagery into the opposite of itself, to no useful purpose.

A similar moralizing tone governs some responses to Hockney's rendering of persons. Present only by implication in *A Bigger Splash,* the hu-

FIGURE 135. *A Bigger Splash* by David Hockney, 1967. Acrylic on canvas, 96 x 96".
© David Hockney.

man figure is altogether replaced by tools in *A Lawn Being Sprinkled* (Fig. 136), which for one critic evokes the "aloneness" in Edward Hopper's paintings and which another describes as "a vacant suburban yard, its automatic sprinklers having usurped the activity of both nature and gardener." We would learn more about these paintings by comparing them to those of Claude Lorrain, where figures are subordinated to environmental design and the setting is more important than any event of the moment. In *A Lawn Being Sprinkled* the artifice of the architecture is so simple

FIGURE 136. *A Lawn Being Sprinkled* by David Hockney, 1967. Acrylic on canvas, 60 x 60". © David Hockney.

and the environmental phenomena—grass, water, air—so artfully organized and so dependent on technologies that no experiential gap exists between the "natural" and the "artificial." This Arcadia is wholly naturalized in a contemporary backyard; Christopher Knight has helpfully drawn analogies with the Greek equivalent of a primal paradise: "Hockney's pictures of swimming pools . . . are contemporary adaptations of the conventional literary and artistic theme of the Golden Age. The voluptuous and sybaritic bather is a primary symbol of that classical myth of origin, a myth that speaks of a lost, pastoral Arcadia of peace and harmony, which stands in sharp contrast to the convulsively animated world of history."

However, it is arguable that Hockney has in fact allowed for that "world of history" and not merely turned his back on it. The classically structured

FIGURE 137. *Portrait of an Artist (Pool with Two Figures)* by David Hockney, 1971. Acrylic on canvas, 84 x 120". © David Hockney.

sequence of bare mountains, lush planting, and architectural water (so to speak) of Hockney's 1971 canvas *Portrait of an Artist (Pool with Two Figures)* (Fig. 137) describes a historical and technological progression like that of the Questa lemon-box label (Fig. 22). A critic describing Hockney's architecture as "a city set in aspic" has in effect recognized (without necessarily endorsing) the tension between the snapshotlike imagery and the marmoreal rendering in acrylic. Terms like *frozen* and *aspic* indirectly acknowledge Hockney's simultaneous representation of time and nullification of its passage. Noon is the pastoral hour, its stillness "a core of suspended energy"; Hockney's Los Angeles is a city of sunshine, not electric lights.

Ruscha's work, like Hockney's, has often been admired for a supposed demystification of Los Angeles, as if his images constituted a telling critique of local values. I think that they tell us something else. Another image from Chapin's promotional collection, *Sunset Boulevard, Hollywood*

FIGURE 138. Sunset Boulevard, Hollywood, from *Art Work on Southern California* by Lou V. Chapin, 1900.

(Fig. 138), for example, must have appeared scarcely less nostalgic to its targeted eastern audience of 1900 than it does to us today: for us, it evokes the past of Los Angeles, for them simply "the past." Ruscha had already observantly documented the length of this boulevard through West Hollywood (Fig. 78) when he conceptualized it as a sign that looks something like an ad for a movie (Fig. 139), though not quite the one with Gloria Swanson. The self-important syntax evokes *A Streetcar Named Desire, A Man Called Peter,* and other period pieces. There is plenty of irony, but within the closed system of Los Angeles self-referencing; there is no irony at all in the recognition that a place can be subsumed in the idea of itself, and that idea summed up in a word or a phrase. As Peter Schjeldahl says of *Every Building on the Sunset Strip,* "There can be no integral experience . . . to match the seductive density of its name." *Arcadia* and *Utopia* are more evocative words than any picture of or narrative about them can

FIGURE 139. *A BLVD. CALLED SUNSET*
by Edward Ruscha, 1975. Blackberry
juice on moiré, 28 x 40".

justify. Both nostalgia and the notion that this image is judging its subject are, like irony, irrelevant.

A BLVD. CALLED SUNSET evokes certain realities of L.A. by way of the artist's training in commercial art. Similarly, his sequence *A Few Palm Trees* (Fig. 33) recalls the cutout technique of advertising imagery. *Real Estate Opportunities* (1970), a volume of photographs of properties for sale (Fig. 140), is a conceptual work masquerading as a promotion, neatly inverting the logic of Chapin's promotional volume, which masquerades as art. Like Chapin, Ruscha renders L.A. as a sequence of empty places waiting to be filled. This expectancy governs *Some Los Angeles Apartments* (1965), *Thirtyfour Parking Lots* (1967), and *Nine Swimming Pools and a Broken Glass* (1968), with this difference from Chapin, that the filling of the documented spaces is to be done locally; there is no special propaganda toward easterners. Ruscha's volumes of serial images define a recognizable and predictable place—for example, a city of apartment buildings, of palm trees, or of pools—by classification and systematization. He thereby creates a mental image of an experiential city whose characteristics are accessibility, multiplication, and dispersal, foregrounding several omnipresent but little-valued sequences of structures that, like the pervasive neo-Hispanic bungalows or the exceptional Case Study Houses, make up the armature of the city.

Many will find the surface of the city Ruscha represents uninviting; in fairness to these parking spaces and pools, however, they are attractive to the extent that they are experienced, not observed. The supporting apparatus for the pools, for example, is harsh: cement, concrete, metal, glass, fiberglass, plastic, and so forth; it includes blunt signage and clunky vend-

Sherman Way & Forbes Ave. (southwest corner) Van Nuys

FIGURE 140. Page
from *Real Estate
Opportunities*
by Edward Ruscha,
1970.

ing machines (Fig. 141). But the intense turquoise of the water is a visual
approximation of the pleasure offered by the pool as energetically *used*.
An empty parking space also has been known to make hearts leap for joy.
In *Los Angeles: The Ultimate City,* Christopher Rand, as if to validate
Ruscha's work, sketches the phenomenological ancestry of Anglo L.A. as
the product of "squares from the North European countries of the rectilinear flags. . . . In the Midwest they planted their squareness on the landscape: gridirons on the settlements; rectangular fields, farms, towns,
counties, and states on the open country. And coming to L.A. they have
planted it wherever possible; an L.A. teenager can spend half his waking
life now on or in concrete rectangles, such as tennis courts, highways, and
swimming pools."

FIGURE 141. Page from *Nine Swimming Pools and a Broken Glass* by Edward Ruscha, 1968.

Taking issue with the received opinion that a swimming pool wastes water and symbolizes empty hedonism, Joan Didion reads it as "a symbol not of affluence but of order, of control over the uncontrollable." The gap between daily life and the Arcadia of Hockney's *A Bigger Splash* is nowhere more evident than when this control is lost, as in the mess left by flooding in a Beverly Glen yard in 1952 (Fig. 142). In calling attention to water, Hockney does more than highlight a suburban pleasure; the most elegant structure in Los Angeles in 1860 was not a church or even a residence but a reservoir (Fig. 143); even a dramatic, romantic photograph of its latter-day equivalent (Fig. 144) does not exaggerate either the importance or the romance of controlling water.

Taken together, these architectural forms, monuments of engineering, intellectual rationalizations, and sensuous renderings constitute a body

FIGURE 142. Flooding in Beverly Glen, 1952.

of Arcadian rhetoric that interprets technological sophistication as the natural extension of primitive and timeless impulses for gratification. By managing both the image and our response to it, Hockney and Ruscha practice explicitly what most photographs do implicitly, even though the photographs (e.g., Fig. 144) may claim to be merely documentary. That L.A. should appear "Arcadian" or "Utopian" is not determined by the objects in the field of vision but by the "take," or imaginative shaping of their appearance. The key to the Arcadian status of Hockney's and Ruscha's images lies in the absence of any apparent and strenuous effort to make them look idyllic; the L.A. they constitute or describe is an act of the mind or a willed perception. They simply leapfrog architects' and planners' self-conscious efforts to fashion an Arcadian environment.

Some architects did, of course, try to make one. The surprising freshness of Irving Gill's buildings (Figs. 70, 114) comes from his cutting away

FIGURE 143 *(top)*. Plaza Reservoir, Los Angeles, 1860.

FIGURE 144 *(bottom)*. Morris Dam, San Gabriel Canyon, 1941.

at the historicist body of Southern California Hispanic architecture to reveal supposedly timeless forms beneath. He was offering a kind of Edenic architecture appropriate to a Paradise Found. Gill's own language is as simple and intimate as a letter to a friend, and very American in its evocation of an innocence that, though lost, is recoverable: "There is something very restful and satisfying to my mind in the simple cube home with creamy walls, sheer and plain, rising boldly into the sky, unrelieved by cornices or overhang of roof, unornamented save for the vines that soften a line or creepers that weather a pillar or flowers that inlay color more sentiently than any tile could do. I like the bare honesty of these houses, the childlike frankness and chaste simplicity of them." In 1916 he called for architecture that would cooperate with, rather than attempt to resist, the effects of time and weather: "We should build our house simple, plain and substantial as a boulder, then leave the ornamentation of it to Nature, who will tone it with lichens, chisel it with storms, make it gracious and friendly with vines and flower shadows as she does the stone in the meadow."

That repeated effect of flowering vines against a stuccoed surface was, however, a local phenomenon that particularly annoyed Frank Lloyd Wright (see chap. 4), who nevertheless shares honors with Gill as an imaginer of a technologically mature Los Angeles faithful to its Arcadian charter. To describe Wright's work as "organic" is a commonplace; however ambiguous the term may be, Wright used it himself and thereby extended a tradition of romantic naturalism that "distinguished sharply between a mechanistic form that is impressed on a material *ab extra* and an organic form that develops from within." The deep sources of Wright's notions of the "organic" include Coleridge, Emerson, Darwin, and Whitman, from whom, the latter two especially, Vincent Scully argues, Wright derived an evolutionary view of culture as continuous with nature: "It was his lifelong intention to form human life into rhythmic patterns which seemed to him poetic and to embody those patterns in buildings. . . . He tried, though in abstract form, to echo the shapes and dominant rhythms of the landscapes in which his buildings were set." These principles, which could serve as the credo for an Architecture of Arcadia, describe the unexecuted Doheny Ranch project (Figs. 84, 86). The significance of Hockney's and Ruscha's work lies in their accepting the city, as Gill and Wright never could, as a system of given or found objects. However trendily "post-modern" such a perspective may appear, it arguably is an ancient way of constructing reality. We come to see what makers of images train us to see; life, as Oscar Wilde said, imitates art.

Many people both within and beyond L.A. are convinced that the art that life will finally imitate is apocalyptic. Los Angeles is not the only city that has come to think of itself as living under a conditional death threat, but, despite the terror of random shootings and of being trapped forever in traffic, L.A. especially fears its most renowned asset, the environment. Earth, air, fire, and water are the horsemen of an apocalypse of quakes, smog, incineration, and mud slides, all of which except the quakes are cus-tomarily blamed on misuse of the land; even the quakes seem like pun-ishment for building in the wrong place. In *Los Angeles: The Centrifugal City* (1981), Rodney Steiner sums it up well: "The ultimate apocalyptic sce-nario calls for Santa Ana wildfire weather to coincide with an earthquake which disrupts communications and water supplies. Unchecked flames cross the city, reaching ruptured oil refineries and nuclear components in military storage and in power plants. The conflagration is finally quenched in torrential floods brought on by an aberrant tropical hurricane, aided by broken reservoirs, sealing the metropolis in mud washed from fire-denuded hillsides." Fire is the worst (Fig. 145). Didion has defined "the city burning" not simply as L.A.'s greatest *fear* but as its "deepest *image* of itself"; in *The Day of the Locust,* Tod takes revenge on everybody by in-cluding them in his painting of the city on fire.

Many have understood Ruscha's huge oil painting *The Los Angeles County Museum on Fire* (1965–68) (Fig. 146) to be a contribution to this esthetic, despite the artist's mild demurrals.* It is difficult, however, to discover much anger in this dreamlike composition. The 1960s museum is an assemblage of pavilions and moats that looks now both insub-stantial and quaint, like other fragile, self-conscious Southern Califor-nia constructions (Figs. 147, 148) that, like Ruscha's museum, sit or float in an indeterminate space. Ruscha characterized the fire as a "coda" to the classical tranquillity of the composition as a whole, hinting that the point is not that the museum is being destroyed but that it is improved by the element of fire. As the surroundings are transformed into an

FIGURE 145 *(top)*. Fire in the Santa Monica Mountains, 1938.

FIGURE 146 *(bottom)*. *The Los Angeles County Museum on Fire* by Edward Ruscha, 1965–68. Oil on canvas, 54 x 132".

FIGURE 147 (top). Joy residence, Seventh and Figueroa Streets, Los Angeles (undated photograph).

FIGURE 148 (left). Hotel at Beaumont, Riverside County, about 1895.

FIGURE 149. Street scene in West Los Angeles with mural, *Isle of California*, by the Los Angeles Fine Arts Squad (photographed in 1996).

Arcadian no-space, the structure itself has no referents to any point in time;* only the fire embodies the principle of change, and it is itself unchanging. Nobody exists in the painting even to be aware of it; it is like the tree falling in the deserted wood. The fire may inevitably lead to the destruction of the museum, but there is no time within which it operates; as with the figures on Keats's Grecian urn, a process has been forever arrested.

Suspension is the key not only to this image but also to L.A.'s characteristic apocalyptic sensibility: fire and other agents of destruction are, imaginatively, *always* present. As such they have to be lived with, rather as, to the oft-stated reproaches of outsiders, Californians "live with" earthquakes. The public work of Terry Schoonhoven and the L.A. Fine Arts Squad expressed this peculiar sensibility in a series of mural paintings throughout the 1970s and 1980s.* The most famous of them, *Isle of Cali-*

fornia (Fig. 149), is an L.A. icon, in part because (as a nonvendible image) it can claim to be a disinterested public work, and further because the artist left it in situ on a wall in West L.A., to fade from exposure (Fig. 149 was shot in October 1996). Rather in the manner of *The Los Angeles County Museum on Fire, Isle of California* presents disaster as an elegant configuration of phenomena rather than a moral lesson, and as a fait accompli rather than a prophecy. As if anticipating Richard Meier, who is reported to have said that he was taking his design cues for the new Getty Center from the mountains and the freeways rather than from the extant architecture of L.A., Schoonhoven, a native of Illinois, has delivered something far more useful to Angelenos than another scolding: *Isle of California* is a synopsis of the "state" of California as collision of elements and technologies. Subjective responses doubtless differ, but the case is not hard to make that the soaring lyricism of this freeway in boldly foreshortened cross-section induces not angst but thrills.

Ruins and the conditions that produce them are the significant dimension that Schoonhoven adds to the iconographies of Hockney's and Ruscha's canonical imagery. Sometimes these ruins are imported, like the classical structures in his mural on the Harbor Freeway, *City Scape,* and sometimes they are L.A. itself, whether in general, as in the masonry ruins that make up the last panel in a sequence in the U.S. Court of Appeals in Pasadena (the old Vista del Arroyo Hotel [Fig. 88]), or specifically, as with the mural of a postdisaster UCLA (Fig. 150). Additionally, Schoonhoven incorporates what could be imagined as the final stage of a cycle into his renderings: *Venice in the Snow,* which deletes L.A.'s most defining feature, its climate; *Ghost Town,* which shows the San Fernando Valley as a semiarid pastoral landscape; and *Downtown Los Angeles under Water,* an unexecuted mural of a submerged downtown for which a canvas study exists at the County Museum. Death by water is usually understood as a consequence of rare deluges on overbuilt and/or burnt hills and mountainsides; the Pacific Ocean, immense as its presence is, and despite the shedding of a pier from time to time, is the least intimidating of the great local phenomena. Nevertheless, water is an alternative imagined final condition. Schoonhoven's Aquarian cityscape embraces Goodhue's Central Library, the California Club, and the lower stories of the early high-rise

FIGURE 150. Interior, Department of History faculty lounge, with detail of mural, *S.P.Q.R.*, by Terry Schoonhoven, Bunche Hall, UCLA.

buildings that now, in a downtown that has become loaded with them, look dated or even quaint.

Were the moment of disaster his subject, Schoonhoven presumably would have been catering to the same tastes that sent people to movies like *Earthquake* or *Escape from L.A.*, but in fact his catastrophes can only be inferred from the ruins, which survive as if for the admiration of a community that enjoys their romance much as eighteenth-century Europeans appreciated classical fragments. Viewing them as if from some tranquil moment well after the "disaster," we are schooled not in anxiety but in nostalgia,* or even mere curiosity, as if the L.A. around us had long ago disintegrated. The points of reference can be subtle. The UCLA mural, *S.P.Q.R.*, for instance, decorates the wall of the history department's lounge high up in big, ugly Bunche Hall; one of the jokes is that the perspective (as Thomas S. Hines explains in a descriptive analysis mounted on the wall) is from the top of either a restored Bunche Hall or a new building on the same site, whose Hispanic tiles negate the unlamented 1960s style of Bunche. In the lower left of the composition, a handbill announcing a concert is written in *Latin,* suggesting, like the tiles and the title of the work itself (the ancient abbreviation for "the Senate and the People of Rome") both the triumph of Mediterranean over Anglo-Saxon culture, and (appropriately for a lounge of the learned) a future that will bring to life a past that we have so thoughtlessly mislaid.

As a body of imagery of Los Angeles, Schoonhoven's murals share with Ruscha's work a large conceptual scale that permits the imaginative reconstruction of L.A. as a place. Schoonhoven's characteristic strategy, like Ruscha's, is a radical realignment of perspective on the surface of the city. The earthquake in his UCLA mural, like the other disasters in his work, is only implicit; of all the usual agents of destruction, it is, in any event, the one about which we can do the least. The L.A. of Schoonhoven's imagination has collapsed its own future into its present; that future has the iconographic properties of various possible California apocalypses, but in the end it is beyond questions of right and wrong, being simply, in the romantic American mode of Poe and Whitman, *Death.*

Helen Hunt Jackson herself contributed to this sensibility, dwelling heavily, in her account of the "primeval peace" of Old Southern California, on descriptions of obsequies and mourning. Arcadia demands to be recognized as spiritually mature when death is accepted into its system; as shown by Erwin Panofsky, Death is the identity of the pronoun in the warning *Et in Arcadia Ego.* An earthly paradise must always be provisional. E. M. Cioran criticizes Utopian schemes ("a mixture of childish rationalism and secularized angelism") for erasing contradiction from human experience: "Life," he pronounces, "is rupture." In classical and Renaissance literary Arcadias, a blissful merging with the environment is invariably thwarted, first by reversals in love and ultimately by death. History, Cioran writes, "always and everywhere asseverates the failure rather than the fulfillment of our hopes." Reminding us that though in the midst of life we are elsewhere, Schoonhoven's visions allow the luxury of weeping at our own funeral. The consciousness of our collective vanity is painted across the face of the city in his message, *memento mori.*

The most embarrassing charge made against L.A., however, is not that it cannot be well represented, but that it is not worth representing: that its "collective vanity" is trivial. In such a light, Ruscha's work will appear opportunistic and Schoonhoven's, except when he is misread as a Jeremiah, unimportant. Hockney's work sits on a similar critical fence: those who grant that it is not a hostile critique or "demystification" of L.A. may disparage it all the more for endorsing hedonism. Jan Morris's remarks on the strenuousness of the local pursuit of "pleasure" and on L.A. as a "charmless" and "humorless" city, though not flattering, should, however, counter the presumption that a Hockney canvas merely mirrors its subject; Didion has also made the case for L.A. as an arena of labor and tragic consciousness. In a 1975 interview, Hockney remarked that when he arrived in L.A. he found a city without a visual image of itself, whose Piranesi he could become. Perfect ease is not so much a quality of Arcadia as its limiting condition, always beyond—even if only *just* beyond—the actualities. When a canvas like *A Bigger Splash* is accepted not as reportage but as an image of the not-quite-accessible, it stands in relationship to an L.A. backyard as an ideal city in a Renaissance painting stood to the towns of its time.

Some may object that because they are idealized, such images are untrue. The philosopher Alfred North Whitehead converted that objection into a paradoxical defense: "That the propositions of the artistic imagination are untrue in terms of the actual organization of the facts belongs to the essence of their truth." An example is Hockney's technique of representing a house as "the conjunction of two flat geometric forms rather than by its attributes such as doors and windows, [which] suggests that the image is a symbolic representation of a place." Herbert Marcuse, in "Phantasy and Utopia," explains the esthetic imagination as the socially sanctioned way to recapture a psychological state of ideal existence, or in Theodor Adorno's words, *ohne Angst leben*, living without anxiety. In the light of this analysis, works of art that compensate for the incompletely achieved or even failed aspirations of Los Angeles culture will seem to some as the final stage of a century of trying to accommodate Arcadian fantasies to Utopian imperatives. To others, Marcuse's identification of productivity ("one of the most strictly protected values of modern culture") as the yardstick by which people in modern societies are judged leads to the conclusion that cultural artifacts are part of the same system that they pretend to transcend.* If this is the problem, painting is not the solution.

What is the city but the people?
CORIOLANUS

For a short time, in the late nineteenth century, Southern California was promoted as "semitropical." This reading of the environment was probably sincere; the climate and occasional examples of fruit and foliage invited an overreading of the "southern" in Southern California. Ferdinand Deppe's 1832 painting (Fig. 79) can hardly be construed as Yankee propaganda, but it includes green mountains, water, a conical "native" hut, and a perhaps anachronistic palm tree. The rejection by American settlers of this lushly imagined landscape in favor of something soberer is well discussed by Kevin Starr, who argues that tropical imagery and associated rhetoric were tainted by overtones of sloth and corruption. Starr might also have included these corrective words of the promoter Lou V. Chapin, so many of whose images, first published in *Art Work on Southern California* (1900), are in the present volume: "In short, southern California is an American Arcadia. The intensely practical and yet intensely idealistic American combines the muscle of the athlete and the brain of the poet. He would never be satisfied in a luxurious tropical country, where his energy would ooze away, and his liver would degenerate. He takes naturally to southern California, where he can gratify at once his love for beauty and his inclination towards thrift, where he can make a living and enjoy life at the same time." His formula is a balance between idyll and labor, which, once the quaint etiology of masculine diseases is put aside, remains the basis for most defenses of Los Angeles. This formula is impervious to satire. Willard Huntington Wright ridiculed Los Angeles in *The Smart Set* in 1913 for offering "illimitable possibilities for making money and eating fruit," and few would have disagreed with him.

Nature reconciled to craft, and ultimately to architecture, has been the basis of formulas for Paradise since the New Jerusalem, as I have argued before, in *The Architecture of Paradise*. The Paradise to come can never be merely a garden; its tree and water of life are enclosed by gates of pearl and walls of gold *like unto clear glass* (Revelation 21:18). The artfulness is open and unashamed. Southern Californians have often responded to their failures to build "a city upon a hill" by calling for a return to the primal garden; the evidence of ecology, alas, is that as layer after layer of interventions are peeled back, little remains of that garden but the ineffable properties of air and sunshine.

On the gross scale, the Utopian habit of mind survives in specific projects like the 1995 Metro complex near Union Station, and in interrelated processes of demolition and erection, as on Bunker Hill throughout the eighties. It operates more subtly, however, by refocusing our perceptions. Patterns as consistent as the reimaging of Pershing Square and strategies as recent as the Getty architect's comments on where he finds his cues are instances of the characteristic will to salvage L.A. by isolating the supposedly essential elements and erecting a conceptual city upon them, a "real" L.A. that imaginatively overrides the pedestrian armature of mini-malls and dingbats.

The Arcadian sensibility, in its turn-of-the-millennium form, accepts those dingbats and rationalizes them in terms of Los Angeles's allegedly unique experiential properties, the kind celebrated by Peter Schjeldahl in his witty 1978 ode to one of L.A.'s least self-conscious arteries:

To Pico

You are one of the shadowless east-west routes
You start or end, or neither, in breezy Santa Monica
You are one off-ramp on the Santa Monica Freeway
(You cede all long distance traffic to the Santa Monica Freeway)
You are the back door of Century City, ass-end of the Avenue
    of the Stars
You point at Beverly Hills, then bend unconcerned away
You skulk past Hillcrest Country Club fences and high foliage, offended
    and offending
You dawdle through the endless, blurry, unnamed reaches of central L.A.

You duck under the Harbor Freeway into so-called downtown, to which
    you lend your irrepressible shabbiness
You consist of asphalt, cement and largely cheapish small buildings
You have a dustily marginal air.

And so on, for a total of seventy-three lines of direct address to a surface
street that is in fact both topographically and psychologically central to a
city that barely acknowledges its presence.* Calling Pico "broad and
dry . . . blessedly unfoliaged," Schjeldahl evokes the L.A. of Ruscha's *Every
Building on the Sunset Strip,* whose essence is that there is no essence except the conceptual one of the take-it-or-leave-it desert town. His ironies—
for example, "You are like a side-street with elephantiasis . . . / You are
the secret of the city, the incision that reveals its heart of stone"—have
nothing to do with the heavy sarcasms of journalism; his is a witty appreciation of the incongruous rather than a triumphant unmasking of the
meretricious.

The value that most distinguishes this way of feeling from the sensibility that produced, for example, Century City, is freedom, which in Arcadia means the power to develop one's capacities or inclinations without
resistance from or being inhibited by prior structuring and controls,
whether designed or conceptualized. In Arcadia, the landscape is a dispersed, unassertive background; particular structures, like individual
lives, ought, in this kind of idealism, not to have to answer to anybody's
notion of zones or codes. The particular L.A. version of this state of mind
is shaped by the characteristics of the place, its climate and its ecology, both
as they are and as they are imagined to be. Conceding in 1970 that the present state of L.A. architecture was unexciting, David Gebhard nevertheless
made the case that Banham would popularize: that in L.A. "only a minimal amount of order and control is introduced (freeways and airports and
so on) and only when these meaningfully expand the private realm of . . .
[the] citizens. In an age which has become increasingly symbolized by
large-scale and impersonal organizations, L.A. stands as a bulwark against
the increased incursion of massive order in the lives of individuals."

To this philosophy, the obvious and legitimate objection, even within
its own terms, is that one order of control is exchanged for another, for

example, as Banham acknowledges, the regimen of solitary driving for the ritual of waiting for and riding the bus. Angelenos, however, at least as part of their public rhetoric, accept self-discipline as the price of living in their special place. For example, when storm drains were reported on National Public Radio as transferring wastes from the surface of streets into Santa Monica Bay, citizens were urged to stop "curbing" their pets and otherwise dirtying the roadways. To the extent that they cooperate, they are trading a not inconsiderable convenience for the more notional pleasure of feeling that they still live by a clean beach, although for many that beach may rarely or never be visited. The idea, or ideal, of a city of pleasure, in this case, promotes self-sacrificing behavior (small wonder it makes a European smile). As against the political argument, however, that equates the rightness or wrongness of the city with the moral integrity and ways of life of its people, students of Los Angeles must acknowledge the roles played by "climate and setting in shaping the character of the metropolis and in making a mark upon the attitudes, styles, and endeavors of its citizens."

Bruce Bliven, who in 1927 penned the visionary account of an L.A. of "bacchanalian" parkways (see chap. 4), remarks confidently that L.A. is a planner's paradise because lack of water would soon force stabilization of the population and because the city is so young that the problems of the past are not so ingrained as to inhibit correction, there being "no other place in America where the social stratification is so little marked, where all classes do so nearly the same thing at the same time." This is the language of an Arcadian constitution, for a society that is stable, atemporal, and democratic. If Bliven fails as a predictor, it is because he fails as a historian, not recognizing that L.A. had for many years before him been energetic and even ruthless in strategies of growth and heir to (or even burdened with) a long and only provisionally Anglo history, some of whose recessive characteristics were soon to reemerge.

In *Pastoral Cities: Urban Ideals and the Symbolic Landscape of America*, James L. Machor distinguishes the "ideal of a pastoral city" from Utopianism, "if by that term we mean a vision of or an attempt to build a perfect society." Invoking Leo Marx's classic study of American sensibility, *The Machine in the Garden*, Machor recognizes a "middle landscape" where conflicting values are resolved and the polarities of savagery and urbanity are avoided. In this conceptual geography, the solving of social problems takes a back seat to the structuring of landscapes according to the requirements of opposing ideologies of community, on the one hand those of country and small-town life and on the other those of technology and progress. These apparently antagonistic attitudes fuse in the national consciousness as a myth of "cultural pastoralism." The frontier shapes American imagination because it is both a regression to a smaller, simpler community and the first step toward a newer, more sophisticated one. Unlikely as the identification may seem, the suburb is the symbolic "West" of middle-class Americans today, their paradoxically settled frontier.

Peter G. Rowe has usefully characterized the America of residential suburbs, strips, malls, and office parks as such a "middle landscape," but one seriously in need of an esthetic theory and a set of practices to pull itself into shape. A lot of Los Angeles falls under his rubric, having developed according to the impulses of, in his term, "modern pastoralism," the desire to possess both the structures of rural experience and the advantages of technology. This is the landscape that, as Lewis Mumford effectively predicted in 1938, accommodates "a collective effort to live a private life." Whatever the faults of the deep structure—capitalist, Faustian, Emersonian, bureaucratic, for example—the problem in the foreground, as Rowe effectively shows, is the degradation or absence of connective tissue between the dispersed systems and structures (shopping centers and zoned neighborhoods, for example) that make the middle landscape one of discontinuous gratifications edged by anomie.

The most influential modern study of Los Angeles's urban form is Reyner Banham's *Los Angeles: The Architecture of Four Ecologies,* which seeks to resolve the region's Utopian/Arcadian dilemma by distinguishing the scales at which the two approaches have operated. Defending laissez-faire growth within the large-scale grids laid down by the authorities of water and power and transportation, Banham argues that at those majestic levels of engineering the Utopian impulse to plan, reshape, and control has worked well; at lower levels, between the lines of the grid, so to speak, he endorses what might be charitably called the free play of imagination and impulse, or—less optimistically—unregulated exploitation.

In *City of Quartz,* Mike Davis attacks Banham for justifying the patterns of capitalistic development that Davis deplores, and praises Peter Plagens for his "principled" condemnation of Banham in *Artforum* (and subsequently in *Architectural Design*). Plagens in fact does call attention to problems about which Banham is not intensely exercised. He fails to engage Banham's reasoning, however, and does not acknowledge that Banham offers answers to this class of objections. Plagens, like Davis after him, lays the ills of Los Angeles at the door of capitalists and their political allies. But if capitalism and politics are the problem, then the discussion is no longer about Los Angeles but about the twentieth century. Banham, in any case, while acknowledging the unattractiveness of the process, defends the product with a telling analogy:

> As against the Utopian one shot plan for the ultimate community, Los Angeles represents processes of continuous adjustment, processes of apportionment of land and resources. They are not very distinguished or morally likable processes, but plain straight-forward capitalist exploitation of land and built structures. They are substantially the same capitalist processes of land exploitation and built structures which produced, for instance, the much admired Georgian London. They are extreme versions of the traditional methods by which cities have been developed and expanded within the Anglo-Saxon context, at least by the "normal" processes of 19th century entrepreneurial activity.

Furthermore, Plagens's articles (see chap. 4) are farragoes of abuse of the city, the freeways, and their culture, for example, "Los Angeles is a dung-heap," "the Santa Ana freeway . . . is a sewer," "Los Angeles is a huge, shallow toilet bowl," "rolling whorehouse interiors [of cars]," and so forth. Such language sounds less principled than passionate. This rhetoric echoes and perpetuates L.A. fiction of the 1960s, which found in the automobile culture simultaneous metaphors for sterility, sex, and decay, like the ones John Rechy mixes in *City of Night* (1963):

> Southern California, which is shaped somewhat like a coffin, is a giant sanatorium with flowers. . . .
> And flowers. . . .
> Roses, roses!
> Orange and yellow poppies like just-lit matches sputtering in the breeze. Birds of paradise with long pointed tongues; blue and purple lupines; Joshua trees with incredible bunches of flowers held high like

torches—along long, long rows of phallic palm-trees with sunbleached pubic hair. . . .
    Everywhere!
    And carpets of flowers even at places bordering the frenetic freeways, where cars race madly in swirling semicircles—the Harbor Freeway crashes into the Santa Ana Freeway, into the Hollywood Freeway, and when the traffic is clear, cars in long rows in opposite lanes, like cold steel armies out for Blood, create a *whooooosh!* that repeating itself is like the sound of the restless windswept ocean, and the cars wind in and out dashing nowhere, somewhere. . . .
    Anywhere!
    Along the coast, beaches stretch indifferently.
    You can rot here without feeling it.

Romain Gary's *White Dog,* set in 1967, similarly implies the incompatibility of technology with the found environment of L.A.: "The sky of dawn was still fresh and pure, filled with that California blue which always carries the suggestion of orange groves, palms, eucalyptus trees, and canyons ringing with a million voices of insects and birds, that shining hour before cars' and factories' exhausts begin their daily murder of air and light, when the yellowish rotten smog raises into the air its flag of pestilence."

Davis breathed new life into these tired tropes when he reformulated them in terms not of the offended sensibilities of fictional straw-men but rather of an extensively documented and ideologically driven polemic. Although he describes Banham's book, with obvious annoyance as well as respect, as having been adopted as *"the* textbook on Los Angeles," that honor now belongs to *City of Quartz* itself. At many points throughout his bracing narrative of greed and folly one may find oneself agreeing with the reviewer of one of his essays that Davis is less clear-sighted about where paradise was found than about where it was lost;* nevertheless, he accounts as nobody else has for how the paradoxical desire for private property and paradisal community succumbed to its internal contradictions. Davis writes with irony of how the "densification" phenomenon of recent years "was perceived to be drowning Edenic landscapes of detached, single-family homes on quiet streets." My effort in these pages has been to show why "Edenic" comes naturally to such writing, and exactly how it sustained itself for so long in the teeth of so much evidence against it.

The Edenic or Arcadian dimension of the Los Angeles landscape required faith in the simultaneity and congruence of private and public
space. The collapse of this cultural fantasy into the neighborhood turf wars
documented by Davis is the local variant on the Closing of the Frontier.
What has been lost, or perceived to have been lost, however, is not empty
space waiting to be filled but a common ambiance made up of the geo-
logical substructure, the atmosphere, and the extensive plantings that collectively override the boundary lines of homesteads and offer the sense
to anyone possessing a corner of Los Angeles that he or she possesses the
entirety. The six conceptual models examined in the previous chapter were
all variations on a central synecdochic proposition: that the part equals
the whole. Anglo L.A.—and, as Davis shows, plenty of the non-Anglo
bourgeoisie as well—has awakened into the realization that the air, the
earth, and what grows from it, those three constituents of a timeless and
communal landscape, are in fact as ecologically and politically malleable
as the zone of the built environment. *City of Quartz* is a "*j'accuse*" directed
to those in authority responsible for the degradation of public space, but
a definition of that space ought to extend beyond the streets and playgrounds to the envelope of climate and nature thought to be the democratic common property of Southern California. This landscape was four-
dimensional, reinventing in the present the terrain and climate of a
sequence of vanished and imagined pasts. That is the "Eden" that has been
largely neutralized in the civic imagination, leaving people secure only
in what their title deeds tell them they possess.

Q

> They shall be afraid of that which is high,
> and fears shall be in the way,
> and the almond tree shall flourish,
> and the grasshopper shall be a burden,
> and desire shall fail.
> ECCLESIASTES 12:5

In the title of his 1959 collection, *The Slide Area: Scenes of Hollywood Life*,
the British author and screenwriter Gavin Lambert equated two allegedly

unstable phenomena, the landscape and the film industry. An opportunistic, careless dispersal of structures and systems across the landscape seems to justify "dissolution" as the condition of the city in classic L.A. fiction, one visible in the periodic collapse of expensive hillsides. We have further become familiar with the transformation of this figure of speech from passive to active, in angry representations of L.A. as a cancer or some other aggressive life-form; such metaphors are the offspring of the once-optimistic conceptual model of L.A. as an unfixed, virtually borderless city, congruent with the traffic that projects it into the desert. In a related but less belligerent form they become images of random conjunctions, as of molecules in a container: the crowds in *The Day of the Locust,* the teenagers of Bret Ellis's Westside.

Less obvious have been the progressive inversions of the image of city as a garden of delights or an arena of achievements into language of hardening, thickening, clouding, and jelling, words that evoke the psychology of depression. These are conditions for which entropy is not the right metaphor. *The Slide Area* opens on a note of paralyzed desire: "About this hour and season, four o'clock in the afternoon and early summer, I find myself looking out of the window and wondering why the world seems bright yet melancholy." When, in the footsteps of the Faulkner of "Golden Land," this narrator pins his malaise upon the insubstantiality and artificiality of Los Angeles, he ceases to have anything new to say, but for a moment he has echoed the sense of contradiction and bewilderment that caused Edmund Wilson to complain about sunlight and Richard Gilbert about the streets being too clean. The problem they describe is not frustration but indifference: in a landscape of desire they feel nothing. This apathy is an ancient and even honorable affliction, as the writer of Ecclesiastes well understood, but as the cultural equivalent of impotence it brings on a severe loss of confidence.

The formulas with which writers attempt to exorcise this demon have ceased to sound persuasive. Hollywood is held by writers like Wilson or Waugh to corrupt or trivialize the achievements of civilization, but "traditional values" of the kind described as breaking down in L.A. were themselves the agents of change. The westward movement from dirt-poverty in Nebraska of the dysfunctional family of "Golden Land" clarifies this

point better than the fixed perspectives of Nathanael West's Yale graduate or Evelyn Waugh's English dilettante. What we see in "L.A." fiction
is less the breakup of a culture than the breakup of the Novel. Many writers on Los Angeles have come, as well, from a socially conscious muck-
raking American tradition. Practicing a literary genre in the process of taking itself apart, they have found in L.A. a convenient mechanism for
producing the alienated citizen of modern literature. Yet their story never
settles anything; it is told over and over again, because, in the case at least
of those who are not opportunists but who write from the heart, there is
a compulsion to say *something*, however mechanical, to account for, or with
luck to dispel, the cloud of anomie to which they bear witness.

For all of that, Los Angeles has not ceased enchanting new generations
of natives and pilgrims hoping for a billet in, as the seventeenth-century
poet Henry Vaughan put it, "that shady city of palm trees." To the extent
that the cultural imagination of L.A. as an earthly paradise survives, it
does so by reworking the old formula by which the advantages on the
grand scale—principally, the climate—are telescoped into local corners,
fragments of Arcadia. One of the best is Victoria Avenue in Riverside, laid
out in 1890, a divided road running nearly the length of the town parallel to the better-known Magnolia Avenue of 1876. "Here," as a local historian states, "it was written into deed restrictions that owners had to plant
and maintain street trees." Today the planting is well past maturity, almost overripe, though carefully maintained. There is little traffic; horses
graze nearly to its edge and the adjacent architecture is unassertive. The
two lanes march ceremoniously through a far less ostentatious neighborhood than a visitor from, for example, La Mesa Drive in Santa Monica or
Sunset Boulevard in Beverly Hills would expect. Something of that pop-
ulist Arcadia of Anglo imagination survives here, where what is planted
and public both overrides and dignifies what is constructed and private.
For the millions who do not live on this lush street, a ten-minute drive
may be their best education in the landscaping of desire.

Afterword

❦

I owe it to the reader to say something about what—other than a number of years of residence in South Pasadena, Beachwood Canyon, Beverly Hills, Encino, Culver City, and Santa Monica—entitles me to say anything about Los Angeles, taking my cue—as so often throughout this book—from Joan Didion, who has described her own frustrating search through layers of idealism, illusion, self-deception, and betrayal for an essential California, a bedrock of fact. She has admitted her failure, as if the narrative of her own Anglo history in the Golden State were one with the problems she identifies in Frank Norris's *The Octopus*, "a deep and troubled confusion . . . a dissonance its author grasped but failed to resolve." Of all the patterns in that lifelong search that speak to me, the most immediate is her identification with Southerners. In "Goodbye to All That," her youthful farewell to first love (that is, to New York), she mentions the Southerners in that city, from New Orleans, Memphis, and Richmond, as fellow "colonials in a far country." She reports, all too briefly, on a month spent in Alabama, Mississippi, and Louisiana, where history, presumably, has the shape and narrative line that is so difficult for an honest eye to discern in California.

Richmond is where I was raised; I have lived in Mississippi, and later New Orleans, for many years. The epigraphs and other remarks by Southern writers in this book no doubt give me away. My childhood equivalents of *Ramona* include, of course, *Gone With the Wind*, but more important were lesser-known fictions like the novels of Thomas Nelson Page and what seems in memory to be a seamless web of stories associating the fortunes of Virginia with the doings of families I either knew or imagined I knew. Eventually I stopped believing in most of these stories, but the structure behind the scenery, in which recognizable men and women shaped, and were shaped by, something that could be objectified and called History, has survived, if not as a philosophical conviction, then at least as a habit of mind.

Southern history has the advantage of capitalizing on its spectacular defeats, both in arms and in social policies, by fixing them within the narrative pattern called "tragedy," with its division of time into a clear "before" and an "after," and its comforting assimilation of the present to an ever-present past. The Californians of whom Didion writes are qualified by experience and temperament for such a legacy, but it eludes them. The fierceness with which people in Los Angeles *affirm* the criminality of the Owens Valley episode and reiterate the conspiratorial account of how automobile companies worked to destroy the beloved Red Cars speaks of a will to construct a comprehensible past, even at the price of wearing a scarlet dollar sign. In accepting guilt, they replace the epic with the tragic sense of life, the guarantor—in modern intellectual circles—of significance. The contrast to the denials cunningly woven into the fabric of Southern memory, as well as to the denials in Los Angeles of that interesting parallel to the Deep South, low-paid, dark-skinned labor (nothing, I learned in Los Angeles, was felt to be in poorer taste than drawing attention to this resemblance), is striking.

For better or worse, the mythological South has proved adept at self-renewal, but in Southern California the romance of place may be over. It has long vanished, for example, from the once intensely imagined towns and fields of New England, although tourists hopefully seek it in Salem or Nantucket. In Los Angeles's secular religion of place, hundreds of thousands of people for about a century could imagine that the envelope of their lives, replicating ancient imagery of timelessness and fulfillment, was, if not Paradise, at least its antechamber, a Promised Land, to exist in which was proof of the road well traveled and the job well done. Perhaps one of several competing cultures in the region, probably neither especially Protestant nor European in its roots, will succeed in rediscovering such a vision. For the culture of Anglo desire, it has nearly vanished.

Explanatory Notes

Q   INVENTING UTOPIA

p. 1   *Although the *Oxford English Dictionary* records the word *smog* as occurring as early as 1905, anxiety in Los Angeles became apparent only after the "brown-out" of 8 September 1943. See John Anson Ford, "Smog Settles over Los Angeles" (1961), in *Los Angeles: Biography of a City,* ed. John Caughey and Laree Caughey (Berkeley and Los Angeles: University of California Press, 1977), 381–88.

p. 7   *Catherine Mulholland, in *The Owensmouth Baby: The Making of a San Fernando Valley Town* (Los Angeles: Santa Susana Press of California State University at Northridge, 1987), disputes received opinion: "I have found no authentic sources or documents to lead me to any other conclusion than that the buying and selling of the Valley proceeded by altogether customary land deals of the kind that have prevailed throughout the history of this country. Unfortunately for the San Fernando Valley, the taint of the often-repeated (and most certainly false) accusation that these five men [Otto F. Brant, Harry Chandler, Harrison Gray Otis, Moses H. Sherman, and H. J. Whitley] conspired with the City of Los Angeles to force the building of the Owens River Aqueduct in order to water their San Fernando Valley lands resulted not only in a blot on their escutcheons but on the Valley's as well, which has long been regarded as a kind of backward foster-child of the City of Los Angeles and has often been treated as such" (131–32). She observes that one effect of this climate of opinion was the changing of the name of Owensmouth to Canoga Park in 1931 (132).

For a detailed and dispassionate account of the public and private conflicts of interest in this matter, see William Kahrl, "The Politics of California Water: Owens Valley and the Los Angeles Aqueduct, 1900–1927," *California Historical Quarterly* 55 (1976): 2–25, 98–120.

☉   CITY OF METAPHOR

p. 45   *Franklin DeKerson Walker, *A Literary History of Southern California* (Berkeley and Los Angeles: University of California Press, 1950), 97–98, states that Taylor wrote his encomium of L.A. with no connection to the Chamber of Commerce or the Santa Fe Railroad.

p. 46   *Walter Wells, *Tycoons and Locusts: A Regional Look at Hollywood Fiction of the 1930s* (Carbondale: Southern Illinois University Press, 1973), 12, usefully sums up the prevailing attitudes of the L.A. novel of that period:

> Dominating the fictions [of the 1930s] and unifying them is a single, over-riding theme. It is a theme of *dissolution,* a generalized breaking down of the old, the traditional, the real, and the substantive—at times replaced by new, less substantive, less meaningful, even deadly substitutes, and at other times replaced by nothing. This all-pervasive coming apart manifests itself variously. Amongst characters, both major and minor, we see repeatedly a loss of innocence; innocence gives way, though, not to sophistication or wisdom but to cynicism, morbidity, or hollow jadedness. In a succession of characters, we also see a loss of motivation and direction; purpose becomes aimlessness, and motivation gives way to listlessness or a compulsive consumption of energy. Traditional values break down and are replaced by new, more superficial and self-serving ones. Personal dreams are shattered, sometimes even the capacity to dream; weary resignation fills the void. Lost too is any sense of belonging; in its place we see transience, impermanence, adriftness. The ability, even the will, to love is destroyed, and with it normal sexuality; callousness, isolation, and perversion fill the void.

Cf. David Galloway's analysis that substantially anticipates Wells, "Nathanael West's Dream Dump," *Critique* 6, no. 3 (winter 1963–64): 46–64.

p. 60   *See Huxley's novel *After Many a Summer Dies the Swan* (1939). Carolyn See's UCLA dissertation, "The Hollywood Novel: An Historical and Critical Study" (1963), which unfortunately has not been published, usefully summarizes the themes, motifs, and strategies of many examples of the genre. In chapter 2, she remarks on such recurrences as the fixed scenario of arrival, the protagonist's near-total detachment from the past, the lack of local relationships (so that all encounters are by chance), the wonder and/or disgust at local architecture and dress, the fixed "sets" such as the courtyard apartments in *The Day of the Locust,* vulgar and/or violent parties, movie premieres, suicides, and funerals.

p. 67   *Jan Morris, "The Know-How City" (1976), in *Destinations: Essays from Rolling Stone* (New York: Oxford University Press, 1980), finds L.A. "charmless" and "humorless" and notes the earnest professionalism of the pursuit of happiness, as in, e.g., surfing (92).

p. 70   *Cf. a hostile summation of Malibu, the closing lines of Lawrence P. Spingarn's "West" (1958): "Plateaus of folly, gulches of neglect / The gin and tonic waves at Malibu"; see *Poetry Los Angeles: I,* ed. James B. May, Thomas McGrath, and Peter Yates (London: Villiers, 1958), n.p.

A USABLE PAST

p. 75   *"As they neared the selected spot a procession was formed, made up of the soldiers, with the governor at their head, the priests from San Gabriel, accompanied by their Indian acolytes, then the male settlers, and, lastly, the women and the children, the former bearing a large banner of the Virgin Mary painted upon it. . . . Prayers and a benediction from the *padres* concluded the ceremony" (cited in Rev. Francis J. Weber, *The Founding of the Pueblo de Nuestra Señora de Los Angeles: A Study in Historiography* [Los Angeles: Archdiocese of Los Angeles, 1970], 6).

p. 85   *Cf. Carl R. Lounsbury's exposure, in "Beaux-Arts Ideals and Colonial Reality: The Reconstruction of Williamsburg's Capitol," *Journal of the Society of Architectural Historians* 49, no. 4 (December 1990): 373–89, of the errors in the 1930s restoration of the colonial Capitol in Williamsburg, Virginia, where evidence of the eighteenth-century building's plainness was slighted or misinterpreted in order to fashion a lavish facsimile of sophisticated Georgian architecture and interior design. The product has proved to be more useful to interior designers in the West End of Richmond than to students of the eighteenth century, although the restoration has itself become a part of twentieth-century

architectural and cultural history. The parallels for California are instructive
and remain to be explored.

p. 85   *The site of the original Plaza, though not far from the present one,
remains uncertain; see Neal Harlow, *Maps and Surveys of the Pueblo Lands of Los
Angeles* (Los Angeles: Dawson's Book Shop, 1976), 14–16.

p. 89   *See *Los Angeles, 1781–1981: Special Bicentennial Issue,* ed. Harry Meyer,
California History 60, no. 1 (spring 1981); and Antonio Ríos-Bustamante and
Pedro Castillo, *An Illustrated History of Mexican Los Angeles,* University of Cali-
fornia Chicano Studies Research Center Publications, Monograph #12 (Los
Angeles: Regents of the University of California, 1986).

p. 91   *Governor John Bigler: "Of what avail is it that our soil is the most productive, and our climate admirably adapted to the culture of all the necessities
and luxuries of life, if flowing vales sleep in native beauty and silence, and expansive plains are but the roaming grounds and rich pasture fields for the unchecked herd. The true wealth of a prolific soil is to be found alone in the hardy
and industrious hand which brings it into subjection—which turns the rich sod
with the ploughshare, prepares it for the rains of winter and dews at nightfall,
and which at harvest season, reaps from fields of bending grain the rich recom-
pense of toil" (cited in David Streatfield, "The Evolution of the Southern California Landscape: 1. Settling into Arcadia," *Landscape Architecture* 66 [1976]: 44).

p. 95   *See Helen Hunt Jackson, *Ramona: A Story,* 2nd ed. (Boston: Roberts
Brothers, 1886), appendix: "Ramona's Home: A Visit to the Camulos Ranch, and
to Scenes Described by 'H. H.'. By Edwards [*sic*] Roberts"; and Charles Fletcher
Lummis, *The Home of Ramona: Photographs of Camulos, the Fine Old Spanish Estate
Described by Mrs. Helen Hunt Jackson, as the Home of "Ramona"* (Los Angeles:
Chas. F. Lummis, 1888), no pagination. The ambiguous punctuation within
Lummis's title implies, but does not actually affirm, that Jackson so "described"
the Camulos rancho. Stanza 8 of the poem "Camulos" in this book reads:

> Untaint by greed of riches,
>   That is our modern shame;
> Unchanged as in those far old days
>   When Padre Serra came;
> Its white adobes face the sun,
>   Its myriad wood-doves call—
> Its heart the heart of mother Spain—
>   Of Spain before the fall.

Lummis supported the "Spanish" metaphor for Los Angeles against the
claims of many who saw Southern California as a new Italy. He wrote *The
Spanish Pioneers* (1893) and argued for the emergence of a Hispanicized Anglo-

Saxon culture from Texas to Southern California. He "styled himself 'Don Carlos,'" lived on Southwestern food, and dressed in a kind of "Spanish" costume (Kevin Starr, *Inventing the Dream: California through the Progressive Era* [New York: Oxford University Press, 1984], 81–86). Lummis's services to Spanish culture were ultimately rewarded by a royal decoration.

p. 99   *David Gebhard, "Architectural Imagery: The Missions and California," *Harvard Architecture Review* 1 (spring 1980), observes that the fact that the first Mission Revival buildings were railroad stations is appropriate to the "selling" or "convincing" aspect of the movement: the creation of a Hispanic California for tourists and potential immigrants (138–39).

p. 103   *See also Alson Clark, "Wallace Neff and the Culture of Los Angeles," in *Wallace Neff, 1895–1982: The Romance of Regional Architecture*, ed. Andrea P. A. Belloli (San Marino, Calif.: Huntington Library, 1989), 15–35. Clark explains that what was copied was "Neff's vocabulary—the egg-shaped arch, silo tower, corbeled balcony running partway across the facade, horizontal stress, and overly low roof pitch—so ubiquitous that Los Angeles would hardly be Los Angeles without them" (27).

p. 105   *Filming in L.A. began as early as 1907 but is often dated from Cecil B. De Mille's arrival in Hollywood in 1913. By 1915 MGM was established in Culver City and Universal Studios in Universal City. All major U.S. producers were in Southern California by 1920; by 1928, expansion across Los Angeles had brought Warner Brothers and Disney to Burbank, Republic to Studio City, and Fox to Westwood. See Howard J. Nelson, *The Los Angeles Metropolis* (Dubuque, Iowa: Kendall/Hunt, 1983), 182.

p. 109   *"The Cloister Way, the Carmel Mission Wing, the Spanish Art Gallery, the Catacombs under the inn, the Music Room of the Spanish Renaissance, the tile-domed Alhambra Suite, the stained glass, hundreds of statues of saints, religious banners, medals, and tapestries and (this for visitors to the Panama-California Exposition of 1915 in San Diego) a life-sized Tussadesque tableau of the papal court of Pius X: it was as if the Midwest Protestant American imagination, disordered with suppressed longing for the luxuriant bosom of the repudiated Mother Church, now indulged itself in an orgy of aesthetic hyper-dulia. Riverside, California, which had not even had a mission in the days of the padres, now became the Southern California center of the mission cult" (Starr, *Inventing the Dream*, 86).

p. 110   *In "The Getty" (1977), in *The White Album* (New York: Simon and Schuster, 1979; reprint, New York: Pocket Books, 1980), Joan Didion observes that it "seems to stir up social discomfort at levels not easily plumbed" (74), but finds it both honest and anti-elitist. Charles Moore, Peter Becker, and Regula Campbell, in *The City Observed: Los Angeles* (New York: Vintage, 1984), call it "not right: the grasp on make-believe is unsteady" (115). Yet a detail of the architecture held pride of place on the cover of David Gebhard and Robert Winter's magisterial *Architecture in Los Angeles: A Compleat Guide* of 1985 (the edition was superseded in 1994 by one whose cover honors Frank Gehry). William MacDonald has commented that although the Getty Museum in Malibu represented for many in the 1970s the failure of Los Angeles to acquire an outstanding new building by a contemporary architect, the Getty Trust's choice of Richard Meier in the 1980s to design their new research institute and museum in Brentwood was equally deplored as a failure to recognize the city's historicist and eclectic traditions (which were presumably enriched by the Malibu villa) (conversation with the author).

ꙮ   THE SHAPES OF L.A.

p. 117   *The notion of Los Angeles as "West" is examined broadly but unevenly throughout an issue of the *South Dakota Review* 19, nos. 1–2 (spring-summer 1981).

p. 126   *A trader working out of Mexico City, Ferdinand Deppe made at least six trips to Alta California between 1828 and 1836 (Jeanne Van Nostrand, *The First Hundred Years of Painting in California, 1775–1875* [San Francisco: John Howell, 1980], 12). The painting is the property of the Santa Barbara Mission.

p. 129   *See Reyner Banham, *Los Angeles: The Architecture of Four Ecologies* (Harmondsworth: Penguin, 1971; reprint, Harmondsworth: Pelican, 1973), 69–72; cf. Brendan Gill, "Reflections: The Horizontal City," *New Yorker* (15 September 1980): "[The Greenes'] houses celebrate wood with a primordial fervor; coming upon a Greene & Greene house, with its shaggy pelt of cedar-shake shingles, its boldly exposed rafters and beams, one imagines that a portion of some distant forest has been carried to the site and imperfectly domesticated (though the energy of its forest nature continues to flow). . . . The house is at rest on its site and yet doesn't pretend that it has always belonged there. An accommodation has had to be made between it and the surrounding landscape by means of terraces, lawns, and gardens—a further stage of domestication" (126).

p. 142   *Colonel Griffith J. Griffith deeded three thousand acres of Rancho Los Feliz to the city in 1896; his many enemies derided the gift as an effort to relieve himself of the taxes. In the next decade he served two years in San Quentin for trying to kill his wife; his subsequent offer of an observatory for the park was refused with much editorial abuse. On his death in 1919 the city accepted his seven-hundred-thousand-dollar legacy for expansion and improvement of the park. See Kevin Starr, *Material Dreams: Southern California through the 1920s* (New York: Oxford University Press, 1990), 111.

p. 153   *Barbara Rubin, "A Chronology of Architecture in Los Angeles," *Annals* *of the Association of American Geographers* 67 (December 1977), states, "As an urban configuration, 'Los Angeles' incorporates a number of communities generally perceived as suburbs but which are, in reality, independent satellite cities: each exhibits a more-or-less developed urban structure comprised of a central business district, centralized civic and political institutions, a comple-ment of variously zoned residential districts and an industrial zone. The origins of this pattern can be found in . . . the 'boom of the 'eighties'" (522).

p. 164   *John Chase and John Beach, in "The Stucco Box," in *Home Sweet Home: American Domestic Vernacular Architecture,* ed. Charles W. Moore, Kathryn Smith, and Peter Becker (Los Angeles: Craft and Folk Art Museum; New York: Rizzoli, 1983), 118–29, assert a continuity between the boxlike structures of the pueblo and the stucco-box apartment house. Their essay goes far beyond the scope of the analyses cited here. Affectionately termed the "dingbat" in Banham's 1971 analysis (175), this building type is also examined by Rubin (1977, 535–37).

Ⓠ   INVENTING ARCADIA

p. 202   *See Andrew V. Ettin, *Literature and the Pastoral* (New Haven: Yale University Press, 1984), 148–49. Ettin describes the pastoral mode generally as "a way of life prior to responsibilities, precluding the complicated social arrangements, formal legal or religious laws, and pragmatic concerns that come with familial responsibilities" (149).

p. 213   *Ruscha says, "What really interested me about that project was its oblique aerial perspective. . . . I actually feel like there's something classical and gentle about that painting[;] . . . the fire is really like an afterstatement—like a coda" (cited in Patricia Failing, "Ed Ruscha, Young Artist: Dead Serious about Being Nonsensical," *ARTNews* 81, no. 4 [April 1982]: 81).

p. 216   *David Bourdon comments, "In Ruscha's idealized view, the museum's confectionery pavilions and reflecting pools are afloat in an atmospheric, non-specific type of space; Hancock Park and the La Brea Tar Pits have been con-verted into murky-looking greenery, and Wilshire Boulevard has shrunk to a narrow, untrafficked path" ("Ruscha as Publisher [or All Booked Up]," *ARTNews* 71, no. 2 [April 1972]: 36).

p. 216   *Terry Schoonhoven and Victor Henderson made up the L.A. Fine Arts Squad from 1969 until 1974, when they separated; Schoonhoven dropped the "Fine Arts Squad" label in 1979. See *Vapor Dreams in L.A.: Terry Schoonhoven's Empty Stage,* ed. Constance W. Glenn and Jane K. Bledsoe (Long Beach: Califor-nia State University Art Museum, 1982), 16 (exhibition catalogue).

p. 218   *The artist is reported as saying, "The term apocalyptic to me doesn't quite apply to those paintings. . . . To me an apocalyptic painting is a wrathful

image perhaps of an earthquake where things are tumbling into the ocean[,] . . .
and I'm really not interested in painting that kind of image at all. . . . The earthquake painting in Los Angeles [*Isle of California*] is actually very calm. It's a post-
apocalyptic painting. It's that charged, serene space after the disaster that has
always fascinated me" (Phyllis J. Lutjeans, "An Interview with Terry Schoonhoven, the Los Angeles Fine Arts Squad, September 8, 1975," in *Terry Schoonhoven: The Los Angeles Fine Arts Squad Paints a Mural for the Newport Harbor
Museum* (N.p., 1975) no pagination (exhibition catalogue).

p. 221   *"This idea expresses perhaps more than any other the existential attitude in industrial civilization. . . . Man is evaluated according to his ability to
make, augment, and improve socially useful things. Productivity thus desig-
nates the degree of the mastery and transformation of nature: the progressive
replacement of an uncontrolled natural environment by a controlled technological environment. However, the more the division of labor was geared to utility
for the established productive apparatus rather than for the individuals—in
other words the more the social need deviated from the individual need—the
more productivity tended to contradict the pleasure principle and to become an
end-in-itself. The very word came to smack of repression or its philistine glori-
fication: it connotes the resentful defamation of rest, indulgence, receptivity—
the triumph over the 'lower depths' of the mind and body, the taming of the
instincts by exploitative reason" (Herbert Marcuse, *Eros and Civilization: A
Philosophical Inquiry into Freud* [Boston: Beacon Press, 1955; reprint, Boston:
Beacon Press, 1966], 155–56).

p. 223   *See, however, Martin Schwartz's witty, thorough, and simultaneous
(though unrelated) appreciation of the architecture in "The Essential Pico
Boulevard," *SCAN* (Southern California Associates News) 10, no. 1 (November
1978): 1–7.

p. 227   *Davis evokes from photographs an "old Downtown" of racially mixed
crowds (231), but Marshall Berman, reviewing another book to which Davis
contributed an essay, asserts that the photographs are confected images of
World War II propaganda, not documents of interracial harmony ("Hitting the
Streets," review of *Variations on a Theme Park: The New American City and the
End of Public Space*, Michael Sorkin, ed., *Los Angeles Times Book Review*, 29 March
1992: 11). A barrage of attacks on the credibility of some of Davis's statistics
and conclusions appeared in late 1998 and early 1999, too late for consideration
in the present volume; see "City of Frauds," *The Economist*, 12 December 1998:
31; Robert A. Jones, "The Truth Squad of History," *Los Angeles Times*, 10 January
1999: B1+; Todd S. Purdum, "Best-Selling Author's Gloomy Future for Los
Angeles Meets Resistance," *New York Times*, 27 January 1999: A10.

Reference Notes

Ɏ   PREFACE

Reyner Banham   Reyner Banham, *Los Angeles: The Architecture of Four Ecologies* (Harmondsworth: Penguin, 1971; reprint, Harmondsworth: Pelican, 1973), 235, 247.

"the all-too-limited literature"   Todd S. Purdum, "More Folly Than Disaster in Paradise," review of *Ecology of Fear: Los Angeles and the Imagination of Disaster,* by Mike Davis, *New York Times,* 31 August 1998: E6.

Ɏ   INVENTING UTOPIA

"came alive in . . . pre-smog Los Angeles"   John Beach, "Lloyd Wright's Sowden House," *Fine Homebuilding* (April-May 1983): 67.

"the sun, strained by"   William Faulkner, "Golden Land," in *The Collected Stories of William Faulkner* (New York: Random House, 1950), 706.

Maps of Los Angeles   References are to the maps of Los Angeles and adjacent counties published by the Thomas Company; to those of the Automobile Club of Southern California/California State Automobile Association; to composite maps based on interviews with residents of Boyle Heights and Northridge, published by the Los Angeles Department of City Planning (*The Visual Environment of Los Angeles,* 1971) and reproduced in David Brodsly, *L.A. Freeway: An Appreciative Essay* (Berkeley and Los Angeles: University of California Press, 1981), 27; and to Mike Davis, *City of Quartz: Excavating the Future in Los Angeles* (London: Verso, 1990), 75.

"halfhidden . . . like the facades of eastern temples"   Faulkner, "Golden Land," 701–2.

"They shall try as far as possible"   Cited in David Gebhard, *Santa Barbara: The Creation of a New Spain in America* (Santa Barbara: UCSB University Art Museum, 1982), 9 (exhibition catalogue).

"planned not for people"   David Gebhard and Robert Winter, *Los Angeles: An Architectural Guide,* photographic consultant Julius Shulman (Salt Lake City: Gibbs-Smith, 1994), 133.

"barren and forlorn"   Cited in Thomas Hines, *Richard Neutra and the Search for Modern Architecture* (New York: Oxford University Press, 1982), 132.

"cheap by the acre"   Julius Shulman, memorandum to the author, August 1998.

"produced varied effects"   Hines, *Richard Neutra,* 133.

"the emergence . . . in favor of the suburbs"   Robert M. Fogelson, *The Fragmented Metropolis: Los Angeles, 1850–1930* (Cambridge: Harvard University Press, 1967), 2.

"The arts and sciences"   Cited in Fogelson, *Fragmented Metropolis,* 12.

"for of all the major products"   Fogelson, ibid., 20.

"This fantastic"   Earnest Elmo Calkins, "The California Legend," *Atlantic* 145, no. 2 (February 1930): 158.

"If there is one characteristic"   Cited in Judith Elias, *Los Angeles: Dream to Reality* (Northridge: Santa Susana Press, 1983), 1.

"posters in the east and in Europe"   Elias, *Los Angeles,* 4.

"practically every means of utilizing"   Glenn S. Dumke, *The Boom of the 'Eighties in Southern California* (San Marino: Huntington Library, 1944), 16.

"the effect of Los Angeles smoke on the surrounding pellucid air"   John D. Weaver, "The Laboratory of Marvels," *California History* 60, no. 1 (spring 1981): 54.

a fee or a commitment to purchase   See John W. Reps, *Views and Viewmakers of Urban America: Lithographs of Towns and Cities in the United States and Canada, Notes on the Artists and Publishers, and a Union Catalogue of Their Works, 1825–1925* (Columbia: University of Missouri Press, 1984), 10; also chap. 9.

"an archaic material"   Cited in Sam Hall Kaplan, *LA Lost and Found* (New York: Crown, 1987), 133.

Described by Schindler as a "camper's shelter"   Cited in David Gebhard, *Schindler* (New York: Viking, 1971), 48.

Schindler appears to have conceived of it   Gebhard, *Schindler*, 53.

"It was a city . . . which never really felt urban"   John Russell Taylor, *Strangers in Paradise: The Hollywood Emigrés, 1933–1950* (London: Faber and Faber, 1983), 16.

"the role taken, in the genesis of events"   E. M. Cioran, "Mechanism of Utopia," *Grand Street* 6, no. 3 (spring 1987): 83 (emphasis in original).

☉   CITY OF METAPHOR

"After winding through the willow"   Ord, *The City of the Angels . . .* , ed. Neal Harlow (1856; reprint, Los Angeles: Zamorano Club, 1978), 9.

"a sort of island on land"   Helen Hunt Jackson, *Glimpses of California and the Missions, with illustrations by Henry Sandham* (1883; reprint, Boston: Little, Brown, 1902), 214. Jackson's essays originally appeared as articles in the *Century Magazine* (1883).

California as an island   John Barger Leighly, *California as an Island: An Illustrated Essay*, Publications of the Book Club of California, no. 14 (San Francisco: Book Club of California, 1972). Leighly suggests that the intention of calling the desolate Baja peninsula "California" may have been satirical (14).

Ramona   Helen Hunt Jackson, *Ramona: A Story* (Boston: Roberts Brothers, 1884).

"Ramonaland"   The term is used throughout Charles Moore, Peter Becker, and Regula Campbell, *The City Observed: Los Angeles* (New York: Vintage, 1984), to account for romantic neo-Hispanic architecture.

"most of our countrymen . . . expected"   Philip tyson, untitled report, in United States Senate, *Report of the Secretary of War, Communicating Information in Relation to the Geology and Topography of California*, 31st Cong., 1st sess., ex. doc. no. 47 (Washington: Government Printing Office, 1850), 49.

"The Puebla [sic] de Los Angeles"   Charles Nordhoff, *California for Health, Pleasure, and Residence: A Book for Travellers and Settlers* (New York: Harper and Bros., 1872), 137.

"Palm trees are as gray as an elephant's ears"   Benjamin Franklin Taylor, *Between the Gates* (Chicago: S. C. Griggs, 1878), 262, 263, 259.

"a reliable purse"   Jane E. Weeden, *Los Angeles: A Descriptive Poem* (Los Angeles: n.p., 1884), no pagination.

Nordhoff . . . wrote on commission   David Streatfield, "The Evolution of the California Landscape: 3. The Great Promotions," *Landscape Architecture* 67 (1977): 229.

the main character "alighted"   Carroll Graham and Garrett Graham, *Queer People* (New York: Vanguard Press, 1930), 11. In her 1963 UCLA dissertation, "The Hollywood Novel: An Historical and Critical Study," Carolyn See describes it as the archetypal novel of its genre.

"ALL ROADS LEAD TO HOLLYWOOD"   Horace McCoy, *I Should Have Stayed Home* (New York: Knopf, 1938), 8.

"Los Angeles . . . bowl of smog"   Alison Lurie, *The Nowhere City* (London: Heinemann, 1965; reprint, New York: Avon, 1967), 335.

"Not too long ago"   Letter in the *Los Angeles Times Magazine* (21 May 1989): 8.

"We who lived here for some time"   Glenn Cunningham, "Comments on Howard J. Nelson's 'The Spread of an Artificial Landscape over Southern California,'" *Annals of the Association of American Geographers* 49, no. 3, part 2 (September 1959): 100.

"I used to like this town"   Raymond Chandler, *The Little Sister* (Boston: Houghton Mifflin, 1949), 181.

love of a place   Eudora Welty, *Place in Fiction* (New York: House of Books, 1957), no pagination.

"Between the veranda and the river meadows"   Jackson, *Ramona*, 21–22.

"In a thousand years or so"   Evelyn Waugh, "Half in Love with Easeful Death: An Examination of Californian Burial Customs," in *The Essays, Articles, and Reviews of Evelyn Waugh,* ed. Donat Gallagher (Boston: Little, Brown, 1983), 331. Originally published in *Tablet,* 18 October 1947, pp. 246–48.

"The area is getting suburban . . . And yet [Los Angeles] will die . . . the lights snap on"   Christopher Isherwood, *A Single Man* (New York: Simon and Schuster, 1964), 25–26, 110–12.

"[One] can draw wholly valid assumptions"   Walter Wells, *Tycoons and Locusts: A Regional Look at Hollywood Fiction of the 1930s* (Carbondale: Southern Illinois University Press, 1973), 125.

"it is not necessary to verify the accuracy"   Tom S. Reck, "Raymond Chandler's Los Angeles," *Nation* 222 (20 December 1975): 661–63.

"My solution is to make everybody in L.A."   Remi Nadeau, *Los Angeles: From Mission to Modern City* (New York: Longmans, Green, 1960), 1–2.

Clichés of Urban Doom   Ruth Glass, "Urban Images," in *Clichés of Urban Doom and Other Essays* (Oxford: Basil Blackwell, 1989), 106–24.

"the belief that happiness can be found"   David Wyatt, *The Fall into Eden: Landscape and Imagination in California* (Cambridge: Cambridge University Press, 1986), 207.

"the whole arabesque and painted world"   Stephen Vincent Benét, *The Beginning of Wisdom* (New York: Henry Holt, 1921), 237–39.

"a hybrid species of Spanish architecture"   Graham and Graham, *Queer People,* 55.

"The terrace, the sundrenched terra cotta tiles"   Faulkner, "Golden Land," 706–7.

"unnaturally clean suburbs"   Richard Gilbert, *City of the Angels* (London: Secker and Warburg, 1964), 19.

"All the houses on the street"   Lurie, *Nowhere City,* 11.

Faulkner in L.A.   See Joseph Blotner, *Faulkner: A Biography,* 2 vols. (New York: Random House, 1974), 2:934, 943; and Ian Hamilton, *Writers in Hollywood, 1915–1951* (New York: Harper and Row, 1990), chap. 10.

"the city in the bright soft vague . . . that city of almost incalculable wealth" Faulkner, "Golden Land," 719.

"the purposes and passions of humanity . . . gigantic and vulgar"   Edmund Wilson, "The Boys in the Back Room. 6: Facing the Pacific," in *Classics and Commercials: A Literary Chronicle of the Forties* (New York: Farrar, Straus, 1950), 45–56.

"[The sun] was still high, still afternoon"   Faulkner, "Golden Land," 725–26.

"numbingly bland"   Joan Didion, "Los Angeles Notebook," in *Slouching towards Bethlehem* (New York: Pocket Books, 1981), 218.

Los Angeles and the Palm Tree   *Los Angeles and the Palm Tree: Image of a City* (Los Angeles: Arco Center for Visual Art, 1984) (exhibition catalogue).

Chez Chance   Jay Gummerman, *Chez Chance* (New York: Pantheon, 1995).

"Squirrels live in the ground"   R. W. C. Farnsworth, *A Southern California Paradise, (in the Suburbs of Los Angeles): Being a Historic and Descriptive Account of Pasadena, San Gabriel, Sierra Madre, and La Cañada. with Important Reference to Los Angeles and All Southern California, and Containing Map and Illustrations* (Pasadena: R. W. C. Farnsworth, 1883), 9.

A Few Palm Trees   Edward Ruscha, *A Few Palm Trees* (Hollywood: Heavy Industry Publications, 1971).

"like Los Angeles weather"   Peter Plagens, "Ed Ruscha, Seriously," in *The Works of Edward Ruscha,* essays by Dave Hickey and Peter Plagens; intro. by Anne Livet, foreword by Henry T. Hopkins (New York: Hudson Hills Press with the San Francisco Museum of Art, 1982), 33.

"There is something uneasy in the Los Angeles air"   Didion, "Los Angeles Notebook," 216.

"The lingering mist of morning fog"   Frank Fenton, *A Place in the Sun* (New York: Random House, 1942), 101.

"For a few days now we will see smoke"   Didion, "Los Angeles Notebook," 216.

"The edges of the trees burned . . . When he noticed that they were all of plaster"
   Nathanael West, *The Day of the Locust* (New York: Random House, 1939), 6–7.
"a nondescript affair called the San Bernardino Arms"   West, *Day,* 8.
"Vista Gardens . . . a great big advertisement for nothing"   Lurie, *Nowhere City,*
   40, 51.
"done partly in the adobe of Indian pueblos"   Liam O'Flaherty, *Hollywood
   Cemetery* (London: V. Gollancz, 1935), 171–72.
*"high up on the slope of the Hollywood Hills . . . I came to a halt . . . God curse
   this antiseptic"*   Christopher Isherwood, *The World in the Evening* (London:
   Methuen, 1954), 11, 16–17, 23.
"All day the heat . . . In that kindly light"   Evelyn Waugh, *The Loved One:
   An Anglo-American Tragedy* (London: Chapman and Hall, [1948]), 1.
"just born, everything moist and fresh"   West, *Day,* 156.
Kaiser's Stoneless Peaches   Waugh, *Loved One,* 74.
"Too many of the Los Angeles women"   Gilbert, *City,* 33.
"Los Angeles has more lovely girls"   Edmund Wilson, *The American Jitters:
   A Year of the Slump* (New York: Scribner's, 1932), 226.
"Which came first in this strange civilization"   Waugh, *Loved One,* 74.
Wells on The Day of the Locust   Wells, *Tycoons,* 53.
"any of the sincere, honest people who work here"   Cited in Wells, *Tycoons,* 63.
"moral decay"   Wells, *Tycoons,* 51.
"something happened in Southern California"   Kevin Starr, "It's Chinatown,"
   New Republic (26 July 1975): 31.
Sontag's devastating critique   Susan Sontag, *Illness as Metaphor* (New York:
   Farrar, Straus, and Giroux, 1977).
"the tacky sleepy slowpoke Los Angeles"   Isherwood, *Single Man,* 14.
"the sunshine mocking the defeated hopes"   Starr, "It's Chinatown," 31.
"Across the top, parallel with the frame"   West, *Day,* 236–37.
Fogelson . . . challenges West's assumptions   Fogelson, *Fragmented Metropolis,*
   198.
"Raymond Chandler's City of Lies"   Liahna K. Babener, "Raymond Chandler's
   City of Lies," in *Los Angeles in Fiction: A Collection of Critical Essays,* ed. David
   Fine (Albuquerque: University of New Mexico Press, 1984), 116, 119, 125, 127.
"We tell ourselves stories in order to live"   Joan Didion, "The White Album," in
   The White Album (New York: Simon and Schuster, 1979; reprint, New York:
   Pocket Books, 1980), 11.
Faye Greener, "who often spent the whole day"   West, *Day,* 88.
"the extraordinary thing about L.A."   Chris Dawson, "The Iconography of the
   Mundane," in *Los Angeles 2: Architecture and Culture, Architectural Design* 52,
   nos. 3–4 (1982): 120.

A kind of instant encapsulization   Jay McInerney, *Brightness Falls* (New York: Knopf, 1992; reprint, New York: Vintage, 1993), 388–89.

"The coast road, at Santa Monica"   Françoise Sagan, *The Heart-Keeper* (*Le garde du coeur*) (New York: Dutton, 1968), 11.

"Ten years ago those scrub-covered hills"   Romain Gary, *White Dog* (New York: World, 1970), 27.

"We took more crystal Methedrine"   Richard Rayner, *Los Angeles without a Map* (New York: New American Library, 1988), 120–21.

"There was a song I heard when I was in Los Angeles"   Bret Easton Ellis, *Less Than Zero* (New York: Simon and Schuster, 1985), 207–8.

Beverly Hills High School   Michael Leahy, *Hard Lessons: Senior Year at Beverly Hills High School* (Boston: Little, Brown, 1988).

"It was one of those clear bright summer mornings"   Chandler, *Little Sister*, 1.

"a landscape of shadows, of mists and exhalations"   Morley Baer and David Rains Wallace, *The Wilder Shore* (San Francisco: Sierra Club Books, 1984), 35.

"There was loneliness and the smell of kelp . . . Far off the purl of motors"   Raymond Chandler, *Farewell, My Lovely* (New York: Knopf, 1940; reprint, New York: Vintage, 1988), 36–37, 39.

"the Great Wrong Place"   W. H. Auden, "The Guilty Vicarage," in *The Dyer's Hand and Other Essays* (New York: Random House, 1962), 151.

"listened to the groundswell of the traffic on Laurel Canyon Boulevard"   Raymond Chandler, *The Long Goodbye* (Boston: Houghton Mifflin, 1953; reprint, New York: Ballantine, 1971), 224 (emphasis added).

for love of the jacarandas   Eve Babitz, introduction to *Los Angeles Stories: Great Writers on the City*, ed. John Miller (San Francisco: Chronicle Books, 1991), x.

"When I was growing up"   Eve Babitz, *Slow Days, Fast Company* (New York: Knopf, 1977), 8–9.

"[Nazimova] suddenly knew that the flames"   Babitz, *Slow Days*, 153. Nazimova's villa at 8150 Sunset Boulevard became the Garden of Allah hotel in 1927; it was demolished in 1959.

Didion has defined "the city burning"   Didion, "Los Angeles Notebook," 219.

Her context is a Malibu   Didion, "Quiet Days in Malibu," *White Album*, 207–21.

"the most aqueous filtered light"   Didion, "Quiet Days in Malibu," 214.

time, *an element essentially absent*   See, "Hollywood Novel," 110.

A USABLE PAST

"Los Angeles is an epic"   Harry Carr, *Los Angeles: City of Dreams* (New York: Appleton-Century, 1935), 5.

"The general theme decided upon for the murals"   Historical Murals in the Los
   Angeles County Hall of Records, Board of Supervisors' Hearing Room. A Federal
   Art Project of the Works Progress Administration Executed under President
   Franklin D. Roosevelt (Los Angeles: n.p., 1939), no pagination (pamphlet).
Carthay Circle Theatre   See the pamphlet *California 1826–1926* (Los Angeles:
   Carthay Center Historical Committee, 1926).
Jackson memorialized the Los Angeles basin   Jackson, *Glimpses,* 164.
a romantic scenario of the Catholic mass   John Caughey, "The Distant Pawn
   of Empire," *California History* 60, no. 1 (spring 1981): 15.
"the twelve devout Spanish soldiers"   Jackson, *Glimpses,* 163.
"the city's . . . Christian character"   Cited in Rev. Francis J. Weber, *The Founding
   of the Pueblo de Nuestra Señora de Los Angeles: A Study in Historiography* (Los
   Angeles: Archdiocese of Los Angeles, 1970), 14.
The settlers were . . . Indian, African, and mestizo   Caughey 1981, 12, 15.
Weber makes the case   Weber, *Founding,* 13–14.
the much-ballyhooed long name   Theodore E. Treutlein, "Los Angeles, California: The Question of the City's Original Spanish Name," *Southern California
   Quarterly* 55, no. 1 (spring 1973): 1–7. See also Harry Kelsey, "A New Look at
   the Founding of Old Los Angeles," *California Historical Quarterly* 55, no. 4
   (1976): 327–39; and Antonio Ríos-Bustamante and Pedro Castillo, *An
   Illustrated History of Mexican Los Angeles,* University of California Chicano
   Studies Research Center Publications, Monograph #12 (Los Angeles: Regents
   of the University of California, 1986), 36–38.
Truman . . . reported   Maj. Benjamin Cummings Truman, introduction to *Los
   Angeles: The Queen City of the Angels* (Los Angeles: M. Rieder, 1904), no
   pagination.
The natural paradise he describes   Maj. Benjamin Cummings Truman et al.,
   From Pueblo to City: 1849/1910 (Los Angeles: Leberthon, [1910?]), 1.
a "lethargic" and "somnolent" population   Truman et al., *From Pueblo,* 1.
the "irresistible glamour" of the place   Truman, *Los Angeles,* n.p.
Nostalgia   From the Greek *nostos* (return to one's native land) and *algos*
   (suffering).
the pamphlet Los Angeles County To-day   (Los Angeles: Los Angeles County
   Chamber of Commerce, 1929).
A Backward Glance   Robert G. Cowan, *A Backward Glance: Los Angeles,
   1901–1915* (Los Angeles: Torrez Press, 1969), no pagination.
*"While the men baled hay they sang together . . . relatively motionless moment in
   history"*   Richard Gordon Lillard, *Eden in Jeopardy, Man's Prodigal Meddling
   with His Environment: The Southern California Experience* (New York: Knopf,
   1966), 49, 52–53, 107.

The myth of an Anglo golden age   Fogelson, *Fragmented Metropolis*, 74–75.

Major Truman's histories prepare us   Truman et al., *From Pueblo*, 1.

Los Angeles Sonnets   Selman Warren Stone, *Los Angeles Sonnets* (Los Angeles: B. N. Robertson, 1953). Introduction by Lyra Lu Vaile, who suggests that Shakespeare may have to take a back seat to Stone. Citations are from sonnets 10, 11, and 13.

Los Angeles: The Metropolis of the West   Frank L. Meline, *Los Angeles: The Metropolis of the West* (Los Angeles: Francis H. Webb, 1929).

"Old Los Angeles," was formerly "a dirty alley"   Carr, *Los Angeles*, 10 (emphasis added).

"During a residence of several years upon the Pacific coast"   Henry Chapman Ford, *Etchings of the Franciscan Missions of California, with the Outlines of History, Description, Etc.* (New York: Studio Press, 1883). Citation from p. [3].

"theme parks"—as loosely defined in a popular architectural guidebook   Moore, Becker, and Campbell, *City*, xv.

"and the priests seldom visited the pueblo"   Howard J. Nelson, *The Los Angeles Metropolis* (Dubuque, Iowa: Kendall, Hunt, 1983), 4.

"a usable past, a revered founding time"   Starr, *Inventing the Dream*, 88–89.

The gradual manufacture of a synthetic "pueblo"   Roger Hatheway, "El Pueblo: Myth and Realities," *Review* (Southern California Chapter, Society of Architectural Historians) 1, no. 1 (fall 1981): 2–3.

the ranchos, primary beneficiaries of the secularization acts   See H. F. Raup, "Transformation of Southern California to a Cultivated Land," *Annals of the Association of American Geographers* 49, no. 3, part 2 (1959): 62.

"Long since gone . . . are the antelope"   Richard G. Lillard, "Mountain Men and Women in the New West of Los Angeles," in *Los Angeles as West*, nos. 1–2 of *South Dakota Review* 19 (spring-summer 1981): 30.

The second was erased by the third   Fogelson, *Fragmented Metropolis*, 139–41.

a tradition of "appreciation of the earth"   Hildegarde Flanner, *A Vanishing Land* (Portola Valley, Calif.: No Dead Lines, 1980), 2, 22.

"to the noblest and richest rewards"   Thomas Farnham, cited in David Streatfield, "The Evolution of the Southern [*sic*] California Landscape: 1. Settling into Arcadia," *Landscape Architecture* 66 (1976): 42.

"requiring protection . . . embellish, realize, and improve"   Streatfield, "Evolution 1," 39.

as Truman gives evidence   For Benjamin Truman's contribution to defining Los Angeles as "semi-tropic" and the problems with the associated imagery, see Starr, *Inventing the Dream*, 45.

Bryant complained   Edwin Bryant, *What I Saw in California, Being the Journal of a Tour, by the Emigrant Route and South Pass of the Rocky Mountains, across the*

Continent of North America, the Great Desert Basin, and through California, in the Years 1846, 1847 . . . (New York: D. Appleton, 1848), 385.

this Arcadia "inspired utopian dreams"   Streatfield, "Evolution 1," 42.

Citrus orchards, first developed commercially   Streatfield, "Evolution 1," 45.

"You pluck an orange"   Taylor, *Between the Gates*, 261.

Seedling oranges . . . the seedless grapefruit   See Raup, "Transformation," 58–78, esp. 71.

citizens "sit on the verandahs"   Cited in David Streatfield, "The Evolution of the California Landscape: 2. Arcadia Compromised," *Landscape Architecture* 66 (1976): 126.

Immigrants to Los Angeles, with their small-town values   Fogelson, *Fragmented Metropolis*, 144–45.

an esthetic impulse   David Streatfield, "The Evolution of the California Landscape: 3. The Great Promotions," *Landscape Architecture* 67 (1977): 230.

72,350 acres platted in 1887–89 alone   Streatfield, "Evolution 3," 230.

"the talismanic fruit"   Joan Didion, "Some Dreamers of the Golden Dream" (1966), in *Slouching towards Bethlehem*, 20.

"Little it mattered [to speculators]"   Cited in Franklin DeKerson Walker, *A Literary History of Southern California* (Berkeley and Los Angeles: University of California Press, 1950), 117.

"The Senora Moreno's house"   Jackson, *Ramona*, 16.

"the heart of mother Spain"   Charles Fletcher Lummis, *The Home of Ramona: Photographs of Camulos, the Fine Old Spanish Estate Described by Mrs. Helen Hunt Jackson, as the Home of "Ramona"* (Los Angeles: Chas. F. Lummis, 1888), no pagination.

The del Valle family who owned the Camulos rancho   See Richard Griswold del Castillo, "The del Valle Family and the Fantasy Heritage," *California History* 59 (1980): 2–15.

Howard J. Nelson cites the completion   Howard J. Nelson, "The Two Pueblos of Los Angeles: Agricultural Village and Embryo Town," *Southern California Quarterly* 59 (spring 1977): 1–11.

"The intellectual justification for this revival"   David Gebhard, "The Spanish Colonial Revival in Southern California (1895–1930)," *Journal of the Society of Architectural Historians* 26, no. 2 (May 1967): 131.

"distinctive architecture in Southern California"   Harwood Hewitt, "A Plea for Distinctive Architecture in Southern California," *Allied Architects Association of Southern California Bulletin* 1, no. 5 (March 1925): no pagination.

"an attempt to embody the romance of old Spanish civilization"   C. Matlack Price, "The Panama-California Exposition. San Diego, California. Bertram G. Goodhue and the Renaissance of Spanish-Colonial Architecture," *Architectural Record* 37 (March 1915): 234 (emphasis added).

gardens . . . were "but a resumption—a return to the earliest precedents"   Cited in Porter Garnett, *Stately Homes of California,* intro. Bruce Porter (Boston: Little, Brown, 1915), ix–x.

"Up to 1915 . . . California was remarkably free"   Esther McCoy, "Roots of California Architecture," *Arts and Architecture* 73 (October 1956): 36–37.

Wallace Neff, the most imitated California architect   Alson Clark in Wallace Neff Jr., ed., *Wallace Neff: Architect of California's Golden Age* (Santa Barbara: Capra Press, 1986), 24–25.

"the frequently played game"   David Gebhard in Neff, *Wallace Neff,* 11.

"Andalusian" in the sense that Carcassonne   Gebhard in Neff, *Wallace Neff,* 12.

"was unusual, something that was impressive"   Alson Clark, "Wallace Neff and the Culture of Los Angeles," in *Wallace Neff, 1895–1982: The Romance of Regional Architecture,* ed. Andrea P. A. Belloli (San Marino: Huntington Library, 1989), 23.

"a Southland archetype . . . the image of our transformed semi-desert"   Cited in Leon Whiteson, "'20s Spanish Style Needs No Revival: Red Tile Roofs, White Walls Endure as Southland Favorites," *Los Angeles Times,* 5 March 1989: VIII, 26.

"stucco-covered wood stud walls"   David Gebhard and Harriette Von Breton, *Lloyd Wright, Architect* (Santa Barbara: Art Galleries, University of California at Santa Barbara, 1971), 27 (exhibition catalogue).

"even more primitive than pre-Columbian"   Gebhard and Von Breton, *Lloyd Wright,* 34, 42.

The first and most influential   Streatfield, "Evolution 3," 229.

Rail lines entered undeveloped areas   Fogelson, *Fragmented Metropolis,* 85–86 et passim; 115.

Busch Gardens   Nelson, *Los Angeles,* 179.

metaphors of L.A. as "theme park" and set of rides   Moore, Becker, and Campbell, *City,* xiii, xv.

The weather in Los Angeles . . . is unpredictable   Didion, "Los Angeles Notebook," 218.

"Academic historicism . . . would be invisible"   Barbara Goldstein, "Los Angeles in Context," in *Los Angeles Now* (London: Architectural Association, 1983), 8 (exhibition catalogue).

Writing in The Craftsman *in 1916*   Cited in Esther McCoy, *Five California Architects* (New York: Reinhold, 1960; reprint, New York: Praeger, 1975), 61, 67–68.

He is described . . . as . . . artful   Denise Scott Brown, "Development Proposal for Dodge House Park," *Arts and Architecture* 83 (April 1966): 16.

. . . and childlike   Streatfield, "Evolution 3," 232.

"The past is never dead"   *Requiem for a Nun,* cited in Noel Polk, *Faulkner's*

Requiem for a Nun: *A Critical Study* (Bloomington: Indiana University Press, 1981), 93.

◎   THE SHAPES OF L.A.

"Los Angeles when viewed from the air"   SITE Environmental Design, Project Description (press release).
"The physical shapelessness of Los Angeles"   Gilbert, *City,* 35.
"Here there is no opposition"   M. Christine Boyer, "The Tragedy of City Planning," *CRIT* 17 (fall 1986): 48.
"the arid and semi-arid lands"   Cited in John R. Milton, "Literary or Not," *Los Angeles as West, South Dakota Review* 19, nos. 1–2 (spring-summer 1981): 3.
Los Angeles's isolation . . . was announced on the map   Harlan H. Hague, "The Search for a Southern Overland Route to California," *California Historical Quarterly* 55 (1976): 150.
a "flat surface leading to riches"   Milton, "Literary or Not," 5.
A surprising visitor in the 1870s   Ludwig Salvator, *Eine Blume aus dem Goldenen Lande: oder Los Angeles* (Prague: Heinrich Mercy, 1878).
writers like . . . Van Dyke . . . and . . . Austin   Cited in Walker, *Literary History,* 185, 190–91.
Some have found . . . perils of fire and mud slides   Lillard, "Mountain Men and Women," 30–36.
distant foothill and mountain development—with occasionally catastrophic consequences   See John McPhee, "The Control of Nature: Los Angeles against the Mountains," *New Yorker* (26 September 1988): 45–78; (3 October 1988): 72–90.
True West   Sam Shepard, *True West,* in *Sam Shepard: Seven Plays,* intro. Richard Gilman (Toronto and New York: Bantam, 1981).
Every Building on the Sunset Strip   Edward Ruscha, *Every Building on the Sunset Strip* (Los Angeles: Edward Ruscha, 1966).
the shallowness thought to inhere in the . . . gas-guzzling cars   Plagens, "Ed Ruscha," 35.
visual experience of the Strip   See Andrew Bogle, introduction to *Graphic Works by Edward Ruscha* (Auckland, New Zealand: City Art Gallery, 1978), 22 (exhibition catalogue); Jonathan Crary, "Edward Ruscha's 'Real Estate Opportunities,'" *Arts Magazine* 52, no. 5 (January 1978): 121; Peter Schjeldahl, "Ed Ruscha: Traffic and Laughter," in *Edward Ruscha* (Lyon: Octobre des Arts, 1985), 49 (exhibition catalogue).
"'all I was after . . . was that store-front plane'"   Cited by David Bourdon in

Linda L. Cathcart, ed., *Edward Ruscha,* intro. Linda L. Cathcart (Buffalo: Albright-Knox Art Gallery, 1976), 5 (exhibition catalogue).

twenty-five thousand palm trees   Kathi Norklun, "The Symbol of a City," *Art Week* 15, no. 8 (September 1984): 3.

"Los Angeles is the palm tree"   Norklun, "Symbol," 3.

Doheny estate . . . (there is little documentation)   For a detailed presentation of the Doheny designs and argument that Wright was probably not commissioned to generate them, see David G. De Long, "Frank Lloyd Wright: Designs for an American Landscape, 1922–1932," in *Frank Lloyd Wright: Designs for an American Landscape, 1922–1932,* ed. David G. De Long et al. (New York: Abrams, 1996), esp. 16–30.

"beautiful in California"   Cited in Bruce Brooks Pfeiffer and Gerald Nordland, *Frank Lloyd Wright in the Realm of Ideas* (Carbondale: Southern Illinois University Press, 1988), 38.

what he would call "organic architecture"   See Wright's *An Organic Architecture: The Architecture of Democracy* (1939), cited in Pfeiffer and Nordland, *Frank Lloyd Wright,* 32.

"wild, sharp ridges fuzzy with chaparral"   Christopher Rand, *Los Angeles: The Ultimate City* (New York: Oxford University Press, 1967), 11. Originally published in 1966 in the *New Yorker.*

the Maryland Hotel's Italianate garden pergola   Kevin Starr, *Material Dreams: Southern California through the 1920s* (New York: Oxford University Press, 1990), 194.

"Strangers, wooed to our city"   Cited in John Baur, *The Health Seekers of Southern California, 1870–1900* (San Marino: Huntington Library, 1959), 39.

In 1910 Griffith J. Griffith strongly urged   Griffith J. Griffith, *Parks, Boulevards and Playgrounds* (Los Angeles: Prison Reform League, 1910), no pagination.

"Old men and females, landladies and cranks"   Myron Henry Broomell, *The City Built on Sand: A Poem about Los Angeles* (Denver: Allan Swallow, 1948), no pagination.

"The idea of a multilayered parking structure under a park"   Gebhard and Winter, *Los Angeles,* 229.

Edward Ruscha captioned his aerial photograph   Ruscha's photograph introduces his series *Thirtyfour Parking Lots in Los Angeles* (Los Angeles: Edward Ruscha, 1967).

Banham dismissed downtown as irrelevant   Banham, *Los Angeles,* chap. 10.

"meant to compress . . . Los Angeles experience"   See John Pastier, "SITE Selected to Redesign Los Angeles' Pershing Square," *Architecture* 75, no. 10 (October 1986): 16.

"because the design represented a new idea"   "Design Awards/Competitions:

Pershing Square International Design Competition," *Architectural Review* 174 (November 1986): 69.

"Sleazy, a bit dusty, very masculine"   Nikos Stangos, ed., *David Hockney by David Hockney,* intro. Henry Geldzahler (New York: Abrams, 1977), 99.

"the resonance of [this] otherwise bland image"   Cited in Marco Livingstone, *David Hockney* (New York: Holt, Rinehart, Winston, 1981), 69.

"L.A. in the flatlands: long straight roads"   Cited in Lawrence Weschler, "A Visit with David and Stanley: Hollywood Hills, 1987," in *David Hockney: A Retrospective* (New York: Abrams, 1988), 83 (exhibition catalogue, Los Angeles County Museum of Art).

metaphor "can be a double-edged sword"   Pastier, "SITE Selected," 16.

a volume of handsome photographs   Lou V. Chapin, *Art Work on Southern California* (San Francisco: California Photogravure, 1900).

availability of good help   Chapin, *Art Work,* fascicle 12, p. 23.

Pasadena attempted to fashion itself   Victoria Padilla, *Southern California Gardens: An Illustrated History* (Berkeley and Los Angeles: University of California Press, 1961), 236–41.

creative Whitley Heights, eclectic Silverlake   Martin Zimmerman, "The Hills: Arts Colony Refuge from Hectic Hollywood," 23 July 1989: VIII, 2+; Evelyn De Wolfe, "Silver Lake: Westside Life Style at Half the Price," 12 March 1989: VIII, 2+; Leon Whiteson, "Olive Hill: Designing East Hollywood Future," 19 March 1989: VIII, 3+; Leon Whiteson, "Watts Towers: Symbol of High Expectation," 26 May 1989: V, 1+.

A character in Evelyn Waugh's The Loved One   Waugh, *Loved One,* 3–4.

"Beverly Hills was—and is—as pretty and artificial"   Brendan Gill, "Reflections: The Horizontal City," *New Yorker* (13 September 1980): 113.

"a sort of Naples"   Cited in Walker, *Literary History,* 118.

Gill compares it to Pompeii   Gill, "Reflections," 146.

"that unmistakable sensation of being in a provincial capital"   V. Barrett Price, "The Ultimate Western City," in *Los Angeles as West, South Dakota Review* 19, nos. 1–2 (spring-summer, 1981): 27. Starr suggests "Toulouse or Nice" (*Inventing the Dream,* 65).

"a windy canyon . . . between bizarrely configured office towers"   Davis, *City,* 190.

"has preserved to a remarkable extent"   Augusta Fink, *Time and the Terraced Land* (Berkeley: Howell-North, 1966), 28. Cf. Davis, *City,* 167, on the politics of Rolling Hills landownership.

"be restored to its former glory"   William Trombley, "Westwood Village Looks to Its Past for Its Future," *Los Angeles Times,* 5 July 1987: II, 1.

facilities in Torrance   McCoy, *Five California Architects,* 86.

Gill, whom Esther McCoy praises   McCoy, ibid., 83.

"the source of a set of design principles"   Streatfield, "Evolution 3," 232.

"Californian ideal of the sanitary, labor saving house"   See McCoy, *Five California Architects*, 61, 67–68.

railway station . . . was . . . used only for freight   McCoy, ibid., 87.

Horatio West Court   McCoy, ibid., 97.

"ideal of instant place"   Stefanos Polyzoides, Roger Sherwood, and James Tice, *Courtyard Housing in Los Angeles: A Typological Analysis*, photography by Julius Shulman (Berkeley and Los Angeles: University of California Press, 1982), 6.

"both concrete and symbolic references"; "egalitarian" ideals and esthetics; "emphasizes urban continuity"; "public realm of streets and squares"   Polyzoides, Sherwood, and Tice, *Courtyard Housing*, 55.

"the symbol, for good or ill . . . It is difficult to know whether"   John Chase and John Beach, "The Stucco Box," in *Home Sweet Home: American Domestic Vernacular Architecture*, ed. Charles W. Moore, Kathryn Smith, and Peter Becker (Los Angeles: Craft and Folk Museum; New York: Rizzoli, 1983), 118, 127.

"increased densification"   Sam Hall Kaplan, "The New Suburbia: Mediterranean-Style Villages Are Replacing Cookie-Cutter Tract Homes in Award-Winning Southern California Developments," *Los Angeles Times Magazine*, 18 September 1988: 31.

in the words of . . . Barry Berkus   Cited in Kaplan, "The New Suburbia," 31.

"what was Californian about California"   Joseph Giovannini, "Gordon Kaufmann," in *Caltech, 1910–1950: An Urban Architecture for Southern California* (Pasadena: California Institute of Technology, Baxter Art Gallery, 1983), 31 (exhibition catalogue).

The look of "a rural hacienda"; "They initiated a strategy"   Stefanos Polyzoides and Peter de Bretteville, "The Caltech Campus in the Twentieth Century," in *Caltech, 1910–1950*, 54.

Kaufmann's wider variety of building types   Giovannini, ibid., 34.

his work depicts a subject . . . the romance of the Mediterranean   Giovannini, ibid., 34.

"drawn from a model of the arcaded Italian town"   Barbara Goldstein, "Los Angeles in Context," in *Los Angeles Now* (London: Architectural Association, 1983), 10, 40 (exhibition catalogue). See also essays by Peter Cook and George Rand, *Morphosis Buildings and Projects* (New York: Rizzoli, 1989), 96–99.

"a miniature historic small town"   Cited in Leon Whiteson, "Santa Monica's Edgemar Improves Upon the Mini-Mall," *Los Angeles Times*, 7 May 1989: VIII, 16.

"Vista Gardens"   Lurie, *Nowhere City*, 1967, 40.

that place is America; it is also Southern California   Louis Marin, *Utopics: Spatial Play*, trans. Robert A. Vollrath (Atlantic Highlands, N.J.: Humanities Press, 1984), 252.

"What is there now . . . is . . . temporary and replaceable"   Introduction to Esther McCoy, *The Second Generation* (Salt Lake City: Peregrine Smith, 1984), xi–xii.

"Forest Lawn, after all, had been built to provide the illusion"   Barbara Rubin, Robert Carlton, and Arnold Rubin, *L.A. in Installments: Forest Lawn* (Santa Monica: Westside Publications, 1979), 55.

"the only thing in California that is not a copy"   Letter to A. D. Peters, cited in Linda Venis, "L.A. Novels and the Hollywood Dream Factory: Popular Art's Impact on Los Angeles Literature in the 1940's," *Southern California Quarterly* 69, no. 4 (winter 1987): 369.

"The great misfortune of London"   Henry James, from *Essays in London and Elsewhere* (New York: Harper and Brothers, 1893), cited in Morton White and Lucia White, *The Intellectual versus the City, from Thomas Jefferson to Frank Lloyd Wright* (Cambridge: Harvard University Press, 1962), 93.

Lummis . . . adobes   Paul Gleye, *The Architecture of Los Angeles* (Los Angeles: Rosebud Books, 1981), 78.

the city he contemptuously dismissed   Brendan Gill, *Many Masks: A Life of Frank Lloyd Wright* (New York: Putnam's, 1987), 266.

"We would take that despised outcast . . . the concrete block"   From Wright's *Autobiography*, cited in *Frank Lloyd Wright in Los Angeles, 1919–1926: An Architecture for the Southwest* (Los Angeles: Department of Cultural Affairs, City of Los Angeles and School of Architecture, University of Southern California, 1988), no pagination (exhibition catalogue).

"California . . . smothers the whole in eucalyptus and mimosa arms"   Cited in Yukio Futagawa, ed., *Frank Lloyd Wright: Monograph, 1914–1923*, text by Bruce Brooks Pfeiffer, Frank Lloyd Wright series, no. 4 (Tokyo: A.D.A. Edita, 1985), 210.

"homely midwest invasion . . . the poetic thing this land was"   Neil Levine, "Landscape into Architecture: Frank Lloyd Wright's Hollyhock House and the Romance of Southern California," *AA Files* 3 (January 1983): 22–46.

"on a crust of earth at the edge of a sea"   John Steven McGroarty, *Los Angeles from the Mountains to the Sea* (Chicago and New York: American Historical Society, 1921), 36.

Yaxchilán   Vincent Scully, introduction to *The Nature of Frank Lloyd Wright*, ed. Carol R. Bolon, Robert S. Nelson, and Linda Seidel (Chicago and London: University of Chicago Press, 1984), 20, xviii, xxi.

to assert a genius of place   Vincent Scully Jr., *Frank Lloyd Wright*, Masters of World Architecture Series (New York: Braziller, 1960), 24–25.

Scully's reading of the designs as a recapitulation   Scully, *Frank Lloyd Wright*, 25.

processional free-standing hollyhocks   Levine, "Landscape into Architecture," 1983, 34.

"imposed itself upon the naked crown of Olive Hill"   Gill, *Many Masks*, 252.

"culture of cities"   Lewis Mumford, *The Culture of Cities* (New York: Harcourt, Brace, 1938).

"in the silhouette of the Olive Hill house"   From Wright's 1932 *Autobiography*, cited in Levine, "Landscape into Architecture," 1983, 34.

Wright rejected L.A.'s characteristic   Jim Tice, "L.A. Block Houses, 1921–24: Frank Lloyd Wright," *Architectural Design* 51, nos. 8–9 (1981): 62.

Olive Hill . . . might have been a kind of gate   Levine, "Landscape into Architecture," 1983, 31.

The main house itself, its interior court   Kathryn Smith, "Frank Lloyd Wright, Hollyhock House, and Olive Hill, 1914–1924," *Journal of the Society of Architectural Historians* 38 (March 1979): 27.

"In 1925 . . . I was young and the city was young"   Cited in Esther McCoy, "Lloyd Wright," *Arts and Architecture* 83, no. 9 (October 1966): 24.

Wright also wedded a Beaux Arts cruciform plan; "the provision for multiple 'speedways'"   Gebhard and Von Breton, *Lloyd Wright*, 46.

Wright was reported at the time   "Comprehensive Plan for Greater Los Angeles Beautiful Offers Maximum Traffic Control at Minimum Expense," *Los Angeles Times*, 30 August 1925: V, 4.

after 1970 it was moved and eventually demolished   Arnold Hylen, *Los Angeles before the Freeways, 1850–1950: Images of an Era* (Los Angeles: Dawson's Book Shop, 1981), 55.

Edward Dimendberg   "Mysteries of Bunker Hill" (paper read at the Society of Architectural Historians 51st Annual Meeting, Los Angeles, 1998).

"lobotomized"   Sam Hall Kaplan, "Lautner Still Ahead of His Time," *Los Angeles Times*, 14 September 1986: VIII, 2.

"psychologically ought to be"   "Under the Hollywood Sign," introduction to *Edward Ruscha: Prints and Publications, 1962–74* (London: Arts Council of Great Britain, 1975), no pagination.

"With the increasing speed . . . a magnificent forefront for the city"   Cited in McCoy, "Lloyd Wright," 24.

A project promoted by Harry Chandler . . . proposed an enormous 230-foot-wide boulevard   Sherley Hunter, *Why Los Angeles Will Become the World's Greatest City* (Los Angeles: H. J. Mallen, 1923).

Hindsight situates this nearly forgotten scheme   It is not mentioned in Starr, *Material Dreams*, or in Scott L. Bottles, *Los Angeles and the Automobile: The Making of the Modern City* (Berkeley and Los Angeles: University of California Press, 1987), or in Douglas R. Suisman, *Los Angeles Boulevard: Eight*

X-Rays of the Body Public, Forum Publication #5 (Los Angeles: Los Angeles Forum for Architecture and Urban Design, 1989).

what would be called the "Miracle Mile"   See Suisman, *Los Angeles Boulevard,* 27–29; and Starr, *Material Dreams,* 81–83.

a route followed by American Indians   Starr, *Material Dreams,* 81–82.

"A great unfolding of a dream"   Hunter, *Why Los Angeles,* not paginated. All emphases in original.

"a new kind of city"   Joan Didion, "Letter from Los Angeles," *New Yorker* (26 February 1990): 88.

They were first conceived as adjuncts   See Brodsly, *L.A. Freeway,* 87; and Starr, *Material Dreams,* 106–7.

"there is no day in the year [in Los Angeles] when it is impossible"   *A Major Traffic Street Plan for Los Angeles,* prepared by Frederick Law Olmsted, Harland Bartholomew, and Charles Henry Cheney (Los Angeles: Traffic Commission, 1924), 9, 11–12, 21.

this "vocabulary and imagery continued to haunt city planning"   Brodsly, *L.A. Freeway,* 87.

In 1925 the Allied Architects Association's proposal   Gardner W. Gregg, "Los Angeles' Bold Plan for a Civic Center," *National Municipal Review* 14 (July 1925): 408.

"badly handicapped by 'Bunker Hill'"   Clarence A. Dykstra, "Congestion De Luxe—Do We Want It?" *National Municipal Review* 15 (July 1926): 396.

"I saw huge boulevards, sixty paces wide"   Bruce Bliven, "Los Angeles: The City That Is Bacchanalian—in a Nice Way," *New Republic* (13 July 1927): 197–98.

"One of the most urgent park needs"   *Parks, Playgrounds, and Beaches of the Los Angeles Region: A Report Submitted to the Citizens' Committee on Parks, Playgrounds, and Beaches, by Olmsted Brothers and Bartholomew and Associates, Consultants* (Los Angeles: The Committee, 1930), 12–13.

"Los Angeles has now . . . become an undifferentiated mass of houses"   Lewis Mumford, *The City in History: Its Origins, Its Transformations, and Its Prospects* (New York: Harcourt, Brace, and World, 1961), 510.

a beloved and efficient network of streetcars   Bottles, *Los Angeles,* esp. 1–4, 22, 48, 88, 159.

Los Angeles was . . . ideal . . . because it was decentralized   Bottles, ibid., 180–81, 284.

Reinforcing these attitudes . . . "comradeship" of L.A. . . . "no place for dilettantes"   Jan Morris, "The Know-How City" (1976), in *Destinations: Essays from Rolling Stone* (New York: Oxford University Press, 1980), 92, 87.

"scarcely anywhere have I found life more difficult"   Cited in Richard G. Lillard, "Problems and Promise in Tomorrowland," *California History* 60 (1981): 97.

"the bright mile or two of the Strip . . . the sudden cool dusk and the drift of wind from the sea"   Chandler, *Farewell, My Lovely*, 87.

"the sports page, the blatting of the radio . . . a boy who really made something out of nothing"   Chandler, *Little Sister*, 77–78.

"The predominance of serpentine imagery"   Brodsly, *L.A. Freeway*, 55.

Plagens's angry attacks   Peter Plagens, "Los Angeles: The Ecology of Evil," *Artforum* 11 (December 1972): 67–76 and "The LA Connection: Pushing Freeways," *Architectural Design* 43 (August 1973): 571–74.

"Los Angeles is a huge, shallow toilet bowl"   Plagens, "The LA Connection," 572.

"every other once-virginal city . . . penetrated by the interstate highway system"   Steven V. Roberts, "Ode to a Freeway," *New York Times Magazine* (15 April 1973): 21. Despite this metaphor, Roberts balances the advantages and disadvantages of freeway culture.

"the logical next step in making the Los Angeles dream a reality"   Brodsly, *L.A. Freeway*, 4.

"The freeways . . . were essential to their vision"   Bottles, *Los Angeles*, 221.

"emphasized Los Angeles's dependence on the car"   Gerald Silk et al., *Automobile and Culture* (New York: Abrams; Los Angeles: Museum of Contemporary Art, 1984), 155.

"Time spent on [the freeways] . . . can be counted as time lost"   Rand, *Los Angeles*, 57.

evidence for their efficiency and their advantages over public transportation   See Banham, *Los Angeles*, 90–91, 215–16; and Brodsly, *L.A. Freeway*, 142–45.

the virtual overlay of the freeways along the routes of the Pacific Electric rail lines   Banham, *Los Angeles*, 75–93.

freeways cut into pieces a previously unified central city   Gilbert, *City*, 19.

"The architectural composition lining the streets is secondary"   Frank Dimster, "Character of the Metropolis," *Architectural Design* 51, nos. 8–9 (1981): 29–30.

"the freeway is not a limbo of existential angst"   Banham, *Los Angeles*, 222.

"a state of heightened awareness that some locals find mystical"   Banham, ibid., 215.

"the only secular communion Los Angeles has"   Joan Didion, "Bureaucrats" (1976) in *White Album*, 83.

"I do not mean 'love' in any colloquial way"   Joan Didion, "Goodbye to All That" (1967) in *Slouching towards Bethlehem*, 227.

"Once she was on the freeway and had maneuvered her way to a fast lane"   Joan Didion, *Play It as It Lays* (New York: Farrar, Straus, and Giroux, 1970; reprint, New York: Pocket Books, 1978), 13–14.

"actual participation, [which] requires a total surrender"   Didion, "Bureaucrats," 83.

The simultaneous experience . . . pursued by early advocates   See Bottles, *Los Angeles*, 221.

"Actual participants . . . think only about where they are"   Didion, "Bureaucrats," 83.

      Q   INVENTING ARCADIA

"Les vrais paradis"   Marcel Proust, *A la recherche du temps perdu*, 3 vols., Editions de la Pléiade (Paris: Nouvelle Revue Française, 1954), 3:870.

Art Work on Southern California   Chapin, *Art Work*.

"the vacancy at the heart of physical pleasure"   Plagens, "Ed Ruscha," 32.

"Part of the attraction that Hockney's work exerts"   Robert Hughes, "Bland and Maniacal," *Time* (29 May 1972): 64.

"In place of a hermeneutics we need an erotics of art"   Susan Sontag, "Against Interpretation" (1964), in *Against Interpretation and Other Essays* (New York: Noonday Press; New York: Farrar, Straus and Giroux, 1966), 14.

which for one critic evokes the "aloneness" in Edward Hopper's paintings   Livingstone, *David Hockney*, 108.

"a vacant suburban yard, its automatic sprinklers having usurped" and *"Hockney's pictures of swimming pools"*   Christopher Knight, "Composite Views: Themes and Motifs in Hockney's Art," in *David Hockney: A Retrospective* (N.Y.: Abrams, 1988), 38 (exhibition catalogue, Los Angeles County Museum of Art).

"a city set in aspic"   Peter Webb, *A Portrait of David Hockney* (London: Chatto and Windus, 1988), 68.

"a core of suspended energy"   Thomas G. Rosenmeyer, *The Green Cabinet: Theocritus and the European Pastoral Lyric* (Berkeley and Los Angeles: University of California Press, 1969), 89.

"There can be no integral experience . . . to match the seductive density of its name"   Schjeldahl, "Ed Ruscha: Traffic and Laughter," 49.

"squares from the North European countries of the rectilinear flags"   Rand, *Los Angeles*, 135–36.

"a symbol not of affluence but of order"   "Holy Water," in Didion, *White Album*, 63–64.

"There is something very restful and satisfying to my mind"   From Gill's "A New Architecture" (1912), cited in Streatfield, "Evolution 3," 232.

"We should build our house simple, plain and substantial as a boulder"   Cited in McCoy, *Five California Architects*, 61.

"distinguished sharply between a mechanistic form"   White and White, *Intellectual*, 195.

"It was his life-long intention to form human life"   Scully, *Frank Lloyd Wright,* 11–12.

"The ultimate apocalyptic scenario"   Rodney Steiner, *Los Angeles: The Centrifugal City* (Dubuque, Iowa: Kendall/Hunt, 1981), 17–18.

Didion has defined "the city burning"   Didion, "Los Angeles Notebook," 219 (emphasis added).

Richard Meier, who is reported to have said that he was taking his design cues   *Los Angeles Times,* 26 September 1988: V, 4.

Jackson . . . descriptions of obsequies and mourning   Jackson, *Glimpses,* 173.

Et in Arcadia Ego   Erwin Panofsky, "*Et in Arcadia Ego:* Poussin and the Elegiac Tradition," in *Meaning in the Visual Arts: Papers in and on Art History* (Garden City, N.Y.: Doubleday, 1955), 295–320.

"Life . . . is rupture"; "always and everywhere asseverates the failure rather than fulfillment"   Cioran, "Mechanism," 87–88.

Jan Morris's remarks on the strenuousness of the local pursuit   Morris, "The Know-How City," 92.

Hockney remarked that when he arrived in L.A.   Cited in Livingstone, *David Hockney,* 70.

"That the propositions of the artistic imagination are untrue"   Cited in Herbert Marcuse, *Eros and Civilization: A Philosophical Inquiry into Freud* (Boston: Beacon, 1966), 149.

"the conjunction of two flat geometric forms"   Livingstone, *David Hockney,* 70.

Adorno's words, ohne Angst leben   Cited in Marcuse, *Eros,* 149–50.

"one of the most strictly protected values of modern culture"   Marcuse, ibid., 155.

"What is the city but the people?"   Shakespeare, *Coriolanus* III, I, 198.

The rejection by American settlers of this lushly imagined landscape   Starr, *Inventing the Dream,* 45.

"southern California is an American Arcadia"   Chapin, *Art Work,* fascicle 12, p. 23.

"illimitable possibilities for making money and eating fruit"   Willard Huntington Wright, "Los Angeles: The Chemically Pure," in *The Bachelor's Companion: A Smart Set Collection,* ed. Burton Rascoe and Groff Conklin (New York: Grayson, 1944), 101. See also Starr, *Inventing the Dream,* 133–34.

The Architecture of Paradise   William A. McClung, *The Architecture of Paradise: Survivals of Eden and Jerusalem* (Berkeley and Los Angeles: University of California Press, 1983).

"To Pico"   Peter Schjeldahl, "To Pico," preface to *Guacamole Airlines and Other Drawings by Edward Ruscha* (New York: Abrams, 1980), 6–7.

"only a minimal amount of order and control is introduced"   David Gebhard, "L.A.: The Stuccoed Box," *Art in America* 58, no. 3 (May–June 1970): 130.

the obvious and legitimate objection . . . is that one order of control is exchanged for another   Banham, *Los Angeles*, 217.

when storm drains were reported on National Public Radio as transferring wastes   All Things Considered, 7 August 1996.

"climate and setting in shaping the character of the metropolis"   Steiner, *Los Angeles*, 55.

Bliven, who in 1927 penned the visionary account   Bliven, "Los Angeles," 198.

Machor distinguishes the "ideal of a pastoral city" from Utopianism   James L. Machor, *Pastoral Cities: Urban Ideals and the Symbolic Landscape of America*, History of American Thought and Culture Series (Madison: University of Wisconsin Press, 1987), 9.

Leo Marx   Cited in Machor, *Pastoral Cities*, 9.

The frontier shapes American imagination because it is both a regression to a smaller, simpler community   Jonas Spatz, *Hollywood in Fiction: Some Versions of the American Myth*, Studies in American Literature 22 (The Hague: Mouton, 1969), 10.

the suburb is the symbolic "West" of middle-class Americans today   Machor, *Pastoral Cities*, 212.

the America of residential suburbs, strips, malls, and office parks   Peter G. Rowe, *Making a Middle Landscape* (Cambridge: MIT Press, 1991).

"a collective effort to live a private life"   Cited in Rowe, *Making a Middle Landscape*, 290.

Defending laissez-faire growth within the large-scale grids   Banham, *Los Angeles*, 139.

Davis attacks Banham for justifying the patterns of capitalistic development   Davis, *City*, 74.

"As against the Utopian one shot plan for the ultimate community"   Reyner Banham, "LA: The Structure behind the Scene," *Architectural Design* 41 (April 1971): 227.

"Los Angeles is a dung-heap"   Plagens, "Los Angeles," cited in Davis, *City*, 74.

"the Santa Ana freeway . . . is a sewer"; "Los Angeles is a huge, shallow toilet bowl"; "rolling whorehouse"   Plagens, "The LA Connection," 571, 572, 573.

"Southern California, which is shaped somewhat like a coffin"   John Rechy, *City of Night* (New York: Grove Press, 1963), 87.

"The sky of dawn was still fresh and pure"   Gary, *White Dog*, 17.

"the textbook on Los Angeles"   Davis, *City*, 74.

the "densification" phenomenon of recent years   Davis, ibid., 173.

The collapse of this cultural fantasy into the neighborhood turf wars   Davis, ibid., chap. 3: "Homegrown Revolution."

The Slide Area: Scenes of Hollywood Life   Gavin Lambert, *The Slide Area: Scenes of Hollywood Life* (New York: Viking, 1959).

"that shady city of palm trees" Henry Vaughan, "The Retreat," *Henry Vaughan,* ed. Louis L. Martz (Oxford: Oxford University Press, 1995), 28, line 26.

One of the best is Victoria Avenue in Riverside The local historian is Tom Patterson, *Landmarks of Riverside and the Stories behind Them,* foreword by W. W. Robinson (Riverside: Press-Enterprise Company, 1964), 42. See also Elmer Wallace Holmes, *History of Riverside, California . . .* (Los Angeles: Historic Record Company, 1912).

AFTERWORD

"a deep and troubled confusion . . . a dissonance its author grasped but failed to resolve" Joan Didion, "The Golden Land," *New York Review of Books,* 21 October 1993: 88.

"colonials in a far country" Didion, "Goodbye to All That," 229.

Illustration Credits

Uncredited photographs are by the author.

Figs. 2, 3, 11, 14, 16–20, 22–24, 26, 31, 32, 34–41, 43, 46, 49, 51–67, 72, 75, 80, 99, 104–9, 111, 112, 124, 128, 130–31, 144, 145: these items are reproduced by permission of The Huntington Library, San Marino, California. For the following, additional credit is due to Otis College of Art and Design: Figs. 37, 38, 66; and to Chapman and Hall, Publishers (Kluwer Academic Publishers, USA): 34, 35.

Figs. 4, 12, 13, 27, 28, 29, 44, 45, 50, 71, 81, 87–92, 98, 101, 113, 115, 117, 121, 132–34, 138, 148: California Historical Society, Title Insurance and Trust Photo Collections, Department of Special Collections, University of Southern California Library.

Figs. 5, 42, 68, 85, 100, 129, 142, 143, 147: Department of Special Collections, University Research Library, UCLA.

Figs. 6, 8: Photos courtesy Dion Neutra Architect and Neutra Papers—UCLA Special Collections.

Figs. 7, 9, 21, 96, 120: © Julius Shulman, Hon. AIA.

Figs. 10, 15: © Disney Enterprises, Inc.

Fig. 25: Courtesy of the Los Angeles Public Library, Rare Books Department.

Figs. 33, 78, 126, 139–41, 146: Courtesy Edward Ruscha.

Figs. 70, 114: © Marvin Rand 1999.

Figs. 74, 76, 103, 110, 135–37: © David Hockney.

Fig. 77: Tim Street-Porter.

Fig. 79: Santa Barbara Mission Archive-Library.

Figs. 82, 83, 93–95, 97: Architectural Drawing Collection, University Art Museum, University of California at Santa Barbara.

Figs. 84, 86, 122: Frank Lloyd Wright drawings are copyright © 1998 The Frank Lloyd Wright Foundation, Scottsdale, Ariz.

Fig. 102: © SITE Projects, Inc.

Fig. 116: Courtesy of the Archives, California Institute of Technology.

Fig. 123: The Mitchell Wolfson Jr. Collection, The Wolfsonian-Florida International University, Miami Beach, Florida.

Index

Compositor: Integrated Composition Systems
Text: 10/14 Palatino
Display: Snell Roundhand Script and Bauer Bodoni
Printer and binder: Edwards Brothers, Inc.